Write More,

SELL MORE

Write More, SELL MORE

Robert Bly

WRITER'S DIGEST BOOKS
CINCINNATI, OHIO

ABOUT THE AUTHOR

Robert Bly has been a professional writer for more than fifteen years, receiving more than $2 million in advances, fees and royalties from more than one hundred publishers, editors and corporate clients nationwide. He is the author of over one hundred articles featured in such magazines as *Cosmopolitan* and *Writer's Digest* and he has also written thirty-seven books, including *Careers for Writers*. Thousands of writers have attended his writing seminars and purchased his instructional cassettes and he is a frequent speaker at writers conferences across the United States.

Write More, Sell More. Copyright © 1998 by Robert W. Bly. Printed and bound in the United States of America. All rights reserved. No part of this book may be reproduced in any form or by any electronic or mechanical means including information storage and retrieval systems without permission in writing from the publisher, except by a reviewer, who may quote brief passages in a review. Published by Writer's Digest Books, an imprint of F&W Publications, Inc., 1507 Dana Avenue, Cincinnati, Ohio 45207. (800) 289-0963. First edition.

This hardcover edition of *Write More, Sell More* features a "self-jacket" that eliminates the need for a separate dust jacket. It provides sturdy protection for your book while it saves paper, trees and energy.

Other fine Writer's Digest Books are available from your local bookstore or direct from the publisher.

02 01 00 99 98   5 4 3 2 1

Library of Congress Cataloging-in-Publication Data

Bly, Robert W.
    Write more, sell more / Robert W. Bly.—1st ed.
       p.   cm.
    Includes bibliographical references and index.
    ISBN 0-89879-816-7 (hardcover : alk. paper)
    1. Authorship. 2. Authorship—Marketing. I. Title.
PN161.B58   1998
808'.02—dc21   98-15816
                                                   CIP

Editors: Jack Heffron and Roseann S. Biederman
Production Editor: Nicole R. Klungle
Cover Designer: Clare Finney

ACKNOWLEDGMENTS

Thanks to the thousands of writers who have read my books and articles, taken my seminars, listened to my tapes and shared their experiences with me. Researching the answers to your questions, concerns, problems and challenges gave me the inspiration—and information—to write this book.

Thanks also to *Writer's Digest* magazine for allowing me to reprint, in slightly different format, portions of some of the articles I've written for them over the years.

I'm grateful to my wife, Amy, for reading the book in manuscript and making helpful suggestions and corrections to every chapter.

I am also grateful to Jack Heffron and Roseann S. Biederman, my editors, for making this book much better than it was when it first crossed their desks, and to Bonita Nelson, my agent, as always.

TABLE OF CONTENTS

WRITING IS *HELL*. ASK ANY WRITER.
—LOIS LANE, IN *SUPERMAN: WHOM GODS DESTROY, BOOK I*

BOOKS STRETCH OUR MINDS. THEY LET US DREAM.
THEY HELP US SEE OVER THE ROOFTOPS OF OUR NEIGHBORHOODS
TO THE WORLD OF THOUGHT THAT LIES BEYOND.
—FROM AN ADVERTISEMENT FOR THE EMERGENCY BOOK FUND

WRITING—FORMULATING AN IDEA, CHOOSING THE WORDS, AND INSCRIBING
THE THOUGHT ONTO PAPER—IS SOMETHING WE TAKE FOR GRANTED AS A
PURE AND SIMPLE EFFORT. BUT THERE ARE THOSE RARE CASES WHERE THE
ENDEAVOR SURPASSES THE ORDINARY AND BECOMES ART.
—NOBERT A. PLATT, PRESIDENT, MONT BLANC

EVEN WHEN WE KNOW WHAT A TOUGH BUSINESS WRITING IS,
WE DO IT BECAUSE WE HAVE TO.
—ERICA JONG, *DAILY NEWS*, SEPTEMBER 4, 1997

INTRODUCTION

Do you want to make more money writing? This book can help you double, triple or even quadruple your writing income.

Reading it just once can put an extra $100, $500, $1,000 or more in your pocket. Following some of the advice on a regular basis can increase your annual earnings by $10,000, $20,000, even $50,000 or more. Does that sound good to you? Then read on.

A BRIEF BIT OF BACKGROUND:
HOW I CAME TO WRITE THIS BOOK

I'm not the most successful writer in the world. Nor the most prolific. I've never written a best-seller. Yet I make a comfortable six-figure income as a freelance writer. Clients and publishers have paid me well over $2 million in fees, royalties and advances since I became a full-time freelance writer in February 1982. Last year, I grossed almost $250,000. Now I want to share with you my techniques for making more money.

Some writers say, "Money is not important; I just want to get published." If you feel this way, this book is not for you. I agree with best-selling author Ted Nicholas, who writes in his newsletter, *Direct Marketing Success Letter*, "Money is very important. The happiest possible life ideally rests on a balance between four elements: health, career, personal relationships and money."

To help other writers increase their sales and earnings, I've been writing occasional how-to articles for *Writer's Digest* magazine for almost a decade. A few years ago, I wrote an article on how writers can work faster, more productively and more efficiently to substantially increase earnings. The article, "To Sell More, Write More," appeared as a cover story in the February 1996 issue of *Writer's Digest*.

Within a few weeks of publication, I received more than five hundred letters from *Writer's Digest* readers asking for further advice on how to increase their writing productivity and income. In dozens of these letters, writers expressed a similar sentiment: "I am a writer, but I don't make enough money. How can I produce more, sell more of what I write and get paid higher fees?"

Obviously the issue of productivity and earnings struck a responsive chord. So the editors at *Writer's Digest* and I thought, "Why not expand the article into a book?" The result is the book you now hold in your hands: *Write More, Sell More.*

Most writing books tell writers how to write better or get published. They concentrate on breaking in. Here's a book to help you take your earnings to the next level by increasing your productivity, efficiency, output and sales. You will learn easy ways to write more in less time, work better and faster and sell more of what you write. The bottom line: The average reader will be given techniques to double, triple, even quadruple writing income from $10,000–$25,000 a year to $50,000–$100,000 a year or more.

HOW THE BOOK WORKS

As discussed in depth in this book, there are four primary ways you can make more money as a writer:

1. **Write faster.** Get your work done in less time so you earn more money on a per-hour basis. Would you rather be a $10-an-hour writer or a $100-an-hour writer? The choice is largely yours.
2. **Increase output.** That is, write more. Isaac Asimov didn't get huge advances for most of his books. But with 475 books to his credit, his prolificity made him wealthy.
3. **Sell more of the output.** Minimize rejections and sell more of what you write. Your lawyer or doctor doesn't give away his time. Neither should you.
4. **Get paid more.** Sell your writing for higher fees, advances and royalties to better-paying markets. Wouldn't you rather be paid $2,000 for an article than $200 or $25? I'll show you how.

Write More, Sell More is organized in four major parts, with each section addressing one of these four areas. Therefore, it is a complete guide to increasing your income as a writer.

In addition, I've included at least one sample book proposal, query letter, article outline, lead-generating letter, a sales lead tracking form, client contract, sales letter, invoice, author's bio and productivity checklist, so you can save even more time by modeling your efforts after those of other successful writers.

A NOTE TO READERS OF
SECRETS OF A FREELANCE WRITER

A few years ago, I wrote a book called *Secrets of a Freelance Writer*. The book shows how to make a lot of money as a writer, but tells how to do so exclusively in the field of corporate writing—business writing, ad copywriting, technical writing, public relations, sales promotion.

Write More, Sell More is for *all* writers, not just copywriters. Here you'll find productivity, efficiency and marketing tips to increase your writing output and income no matter what you write. The advice can be applied to multiply your earnings whether you're a "traditional" freelance writer doing books and articles; a journalist; a novelist; a poet, playwright or other "literary" writer; a scriptwriter; a screenwriter; a ghostwriter or whatever.

No matter what you write, you can make more money and earn $1,000 a week or more from your writing. *Write More, Sell More* shows you how. Let's get started.

HOW TO USE THIS BOOK

Write More, Sell More can be read in sequence from start to finish. Or, you can skip around from chapter to chapter, reading only about those subjects that interest you. It's not necessary to read all the chapters or read the chapters in sequence to benefit from the information in the book. Feel free to skip topics that aren't of interest. For example, if you are most concerned with getting more assignments and more of your work published, go straight to part three, "Increasing Your Sales." You can always go back and read or reread a chapter later, as the mood strikes you.

I do have a favor to ask. When *Write More, Sell More* helps you make more money writing, will you let me know of your success? I can be reached at

Bob Bly
22 East Quackenbush Avenue
Dumont, NJ 07628
phone: (201) 385-1220
fax: (201) 385-1138
E-mail: Rwbly@aol.com

PART ONE

WRITING FASTER

The first section focuses on how to write faster. The logic is simple: If you can do a $100 writing job in four hours, you earn $25 an hour. If you can do it in half an hour, you earn $200 an hour. This section shows how to double, triple or quadruple your writing speed without sacrificing quality—thus dramatically increasing the amount of money you earn for each hour spent at your keyboard.

CHAPTER 1

Work Habits That Speed You Up

THE LYF SO SHORT, THE CRAFT SO LONG TO LERNE,

TH'ASSAY SO HARD, SO SHARP THE CONQUERING.

—GEOFFREY CHAUCER

There's an old saying among dentists: The faster you drill and fill, the more you bill. Dentists, although highly paid, are still in essence hourly workers—they get paid only when they work. We writers, like dentists, attorneys, computer programmers and many other professionals, earn money proportional to the amount of work we turn out.

Most writers charge a project fee—so much for an article, so much for a book, so much for a resume, so much for a press release. If you charge by the project, you can earn more money by working faster.

Think about it. If you get paid $200 to write a press release, and it takes an entire eight-hour day, your earnings are $25 an hour. Now imagine being able to turn out a correct, effective press release in half a day. Your earnings jump to $50 an hour. Writing faster increases your income potential. If you can do one $200 project a day, and you work five days a week, your income is $1,000 a week, or $50,000 a year. On the other hand, let's say you can work twice as fast. If you can do two $200 projects per day, and work five days a week, you will complete ten projects for a weekly income of $2,000. That's an annual income of $100,000—not bad by most standards.

Fast writers have certain work habits that aid productivity. These productivity tips are easy to implement and require no special knowledge or skills. This chapter covers some of the basics of writing faster and more efficiently.

SETTING YOUR DAILY SCHEDULE

Productive writers have schedules and stick to them. Yet most writers don't schedule their daily activities.

It's not enough to know the projects you're working on. You should break your day into segments—I suggest using increments of an hour, although quarter and half days can also work—and write down on a piece of paper the project you will work on during each of those segments.

Do this every day, at the beginning of your workday (or if you prefer, do it in the evening right before you stop work for the night). Tape your hour-by-hour schedule for the day on a wall near your desk, or pin it to a nearby bulletin board. Note that although you may work on a project for more than one hour a day, you need not schedule these hours consecutively.

As you go through the day, consult your schedule to keep on track. If priorities change, you can change the schedule, but do this in writing: Revise the schedule, print the new version, remove the old schedule and post the new one.

It's OK to redo the schedule as long as you don't miss deadlines. Some days I redo the daily to-do schedule two or three times, depending on deadlines and inspiration. Why not? As long as you are organized, keep track of deadlines and allow enough time to finish each job, you will increase your productivity by working on things you feel in the *mood* to work on.

DETERMINING PRIORITIES

Can you always work on what you want to, when you want to? No. Sometimes, a pressing deadline means putting aside a more pleasurable task for something more formidable—even if you don't feel like doing it right then.

On the wall of my office near my desk, I have posted a list that I update weekly. It's called "Rules of the Office," and it reminds me what I have to do to be successful in my business. Rule number one is "First things first." This means you must set priorities and meet deadlines.

For instance, if I am burning to work on a book but have a press release due the next morning, I write the press release first and fax or E-mail it to the client. Then I reward myself with a morning spent on the book. If you do the book first, you may not leave yourself enough time to get the press release written by your deadline.

THE THREE TYPES OF TO-DO LISTS
EVERY WRITER SHOULD KEEP

The key component of my personal time-management system is a series of lists I keep on the computer. In fact, I have so many lists that I have a file called LISTS to keep track of them!

Every morning, after checking my various online services (the Internet, CompuServe, America Online and AT&T Mail) for E-mail, I open the LISTS file; it tells me which lists I must read and review to start my day.

The most important lists on the LISTS list are my to-do lists. I keep several, but the most critical are my daily to-do list, projects to-do list and long-term to-do list:

1. **Daily to-do list.** Each day I type on my PC, print and post a list of the items I have to do that day. From this list, I create my hour-by-hour schedule. I enjoy work and like to work long hours, so I take on a lot of projects that interest me. But I never take on more than I can handle so I can continue to meet all deadlines.

2. **Projects to-do list.** In a separate computer file, I keep a list of all of my writing projects currently under contract, along with the deadline for each. I review this list several times a week, using it to ensure that the daily to-do list covers all items that have to be done right away.

3. **Long-term to-do list.** This is a list of projects I want to do at some point but are not under contract (such as learning new software or organizing files) and therefore do not have any assigned deadlines. I check this list about once a week and usually put in a few hours each week on one or two of the projects that interest me at the time.

HOW TO OVERCOME PROCRASTINATION
AND WRITER'S BLOCK

Having a daily to-do list—and assigning various tasks to yourself throughout the day in one-hour increments—helps you stay on track and avoid putting things off.

Breaking tasks into one-hour sessions and juggling the schedule to work on what interests you most right now help overcome writer's block: When you get tired or run out of ideas on one project, just switch to another. As long as you have your short-term deadlines and long-term goals in mind, you can be somewhat flexible in your daily schedule, adjusting tasks and time slots to match your enthusiasm for each project.

Give yourself rewards for accomplishing tasks. If you work for a solid hour on a technical manual that's slow going, reward yourself with a break to read your mail or walk around the block. If you stick with your schedule for the whole morning, treat yourself to your favorite food for lunch.

The best way to make every hour of every day productive is to have an hour-by-hour schedule. People who have such a schedule know what they should be doing every minute, and therefore do it. People who don't set a schedule tend to drift through the day, stopping and then starting tasks, jumping from job to job without getting much done.

BEST WRITING STYLES FOR PROLIFIC WRITERS

"I never use a long word when a short one will do or an involved construction when a simple one will do or literary trickery when plain-speaking will do," wrote Isaac Asimov in *Yours, Isaac Asimov.*

Unless you're naturally poetic, don't force yourself to be poetic in your writing. Write in your natural voice. When you write in your natural style, you write quickly and well. When you try to force yourself to write in a way that is not natural or comfortable, the work becomes agonizing and you'll slow to a snail's pace.

Prolific science fiction authors Robert Heinlein and Isaac Asimov wrote first drafts that were pretty close to final copy: Heinlein sent out his first drafts unrevised, while Asimov read them once and made revisions affecting maybe 5 percent of the text. Asimov said having a plain and simple style contributed to his being one of the most prolific writers of this century.

Georges Simenon also used a spare, lean style, enabling him to write each of his novels in less than one week. In a single year—1928—Simenon wrote and published forty-four novels.

Write in a natural, plain style. Your writing should sound like you and reflect your personality. Do not imitate or copy the styles of other writers—even those you admire. Imitation sounds easy but is in fact difficult, unnatural and slow. When you write as if you are talking to the reader one-on-one, you write quickly and productively.

Write simple prose: short words, short sentences. Write to express, not to impress. Care about words and be a careful editor, but don't agonize over every comma to the *n*th degree.

Don't be afraid to write quickly. "Fast writing is good writing," insists Milt Pierce, a New York City freelance writer who has written dozens of articles, books and direct mail packages. Pierce says the pieces he writes quickly are usually the best; if he finds himself agonizing, he knows the writing is not his best.

Actually, there is no direct correlation between writing speed and quality. It depends on the assignment and the author. If you're fortunate enough to be a fast writer, take advantage of your gift. Don't believe those who tell you that if you did it fast, it can't be good. It can. I recently read that Robert James Waller wrote *The Bridges of Madison County*, the best-selling novel of all time, in fourteen weeks. Many critics panned the book, but millions of readers loved it. I cheerfully admit to being one of those readers!

At the same time, don't let editors and clients know how quickly you write. Steve Manning, a Toronto-based freelancer who has written and sold as many as 132 articles in a year, says he never lets editors know how slowly or quickly he wrote a given piece. "It can take me anywhere from two hours to two days to do an article, but I never tell the editor," says Manning. "Editors assume that if the article was written quickly, it's inferior. If I let them think it took two to three weeks, they're more delighted."

TWELVE STEPS TO WRITING BETTER AND FASTER

1. **Use a computer.** You don't have to use a computer, although many corporate clients and editors are pressuring writers to submit copy on disk. But in my opinion, every writer who wants to be productive should use a modern PC with the latest software. Doing so can double, triple or even quadruple your output. Chapter seven guides you on the technology you should acquire and how to use it.

2. **Get multiple assignments on a single topic.** If you do a lot of research on holistic medicine for a magazine article, you may use only 50 percent or less of the material you gather. Instead of wasting the other 50 percent, use it to create additional queries, articles, book chapters and other materials you can sell at a profit. This allows you to "amortize" your investment in research on a topic over many assignments.

3. **Get multiple assignments from a single editor or client.** Most writers concentrate on selling queries and proposals to editors they pick out of *Writer's Market*, ignoring an audience more likely to buy from them—editors they've already worked with.

   In business, it is five times more difficult to make a sale to a new customer than to get another order from an existing customer. Send your queries, proposals and promotions to the editors and clients you already do business with first, and your acceptance rate will be higher.

4. **Get multiple assignments in the same format.** Whether it's biographies for readers age eight to twelve or direct-mail fund-raising packages, once you learn a format, you can work more quickly than when it's new to you. Also, people are more likely to hire you, based on having the first sample in your portfolio. Seek repeat assignments within a given genre or format. The work will be easier to get, and you'll be able to do it faster.

5. **Don't be a perfectionist.** "I'm a non-perfectionist," said Isaac Asimov, author of 475 books, in a letter. "I don't look back in regret or worry at what I have written." Be a careful writer, but don't agonize over your writing to the point when the extra effort no longer produces a proportionately worthwhile improvement in your final product.

   When it comes to writing, my goal is to be good but not perfect. Clients do not have the time or budget for perfection, and for most projects, 95 percent of perfection is good enough. That doesn't mean you deliberately leave in errors or make the piece incomplete. It means you stop polishing the piece when it looks good to you and don't agonize over the fact you're not spending another hundred hours on it. Write it, check it, then let it go.

"I don't think any writing is perfect, ever," says Ronald D. Smith, a children's book author, in an interview in *Children's Writer*. "You can really hang yourself up by trying to get into that perfectionist mode, as if we think anybody can write something that's perfect." In an article in *The Writer*, best-selling novelist Sidney Sheldon says, "Even though I do many rewrites on each book, when I see the printed copy I always want to do one more."

Some writers spend years on a single piece or decades on a novel. May Sarton says she does thirty to sixty drafts on her poems, and Donald Hall said he revised one poem more than six hundred times. But you reach a point where the changes you are making do not materially improve the work or its value to the reader. This is the point when I stop. To go on would not improve the result, and many writers who are perfectionists don't produce or sell much work. Or make much money.

6. **Free yourself from the pressure to be a genius.** As writer Cameron Foote observes, "Clients are looking for good, not great." Do the best you can and write to meet the clients' requirements. They will be happy. Do not feel pressured to be original or present a great truth. Most successful writing takes thoughts, ideas and concepts people already know and believe and presents them in a clear, crisp and compelling way. If you have some new ideas or insights you can give the reader, that's a bonus, but it's not expected or required.

Don't be held up by the false notion that you must uncover some great truth or present your reader with revolutionary ideas and concepts. Most people read more for reinforcement than anything else, so if you tell them things they already know, they won't be disappointed; rather, they'll admire you for your insight and knowledge. (They'll also feel smug that what they believed to be true was validated in print.)

Eliminate performance pressure. Don't worry about whether what you are writing is different or better than what others have written on the subject before you. Just write about the subject the best you can. Others will be interested and enthusiastic; remember, they haven't read 99 percent of the material written on that topic.

7. **Write things you enjoy.** In advising creative people on

choosing their life's work, copywriter David Ogilvy quotes a Scottish proverb that says, "Be happy while you're living, for you're a long time dead." When you enjoy your work, it really isn't work. To me, success is being able to make a good living while spending the workday in totally pleasurable tasks. When you write things you enjoy, you achieve this level of success. You won't love every project equally, of course, but try to balance "must-do" moneymakers with things that are more fun for you. Even better, find lucrative areas that are also exciting to you.

Write what you know. Write what interests you. If you're fascinated, the work will go faster and be more pleasant. If you already know the topic, lack of understanding or data won't bog you down.

On the other hand, if every piece you write is on a new or unfamiliar topic, research will be more time-consuming, and you won't be able to produce a finished writing project as rapidly.

8. **Switch back and forth between multiple assignments.** Florida freelancer David Kohn says, "If you write the same thing a thousand times, no matter what it is, you will get bored." Even if you consider yourself a specialist, do projects outside your specialty. Inject variety into your project schedule. Arrange your daily schedule so you switch from one assignment to another at least once or twice. Variety, as the saying goes, is indeed the spice of life.

9. **Get contracts.** Magazine editors should send letters of agreement; book publishers, contracts; corporate clients, purchase orders. If they don't, write a simple letter of agreement or contract (see Appendix A), sign it and have your client sign it. A written contract makes the assignment real and firm so you can proceed at full speed knowing you have been officially hired.

10. **Make deadlines firm but adequate.** Often you will collaborate with your clients in determining deadlines. Set deadlines for a specific date and time, not a time period. For example, "due November 23 by 3 P.M. or sooner," not "in about two weeks." Having a specific date and time for copy submission eliminates confusion and gives you motivation to complete the work on time.

At the same time, don't make deadlines too tight. Try to build in a few extra days for the unexpected, such as a missing piece of information, a delay doing an interview or a rush revision on another assignment.

11. **Write what you know.** Want to be prolific? My best advice: Write about subjects of which you already have some knowledge. The most prolific authors write as experts, not journalists. Dan Poynter, for example, was able to write dozens of books on parachuting and hang gliding because he is an active participant in these sports.

Specialize in one or several areas of knowledge, then write about them from many different angles. As your familiarity with a topic grows, the quality of your writing will improve and you'll get more done in less time. Interested in money? Become a financial writer. Hypochondriac? Specialize in medicine and health care.

Your writing will be more authentic and valuable when you write what you know. You'll have an easier time making sales. And you'll be able to write rapidly.

An excellent piece of advice for writers is, "Start where you are now." If you are a nutritionist, write about health, diet and nutrition. There's a huge market, and you have a leg up on other writers who don't have your expertise.

12. **Use the 80/20 rule.** The danger of writing the same thing all the time is that while it may be profitable, you can get bored. On the other hand, if every single assignment is completely new and different, your income per hour will be low.

My solution is to apply the 80/20 rule to my project schedule: Approximately 80 percent of what I am doing at any time is in familiar genres and formats within my area of expertise. This keeps me highly profitable. The other 20 percent is in new formats or media outside my area of expertise. This keeps me fresh and allows me to explore things that captivate my imagination but are not in my usual portfolio of assignments.

HOW TO ELIMINATE UNNECESSARY ACTIVITIES THAT SLOW YOU DOWN

In one of his excellent small business how-to books, my friend, author Dr. Jeffrey Lant, mentioned he had a full-time houseboy.

While at the time I thought, "He's crazy—why should an able-bodied young man have a houseboy?" I've now come around to his point of view.

Writing is a skill or service practiced or rendered by the hour. The more hours you spend doing nonwriting activities, the fewer hours you have for writing.

Part of being a productive writer is avoiding interruptions and putting in the necessary hours. You can't do those effectively if you are dividing your time between too many things.

Since you have multiple responsibilities, the solution is to get other people to do as many of the nonwriting activities as you are willing to give up or able to afford.

For instance, instead of picking up the kids after school each day, maybe you can have a neighbor who has children in the same school give your kids a ride, and pay her a few dollars each week for car service. She might be thrilled to earn the extra money!

My approach is to "off-load" nonwriting tasks, getting them off my list of responsibilities so I can concentrate on being a productive, profitable writer. This strategy of "outsourcing"—asking or hiring others to do these nonwriting tasks—is covered in detail in chapter eight.

With an average life span of seventy-five years, we have only 27,375 days from the time we are born until the time we die. And since we're asleep for a third of that time, we have only 18,250 days we're actually awake and active.

How you spend this finite amount of time is mostly up to you. To maximize your productivity, income and output as a writer, writing must be a priority.

If you prefer to garden, that's perfectly fine; but don't complain that your colleague who spends those hours in front of the PC is getting more work done than you are. It's your choice.

ELIMINATING BAD HABITS THAT WASTE TIME

First, identify any bad habits you have that waste your time. For me, it was sleeping an hour after I first woke up in the morning. Since the morning is the most productive writing time for me, by forcing myself to get dressed and go to the office when I awaken, I increased my productivity tremendously.

For you, it may be watching a soap opera in the middle of the day, spending too much time surfing the Web, talking in chat rooms or on the phone, doing housework or staying up late at night to read or watch television.

After you have identified the bad habits, list them, phrasing each item in the imperative voice. For example, if your worst time-wasting habit is procrastination, this should read as "Don't procrastinate" on your list. If you take on too many ancillary responsibilities because you hate saying no, this item should appear on your list as "Learn to say no."

Post this list in your office in a place where you will always see it, such as on the wall in front of you or on your bulletin board or door. With the list of bad habits visible, you will be constantly reminded to avoid these bad habits and correct behaviors that waste time. Before long, you'll see a big improvement and will be getting more done in less time. Try it!

SETTING AND ACHIEVING
REALISTIC PRODUCTION GOALS

If your goal is simply to be busy, be productive, write as much as you can and get it all published, you don't need to set a production goal, because your goal is to produce as much as you can. I'm not suggesting you live this way, but many prolific writers do.

However, I realize that for many of you, productivity is not the end but, rather, is a means to an end, the end being greater earnings. If that's true with you, you need to create a business plan for your freelance writing activities.

The key to a successful plan is to decide how much money you want to earn and then determine what you must do to reach your income goal.

CREATING A BUSINESS PLAN

Most writers have no idea how much effort they must exert to earn a given amount of money. Many do not even have an income goal. If you don't know how much money you want to make or what you have to do to make it, you'll have a difficult time achieving your financial objectives.

You can make a good living at freelance writing, but you have to work at it. Tradition conspires against you.

Here's how to create a simple plan for your freelance writing business:

1. Determine the amount of money you want to earn this year. I'm amazed at how many freelancers have no financial goal. If you don't know how much money you want to earn, how do you know how much work you have to do, and what you must charge, to make the living you want to make?

   The average freelance writer in the United States doing editorial or literary writing earns about $25,000. According to Cameron Foote, publisher of the newsletter *Creative Business*, the average advertising and corporate freelance writer earns $50,000. I would think setting an income objective for your first year of $25,000 to $50,000 is reasonable.

2. Determine how much you must make daily, weekly or monthly to reach your annual income goal. If your goal is $50,000 a year, and you work fifty weeks a year, you must make $200 a day, $1,000 a week, $4,167 a month. Knowing what you must earn each day, week or month tells you whether you are on track to make your goal.

3. Determine your average project fee. Project fees will vary, of course, but how much will you earn for each project on average? If your average fee per article is $1,000, you must write and sell one article or pamphlet per week to achieve your $50,000 annual income goal.

4. Determine the level of sales and marketing activity needed to make your sales goal. If you must write and sell one article a week and your sales closing rate is one assignment for every five query letters, you must write and send five query letters a week, or 250 queries a year.

Only when you have worked out these numbers for your own freelance business will you have a realistic idea of the effort required to earn a living as a freelance writer.

CHAPTER 2

Lucrative Assignments
You Can Do
Rapidly and Easily

A PROFESSIONAL WRITER IS AN AMATEUR WHO DIDN'T QUIT.
—RICHARD BACH

F ast writers tend to take on only those assignments they can complete quickly; they avoid assignments that would take them a long time.

Often, pay is not proportionate to either the degree of difficulty or time needed for completion. This week, for example, I wrote a $3,500 script for one client, in one day, in the morning. A project for another client took me all of the next day and earned me only $400. By selecting the former and avoiding the latter, writers can do more work in less time—and make more money in the process.

This chapter shows you what some of these fast-writing assignments are, where to find them, why these projects can be done so rapidly and how to get them. Also included: how to find assignments you can do while moonlighting from your regular job, if you have one.

SHORT ARTICLES AND LITTLE BOOKS

Write short articles and books instead of long ones. The trend is toward shorter articles and books, so editors and publishers will be receptive. You'll produce more articles and books in less time, and your income will increase: You'll be paid more to write three 1,500-word articles than one 5,000-word article, in most instances. You'll get more advance money for two 75,000-word books than one 150,000-word book.

Service articles can be written quickly from printed materials without extensive interviews or on-site visits. The two basic service articles are the how-to and the where-to.

The how-to tells readers how to do something—for example, how to ask for a raise, find day care for the kids, change the oil in your car, browse the Internet or grow roses. Ten years ago, I wrote a short article aimed at business travelers who read *Amtrak Express*, the "in-train" magazine of Amtrak. The title was, "How to Write Business Letters That Get Results." The 1,500-word article took only a few hours to write, with no interviews or research. The magazine paid me $400.

The where-to article tells readers where to get something—for example, where to buy gourmet food by mail, find day care centers, get a mortgage, attend Star Trek conventions, see new boating equipment or take pottery classes. For *New Jersey Monthly*, I wrote an article describing the various places in the state offering PC training courses. The article was written quickly based on telephone interviews and course materials mailed to me by the schools. I earned a quick $750 for my effort.

How-to is also a popular topic for books. The *New York Daily News* reports that there are approximately two thousand new self-help books published each year, worth $460 million in sales. If you know the topic well, a how-to book shouldn't be too difficult to write. As Ann Landers observes, "You can't beat wisdom born of experience."

Self-help and how-to materials are in demand, and virtually everyone has some experience or knowledge that can be the basis for marketable how-to writings. "The secret to getting a personal experience article published is to use your experience as a stepping-stone to help others who have faced similar situations," writes Judy Boomer in an article in *The Writer.* Tony Seideman, a freelance magazine writer based in New York City, says, "Magazines are hungry for good copy, especially when someone has specialized expertise."

Write for children. Many people are negative about children's book publishing, citing the lower advances and the fact that royalties must be split with an illustrator. But most children's books are only a few hundred words compared with 80,000 words or more for the average adult nonfiction book or novel. Even though the advances on children's books are only a few thousand dollars, they're actually quite high when figured on a dollars-per-word basis—higher than for most adult books.

A friend recently published a children's book with Scholastic. It's a hardcover picture book selling for $14.95. The text portion is less than 500 words; every time someone buys those 500 words, she gets a royalty on $14.95. My books, typically adult nonfiction trade paperbacks, contain 100,000 words each—two hundred times the length of the picture book—yet I actually get a smaller royalty payment for each copy sold (the cover prices are less, and paperbacks pay lower royalties than hardcovers). So to me, at least, children's books seem like a good deal.

"There seems to be some trend back to traditional children's books," said Richard Scott, managing editor of *American Bookseller*, in an interview with *Children's Writer* newsletter. "There is a more uplifting context to the books now coming out, and I see those as a steady, growing category."

If you have a feel for the work and are a fast writer, you can turn out a children's book in a month or even a week—especially a short nonfiction book with a well-defined subject. Try to connect with a publisher that does series books for children with many volumes in each series. Regular assignments could result.

Many adult publishers also do series books. Since these are often written to a formula, you can do them rapidly to fit the publisher's specifications. Editorial acceptance will come more quickly, and with the format laid out, you can "fill in the blanks" and get the book written faster.

Despite the rise of electronic media, publishers continue to contract with writers to produce lots of books—around 50,000 a year. According to Dan Poynter, author of *The Self-Publishing Manual*, there are more than one million books currently in print. This doesn't include thousands of out-of-print books being sold through various catalogs and bookstores. Today a typical "superstore," such as Barnes and Noble or Borders, will have at least 100,000 different titles on its shelves.

TRADE JOURNALS

If you're concentrating on trying to sell your manuscripts to *Redbook, Esquire, Reader's Digest, Travel and Leisure, Sports Illustrated* and the other "consumer" magazines, you should know about a larger, less competitive and potentially more lucrative "other world" of magazine markets: trade journals.

I got my start in writing for the trades with no previous publishing experience. I made sales to such publications as *Audiovisual Directions, Industrial Marketing, Chemical Engineering* and *Direct Marketing* before breaking into consumer magazines (including *Cosmopolitan* and *New Woman*) and books. Today I still write trade articles, because they pay well when compared with other writing assignments on a dollars-per-hour basis.

R.L. Stine, best-selling author of the Goosebumps books, started out as a writer for the trade journal *Soft Drink Industry*, writing articles with titles such as "Squirt Co. Now Using Full-Color Billboards" and "New American Flange Hopper Speeds Feeding of Rip Cap Closures." In his autobiography, *It Came From Ohio! My Life as a Writer*, Stine writes, "Magazine writing was the perfect training for me. I learned to write fast—and move on to the next piece." As of this writing, Stine has written more than 250 published books and currently writes 24 books a year!

You'll find breaking into these specialized magazines easier than breaking into the big-name, general interest publications, too. Be aware that per-article pay rates don't rival *Playboy*'s or *Family Circle*'s, but neither does the competition among freelancers. Since trade journals accept a larger percentage of the articles proposed by writers, you may be able to make more money writing for the trades than for consumer magazines. Consumer magazines may pay more per article, but you can waste a lot of time on queries that don't sell before finally getting a go-ahead—if you get one at all.

Trade magazine editors often rely on "outsiders" for much of what goes into the magazine—sometimes as much as 60 percent of the copy. Because the trades have smaller staffs and a strong feeling of loyalty to their readers, they often welcome new ideas from those familiar with their fields.

I've had many pleasant and rewarding experiences writing for the trades. For example, an editor at *Computer Decisions* obtained material from my seminar on technical writing. The editor asked me to turn it into a 1,200-word article on how to write user's manuals. Using the material already at hand, I wrote the piece and had it in the mail in under an hour. A week later, the magazine sent a check for $750. In one year, I added approximately $6,200 to my annual income writing articles and columns for trade journal editors.

Before you attempt to make your own profits in this market, it's essential to understand just what these magazines are about. Trade magazines serve the needs of a special interest market. They exist in just about every field. Whether you're interested in aviation (*Aviation Daily, Aviation Engineering and Maintenance*), fertilizer (*Fertilizer Progress, Farm Chemicals*) or turkeys (*Turkey World*), there's at least one appropriate magazine for you to approach.

Trade journals exist to keep professionals up-to-date on developments, conferences, trends and practices in their fields. Readers need the information the journals provide to help them perform their jobs better. As a result, trade articles are practical and specific and, depending on the magazine, can be in-depth or technical.

All provide straightforward coverage of a specific industry. Unlike their consumer cousins, these magazines don't strive to be flashy or singularly entertaining. They look different, too— generally less slick than the mass-market magazines. Visuals are used to communicate information, not to add glitz or lure readers.

Trade journals usually pay less than consumer magazines; in fact, some don't pay at all. And among those that do pay, rates vary widely.

For a 1,500-word article on improving technical writing, published in *Chemical Engineering,* I received only $100. The next month, a corporate client asked me to ghostwrite a 1,000-word article on computers. The writing took only a few hours, and the corporate client paid $1,500. In general, rates paid by trade journals range from $50 to $400 per magazine page. But some pay more; others less.

Editors and fees are flexible. I know of one freelance writer who insisted on payment for an article he submitted to a strictly nonpaying magazine. His steadfastness earned him several hundred dollars.

The time to talk about money is after you've received an assignment letter from the editor. If the letter doesn't mention payment, write the editor, asking what fee she is offering.

Seasoned writers with long lists of credits or writers with exclusive stories of particular interest to editors may be able to negotiate higher fees. But beginners may not be able to negotiate such treatment, and may have to settle for bylines that can lead to future sales.

Trade journals represent one of the easiest markets for novice writers to crack. They're also a reliable market for veteran writers. You probably won't get rich writing for the trades, but you *can* generate a steady income year after year.

LETTERS

Every once in a while you read an article in the paper about a local writer who cleverly makes a business writing letters for people, often letters of complaint or love letters. While this sounds nifty, the problem is that people are not going to pay a lot of money for you to write a letter that will be sent only to one person. One writer in my county, for example, gets $150 to write a one-page complaint letter. Not bad, but you won't get rich.

A customer will be willing to pay much more for a letter that is mailed to many people. If someone pays $150 for a love letter sent to one person, the cost is $150 per recipient. On the other hand, a local animal shelter may send its fund-raising letter to all ten thousand adult residents in your town. Even if you charged $1,000 for the copy, that comes to only $.10 per recipient.

What type of customers would mail a letter you write for them to many people? Businesses of all sizes. A local oil company might pay you $400–$500 or more to write a short collection letter to send to residents who haven't paid their heating oil bills. A corporation might pay $500–$1,000 or more for a one-page letter to send to customers and prospects to announce a new product.

No matter what your level of experience as a writer, you've written many letters in your life already. We all have. How long does it take you to write a one-page letter? Businesses are paying $500–$1,000 or more for such letters every day. That's a nice fee for a job that is not labor-intensive. You do, of course, need to have a knack for writing snappy letters, but this can be learned through experience. Remember, this is letter writing, not brain surgery.

THE PER-WORD MYTH

How do you define an assignment as "lucrative"? Since so many magazines set rates by the word, freelance writers judge whether an assignment is well paying by the word rate.

At the low end, for example, science fiction magazines pay a pittance—anywhere from $.02 to $.08 per word. For a ten-page, 2,500-word short story, a fee of $.08 per word earns you a check for $200.

On the high end, some national magazines pay $1–$2 a word or more. One writer told me that she earned $1,600 for a short quiz for *Cosmopolitan*.

However, what counts is not just how much per word you get, but how long it takes you to write those words for the editor or client. The real key to measuring profitability on any assignment is dollars per hour, not dollars per word.

A lucrative assignment, therefore, is not necessarily one that pays a high per-word rate. If the project demands a lot of research, meticulous writing and lots of rewrites, your dollar rate per hour may be low, even though the total project fee is respectable.

By the same token, just because an assignment has a low project fee doesn't make it unprofitable. Recently a publisher asked me to write jacket copy for paperback books at $300 per book. While at first I was turned off by the low project rate, I gave it a try. On average, including revisions, each assignment took me two hours to complete, with none of the jobs taking more than three hours. Therefore, I was earning between $100 and $150 per hour on every assignment. I'll take that work any day of the year.

MEASURING PER-HOUR
PROFITABILITY ON ASSIGNMENTS

Even if you do all or most of your work on a project-fee basis, keep time sheets and track how many hours each job takes. Then divide by your fee to calculate your earnings on a dollars-per-hour basis.

A pattern will begin to emerge: You will find that some assignments you thought were paying well actually didn't when figured on a per-hour basis, and that some assignments with smaller fees are actually quite profitable.

Based on your experience, your skills and the kind of writer you are, you'll find yourself faster on some types of assignments, slower on others. Although I can charge large fees for direct-mail packages selling subscriptions, these assignments take a long time to produce. On the other hand, I can only get a few hundred dollars for a short press release but can write such releases rapidly.

As a rule of thumb, you can maximize profitability by gravitating toward those assignments that yield the highest dollars-per-hour pay and avoiding those with a low dollars-per-hour pay. Book reviews, for example, have to be one of the least profitable types of writing ever: Just reading the book takes many hours for a project that probably pays $10–$25, if that. But I personally am facile when it comes to writing short sales letters to generate leads or announce products; and at $1,000–$1,600 per letter, my hourly rate on these projects—most of which take less than a day, and many of which take less than half a day—is considerable.

Some writers specialize only in those assignments that make them the most money. For example, I know one writer who does nothing but write direct-mail packages to sell subscriptions to medical and financial newsletters—because these copywriting jobs are so lucrative.

Other writers prefer more of a mix to their work. They may take on some larger, long-term assignments as well as small, quick assignments. Switching back and forth keeps them fresh and prevents boredom.

Importantly, it also maximizes the number of billable hours you log each week. A "billable hour" is any time you spend on paying assignments.

"But isn't all of my time billable time?" you may ask. Not at all. You don't get paid for thinking of ideas for new articles and books, researching topics you may want to write about, writing query letters and proposals, mailing and phoning editors and agents to sell them your ideas, having lunch with editors, making sales calls on potential clients or coming up with and presenting cost estimates to potential clients.

You also don't get paid for going to the post office, making photocopies, filing, learning a new software program, shopping for office equipment, taking a seminar, reading trade magazines, and performing numerous other nonwriting tasks involved in running a freelance writing business. We call these tasks "nonbillable time."

For most freelance writers, between 50 and 75 percent of their time is billable. That means if you work a forty-hour week, anywhere from ten to twenty of those hours are spent doing activities for which you cannot charge a client or publisher.

You can obviously maximize your income by increasing the ratio of billable to nonbillable hours. Having a mix of assignments enables you to do this. For example, if you handle only large projects, you may have some unproductive "downtime" between assignments, which adds to your year's total of nonbillable hours.

But if you have a mix of projects, you can switch back and forth, filling up more hours in your day with billable activity. During the lull between big assignments, you can knock out two or three small projects, or perhaps make significant progress on one medium-size job, thus using the time to do billable work instead of idling it away.

How important is it to use your available time efficiently? A freelance writer who works forty hours a week fifty weeks a year and spends half those hours on billable work has gross income of $100,000. If that writer can use her time more efficiently and increase the percentage of billable hours to 60 percent, she will earn $120,000—an extra $20,000 annually—without putting in any more hours at the office.

SPECIAL CONSIDERATIONS FOR MOONLIGHTERS

If you moonlight—that is, you do your writing projects in your off-hours, before or after you have completed the workday for your regular job—projects that either are short or can be done in small increments will fit your schedule. With a limited number of hours to work on writing, you want to avoid labor-intensive projects under tight deadlines.

Is moonlighting feasible for you? It is if the following conditions exist:

- You can conduct your moonlighting activities without letting your boss or co-workers know what you are doing.
- You have enough flexibility in your schedule that you can occasionally contact clients during business hours either in person or by phone.
- You can take an occasional sick day or vacation day to meet with a client if absolutely necessary.
- You have the time and energy to do moonlighting assignments mornings, evenings and weekends—and you don't

mind giving up part of your free time to do so.
- You are able to find clients willing to work with you on a moonlighting basis.
- You are not uncomfortable with the idea of moonlighting—of doing things "behind the back" of your corporate employer.
- Moonlighting does not add so much stress that it becomes a miserable experience.

Many people who moonlight don't actively seek assignments, and probably 95 percent didn't go out and get their first assignments. Instead, the assignments came to them.

If you're a writer, eventually somebody is going to ask if you can do a writing assignment. Accept, and you have secured your first moonlighting project. It's that simple.

My first moonlighting assignment came while I was working as the advertising manager of an industrial firm. One day, after a meeting in my office, the owner of a PR firm doing some work for me said, "Do you do any moonlighting?" I asked what he had in mind. He said one of his clients, Dow Chemical, needed an article on the advantages of magnesium as a design material for use in aircraft, automobiles, etc. Would I be interested in writing it? I said yes and had my first moonlighting assignment.

Because I didn't know what to charge, I asked him what he would pay. He offered $250 for a 2,000-word article to be written from technical papers, brochures and other printed background material supplied by the client. Even by 1981 standards, I was underpaid. But I didn't know any better and was happy to do the work!

Months later, a graphic arts design studio I was using to produce one of our brochures asked me to write ads for one of its accounts. This was my second moonlighting assignment.

All in all, it never amounted to much moonlighting (I went full-time freelance shortly after the second assignment), but it was some nice extra money in my pocket and, more important, gave me a little experience in the "real world" of self-employment before I took the full-time plunge.

There are some major differences between writing as a moonlighter and promoting yourself as a full-time freelancer. As a moonlighter, you cannot use any marketing technique that would reveal your moonlighting activities to your full-time employer. This excludes the use of print ads, directory listings, publicity or writing articles or giving speeches as a freelance authority in your field.

Another thing you want to avoid is sending resumes or sales letters to "blind" ads (i.e., ads with a box number). Once, when I was employed as an advertising manager, I responded to a blind ad from an ad agency looking for part-time and freelance copywriters. It turned out to be *my* ad agency. They wisely didn't inform my boss (I would have been furious), but they were embarrassed about it. They were also concerned that I was looking for a new job, which might mean the loss of my company's business when I left. (This turned out to be true.)

Also, the moonlighter will market and promote his services on a more limited scale than the full-time freelancer. Why? It's obvious. First, the moonlighter can only take on one or at most two jobs at a time, because he must also spend forty to fifty hours a week at his regular job. The full-time freelancer, on the other hand, is hungry for all the work she can get—especially at the beginning.

Second, you as a moonlighter do not want to generate too many sales leads, because you do not have the time to follow up on all of them. To spend your time productively, concentrate on generating quality prospects rather than quantity leads. Send out fewer sales letters, but target them to the right prospects. Visit only those prospects who have a job and are ready to hire. You simply cannot afford to spend what limited extra time you have chasing down casual inquiries and dead ends.

Should you tell potential clients that you are a moonlighter and not a full-time freelancer? I can't answer that for you. Only you can decide. But I can describe the two schools of thought on the subject.

The first holds that you should not tell the client you are a moonlighter. The reason—and it is a valid one—is that some clients do not want to deal with moonlighters.

Their objections are these:

1. Moonlighters do not care as much about the assignment as a full-time freelancer because the moonlighter has a job and the assignment is just extra pocket money. Full-time

freelancers, on the other hand, must do more to please the client, because their survival depends on it.

2. Moonlighters may abandon the assignments or not be available to handle revisions or additional work if they are called away because of their regular jobs, while the full-time freelancer is always available.

3. Moonlighters are difficult to work with because they can't meet with you or accept your telephone calls except at odd hours. Many clients find this inconvenient.

To avoid being the victim of this prejudice, you simply omit the fact that you are a moonlighter from any client discussion. You don't lie about your moonlighting, if the client asks. But you don't *volunteer* the information, either.

It is not easy to maintain the illusion that you are not a moonlighter. But if you attempt it, keep the following in mind:

1. Give the client your home telephone number, not the telephone number of your company.

2. Have an answering machine or voice mail to take the calls when you are at work.

3. Check in with your machine (via remote beeper) or answering service at least twice a day to get messages and return phone calls from prospects and clients.

4. About returning calls: Make sure you have a telephone at your place of business you can use in privacy to return client calls. If you don't, the client will quickly realize you can never return calls during business hours and you must be a moonlighter.

5. Use an occasional vacation day to arrange meetings with clients so they see you are up and about on your own during the day.

The second school says it is best to be honest and state up front that you are a moonlighter. This is what I would do if I were moonlighting today, and here are the reasons:

1. I believe honesty is the best policy, dislike deception and sleep better knowing I am telling the truth at all times.

2. I also believe that people can spot deception, that telling a lie always comes back to do you damage, so it's better to be truthful from the start.

3. While it's true that many potential clients are prejudiced against moonlighters, there are many others that don't give a hoot and would just as readily hire a moonlighter as any other freelancer.

4. Once clients know and accept that you are a moonlighter, they accept the conditions and limitations involved and will actually bend over backward to accommodate your part-time schedule, making things infinitely easier for you.

Because the moonlighter is chained to a desk from 9 A.M. to 5 P.M., Monday through Friday, fifty weeks a year, he necessarily must conduct most client contacts for moonlighting business over the telephone.

The ideal situation (assuming the client knows and accepts your moonlighting status) is to agree to handle telephone contact during the weekends or evenings. Most clients will prefer evenings.

While your main contact at the client organization will accept this, some of the people in her company may not want to be bothered evenings or weekends to deal with a freelancer.

If this becomes a problem, the client may be forced to hire a full-time freelancer who is more available.

The solution is to try to take on projects for which minimal client contact (e.g., interviewing staff to gather information) is needed and most of the assignment can be written from study of existing materials that may be mailed to you and read at your leisure in the evening.

Writing an ad for a trade journal, for example, is an ideal moonlighting project, because you can do it without assistance from or contact with the client.

Writing an employee newsletter, on the other hand, might not be a suitable project if it requires extensive interviews with various employees to gather information for news stories. So you must pick your assignments carefully with this in mind.

If you moonlight, you will be sorely tempted to conduct some of your client contact work during office hours using your office telephone.

Is this OK? Only you can answer whether such activity goes against your own ethical system.

When I was moonlighting, I did occasionally use my office telephone to talk with my moonlighting clients during office hours. However, all calls were local, conversations were kept short and I did this only during my lunch break or other times when activity was slow and I had spare time on my hands.

I found this to be acceptable personal use of the office telephone. Would my employer have agreed? I don't know. But I was comfortable with it. As for you, you'll have to make your own decision.

What about meeting moonlighting clients when you hold a nine-to-five job? It's difficult, but sometimes necessary. Here are some suggestions:

1. Tell the client up front that you are a moonlighter and not generally available for meetings during business hours. If the client accepts this and hires you, she will generally work to accommodate your schedule.
2. Try to handle most of your work by phone and mail. Do not accept assignments that you feel necessitate extensive face-to-face meetings.
3. If meetings will be required, make sure the client is located near your office or home. Don't handle clients who are more than a half-hour's drive away.
4. Schedule client meetings for evenings, weekends, early morning—anytime except during the hours you are working.
5. Meet with the client at a mutually agreed-on location other than her office. The meeting will go much faster if it is held off her premises. A restaurant where you can do business over breakfast, lunch, dinner or even after-work drinks is a good choice, provided it is not too crowded or too noisy.
6. If the client insists on meeting with you during business hours, try for 11 A.M. or 1 or 2 P.M. and then take an early or late lunch.
7. If a long lunch is not enough time or the meeting cannot be held during these hours, you may have to take a vacation or personal day. Tip: If your employer will allow it, use vacation or personal days in *half-day* increments. This enables you to schedule more meetings on your limited number of off-days.

Another issue for moonlighters: Is it OK to use company facilities and supplies to conduct your moonlighting business? Here again, the answer can be supplied only from your personal ethical code.

Obviously, it would not be OK with company management, if they knew. On the other hand, employees have been known to make a personal call or two on the WATS line or run off fifty copies of their daughters' resumes on the office copier.

But whatever you do, don't abuse any privileges. Remember, your moonlighting venture is for *your* personal gain. Your employer gets no benefit from it. And I'm sure if *you* were running your own company and had people on your payroll, you wouldn't want them stealing your supplies, running up your long-distance phone bills or operating second-income businesses using your facility as their office, right? So do unto your employer as you would have others do unto you.

How much moonlighting work should you take on? It depends, of course, on the nature of the assignments you get and how busy you want to be. In general, I would say one or two medium-size projects per month is about right. This way, you are only dealing with two clients at any one time, so the moonlighting is not unmanageable. And four weeks should be plenty of time to do the work. Try this for a few months. Then you can cut back or increase your workload as you desire.

Finally, what about income? How much money can you make moonlighting? It depends on how much work you take on plus the rates you charge.

My former boss at Westinghouse, Terry Smith, makes a nice second income giving private seminars for corporate clients. Although employed full-time as a communications manager at Westinghouse, Smith—an old-timer who has been with the firm for many years—gets five weeks vacation each year and spends most of the time operating his lucrative seminar business.

And what about you? Let's say you write booklets and ads for local businesses, charging $1,500 for a booklet or brochure and $500 for an ad. Do two assignments per month (one booklet and one ad, for example), and you earn $2,000 a month in spare-time income. Not bad.

Do that ten months of the year and that's an extra $20,000 in your pocket. Who couldn't use that? Even if you do only one small $500 assignment a month for twelve months, that's an extra $6,000 a year.

That $6,000 can buy a lot of things. A new PC. A fax machine. A photocopier. A nice used car. As for $20,000, it can be a wonderful nest egg, giving you financial freedom to start your own business—whether it's full-time commercial freelance writing or something else.

CHAPTER 3

Quick Tips and Shortcuts to Help You Write Better and Faster

BLESSED IS HE WHO HAS FOUND HIS WORK;
LET HIM ASK NO OTHER BLESSEDNESS.
—THOMAS CARLYLE

This chapter presents a miscellany of tips, techniques and methods you can use to write more in less time.

"EARLY TO BED, EARLY TO RISE"—DOES KEEPING NIGHT-OWL HOURS HURT WRITERS' PRODUCTIVITY?

Some people cannot control the hours they favor. So if you are a night owl, burning the midnight oil may result in maximum productivity for you. If you are an early bird, get up early and start writing while everyone else in your house is still asleep.

Other people find they can alter their biorhythm patterns deliberately, by controlling when they go to bed and get up. If you have a choice of whether to be an early morning person or a late nighter, and can do either, pick the one that works best for you.

If all else is equal, choose the morning. When you start early in the morning, as I do, you have the benefit of having completed a significant amount of your day's work quota by the time others are first stumbling into their offices. Early starters finish the day's work early and have the rest of the time to do more work or play. Late starters are behind from the moment they get up and feel increasing pressure to get their work done as the hour grows even later.

The easiest productivity tip in the world is to get up and start working an hour earlier than you normally do. Freelance writer

Charles Flowers says whenever he has a deadline or a lot of work on a given day, he gets up as early as he must to meet that deadline, even if it means rising at five in the morning. I have, on some days, been at the office as early as 3 or 4 A.M., although this is rare.

A SUREFIRE TECHNIQUE FOR MAINTAINING PEAK ENERGY THROUGHOUT THE DAY

Energy is a function of many factors, one of them being enthusiasm. When you are enthusiastic, your energy can remain high, even if you are physically tired. When you are bored, your energy drains, and you become lethargic and unproductive.

To maintain peak productivity and energy, maintain peak enthusiasm and avoid boredom. The main cause of boredom for writers is not doing what they want, when they want to do it. Therefore, you should structure your work so you are spending most of your time doing what you want, when you feel like it.

Obviously, you should avoid assignments that bore you. Forcing yourself to work on these will drain your energy. But even those assignments that interest you can get boring if you work on them too long or you don't feel like doing them at the time. The solution is to have many different projects and to work on the one you want to work on at the time. Since you set your own schedule and no one is supervising you, you can do tasks in the order that pleases you.

Of course, when a deadline is looming, you may have no choice but to put aside work you want to do and focus on what has to be done to meet that deadline. But even this is avoidable if you negotiate sufficient deadlines and then plan your time so you get started early, rather than waiting to the last minute as so many authors do.

Everyone finds something that can help revitalize him throughout the day. When you find what works for you, do it. My rented office has a private bathroom, and when the heat gets to me in summer months, I wash my hair and feel better—perhaps the wet head of hair cools my overheated brain. In the winter, I enjoy a cup of homemade soup from the bagel shop across the street as a pick-me-up during the day.

The One-Hour Module Method
Breaking large tasks into small increments makes them easier to handle. In chapter one, I discussed scheduling your daily to-do projects into one-hour increments. Even if you are working on just one project, break the day into one-hour modules and assign a different task to each module. Nine to ten in the morning might be for answering E-mail and reading the previous day's pages. Ten to eleven might be for writing new material. Eleven to noon, for doing research. And so on.

Breaking the day into one-hour segments makes it go faster, gives you more of a feeling of accomplishment at each segment's end and results in your making better use of available time.

The Index Card Method
Another system for breaking large tasks into easier-to-manage segments uses index cards. Unlike regular notepads, index cards are ideal for making information and ideas modular, with one fact or concept per card.

I often use index cards when doing research and when making outlines. In research, list one fact per card, and be sure to note the source. So you don't have to write all the source material each time, note the full source citation on a master reference list, number the sources and then just use the source number on the individual index cards.

To use index cards when making outlines, write on the cards—one topic per card—all topics dealing with your subject matter. For an article on buying a wireless phone, for example, your topics might be PCS vs. cellular; advantages of digital; types of phones; where to buy; costs; uses and applications. You can also write subtopic ideas on separate cards.

Arrange your topic cards in logical order on your desk, from left to right. Put the appropriate subtopic cards under each topic card. Then arrange the subtopic cards in order. Now you have a completed outline you can type up for permanent reference.

DESIGNING YOUR WORK SPACE FOR MAXIMUM PRODUCTIVITY
A computer tech I recently hired to do some work for me commented, "I really like your computer system—everything is in easy reach." He then mentioned that in many personal computer

systems, the owners put vital components, such as the CPU or disk drive or printer, on the floor, under a desk or otherwise out of reach. I've seen that and feel it wastes effort and time. My philosophy is that everything you need—computer systems, office equipment, the telephone, supplies, reference materials, files—should be reachable just by swiveling in your chair and reaching out to the appropriate cabinet, shelf, or drawer—without having to get out of your seat. This is the way my office is organized, and while the lack of exercise does my increasingly fat stomach no good, this arrangement saves time and contributes to my high degree of productivity.

Paper Filing Systems That Work

Avoid using manila file folders stacked in file-cabinet drawers. These flimsy file folders are difficult to find and separate and often slide under one another, making them easy to lose. Use sturdier hanging file folders and file cabinets with high-walled drawers designed to hold these folders. If your file cabinet has regular low-walled drawers, you can buy and easily put in adapter brackets to hold the hanging files.

Don't get fancy with file labeling. Use commonsense labeling and file in alphabetical order. Don't cram files in drawers; this makes them difficult to find and discourages you from even looking. When space gets tight, go through your files and throw away old and obsolete material. Or buy additional file cabinets.

Handling Paperwork and Work Flow Efficiently

Set up a double- or triple-decker in-basket or a separate small set of files for handling incoming paper. I plan my day so I have time every day to go through incoming papers. This way, I can take care of each piece of paper on the spot. If you let papers pile up in in-baskets or to-do files, you may find yourself missing deadlines, payments and other commitments. Many of the papers will become too old to be meaningful by the time you get to them. And the growing stacks of papers to attend to will become depressing and disheartening. Handle each piece of paper as it comes in, and you'll get things done faster, on time and with less stress.

When you have to store papers, use hanging files and file cabinets. Avoid heaping file folders on desks, chairs and other surfaces. Keep working surfaces clean. For the writer, better organization translates directly into getting more done in less time. Poor organization wastes time and can result in loss of important materials.

ELECTRONIC FILING SYSTEMS THAT WORK

Electronic files are as important as or more important than paper files. Your hard disk files, containing your writing and research from many projects, are some of your freelance writing business's most important resources. Here are some tips for managing these files more productively:

1. Keep a set of "boilerplate" files. These are pieces of text you've written for one job that you can reuse in other jobs. If you write articles, for example, one boilerplate file might be your author's bio that appears at the end of each article. If you write grant proposals, much of the language might be similar or even exactly the same from proposal to proposal. Why reinvent the wheel each time? Name these files and keep a master list of them so you can find them easily when you need them.

2. Get a scanner. Many times, you'll be lifting (with appropriate permission, of course) sentences and paragraphs from other documents. It's a waste of time to key this into your computer. Scanning saves a lot of time. You can buy a decent scanner today for under $500. Better still is to have an assistant who can do the scanning for you. Just tell your assistant what material you need; she scans it and E-mails it to you for downloading onto your hard disk.

   If I find good material for a project, I give it to my assistant to scan early. That way, when I'm up against a deadline, it's right there for me to use. If I wait until the last minute, there may not be time to scan it and I'll have to rekey it myself or not use it.

3. Seek and build a library of copyright-free material on subjects you write about. This material can also be scanned and dropped into your text as needed. Hint: The U.S. government is one of the country's largest publishers, and most of its material is copyright free. This means you can lift and use it in your own writing without asking permission. For a free catalog of some useful government publications, write

Consumer Information Center, Pueblo, Colorado 81009, or phone (719) 948-3334.

4. Use logical filenames—JSMEM1, for example, for memo number one to John Smith, or OUTSART1 for an article on outsourcing.

5. Always type the filename at the top of page one of the document, as follows: "filename: OUTSART1." Often you find something you've written in a file folder and then want to find the electronic file for it on your hard disk. Putting the name of every file on the first page of the document makes it easy to find the electronic file. If you can't, you have to scan or retype the material, which is boring as well as a waste of your time.

6. Use your word processor's cut and paste feature to quickly and easily move sentences, paragraphs and even pages between different files. When possible, recycle and reuse material in multiple projects. Again, why reinvent the wheel? If you are going to be writing a short description of crystallography in many different books and articles, have a standard one- or two-paragraph write-up you cut and paste wherever you need it.

7. Manage your hard disk files as a resource, just as a mining company would consider gold ore its resource. Recycle and reuse material as much as you can. You save time and multiply your profits many times over. Of course, you must follow copyright laws when using existing material (see Appendix B).

8. If you have boilerplate text you want to use in a book, copyright that text in your company name, if you have one. Then have your company give you, as an individual, permission to reprint the material. This way, your company retains the copyright and can reuse the material in many places, even though it appears in a book where the reprint rights are controlled by the publisher.

9. Whenever you have a writing project, immediately create a file for it. Fill in all the routine information you can, including title, byline, headers, footers, page numbers, subheads, references, author's bio. If you've prepared an outline, add it to your document file. Then writing simply becomes a matter of filling in the blanks under each heading and subhead.

Having the basic file for your document set up and ready to go in this fashion gives you the electronic equivalent of what Stephen King calls in *The Dark Tower: The Gunslinger* the "unholy exhilaration of blank paper." By getting the mechanics of writing out of the way, you can more easily concentrate on the fun part and progress faster. When the document file is open and ready before you, you can't help but start writing. It's a great tool for overcoming procrastination and writer's block.

BUILDING YOUR REFERENCE LIBRARY

Every freelance writer should start building a reference library of books on the subjects he most frequently writes about. If you are a medical writer, for example, buy books on health care and medicine. If you specialize in travel, collect the Fodor's guides. It's not essential to have a complete reference library when you're starting out; building one is something you can do gradually.

As a writer, you can improve your productivity tremendously by having the information you need at your fingertips. If you have to run to the public library to get missing facts, you will waste an enormous amount of time—time that could be spent writing.

A good reference library puts needed facts at your fingertips. For example, I specialize in computers, so I have more than twenty books about computers. I also have a lot of books about business, chemistry, energy, alternative and mainstream medicine, and investing because I do a lot of work in these fields.

The best way to acquire a good library without spending a lot of money is to frequent used book sales sponsored by local libraries. Here you will find incredible bargains. I recently purchased the 950-page *Encyclopedia of Banking and Finance* for $.50 and the twenty-volume *American Peoples Encyclopedia* for $20. Granted, you won't get new editions or mint-condition books at these sales, but older editions are fine for your purposes. I also bought last year's *Books in Print* for only $1 per volume.

The Barnes and Noble mail-order catalog is loaded with fantastic reference books at bargain prices. For a free copy of this catalog, call Barnes and Noble at (800) THE-BOOK. Become familiar with your local secondhand bookstore; often the proprietor will locate items for you if they are not in stock.

Keep your reference library small and up-to-date. Every year or so, go through the books. If a book is outdated because the information in the field has changed, throw it out. Also get rid of books you haven't looked at over the last few years; chances are, you will never open them again.

You should start a clipping file of articles related to the industries and subjects you write about. I have thick files labeled Chemical Industry, Computers, Telecommunications, Energy, Health Care, Careers and Finance because I regularly handle assignments in these areas. My files include article clippings, booklets, ads I've torn out of magazines and brochures I've collected at trade shows and conventions.

I also keep extensive files for all of my clients. These files include the clients' ads and brochures as well as ads and sales literature produced by their competitors. Be sure to update such files regularly. Otherwise you risk extracting information from them that is out-of-date, which can introduce errors into your copy.

Build your article file as you build your book library. Keep organized clipping files on all subject areas in which you write. Spend at least fifteen to thirty minutes a day reading newspapers and magazines. Scan them for pertinent articles; clip and file information you can use in articles and books. Stay in this scanning mode; avoid the trap of getting caught up in miscellaneous reading, which can cut into your productive hours. Always jot the source (magazine or newspaper, issue date and page number) on clippings. This saves time tracking sources later.

USING THE INTERNET TO CUT YOUR RESEARCH TIME

Although the how-to's of mastering the Internet are beyond the scope of this book, any Internet skills you gain will be worth the investment you make to gain them a hundred times over or more.

You can cut your research time substantially by using the Internet as a research tool. Although there are many ways to do research on the Internet, the most important one for you to learn is how to do subject-matter searches of the World Wide Web using search engines.

Search engines are tools that automatically find and tell you about Web sites containing information on the topic you're interested in. The search engine goes through Web sites by keyword and matches selected Web sites as closely as possible to the topic you want searched.

The Internet access provided by your online service or Internet services provider (ISP) has an icon or button you can click on to do a search. Call tech support if you're not sure which one it is.

Click on that button. You will be asked to type in the name of the search subject. The more specific you are, the better the matches. So it's better to type "software asset management" if that's what you want to learn about, rather than just "software."

You will be asked which search engine you want to use. You can run the search with one search engine or multiple search engines. But each search is performed sequentially, not simultaneously. So if you want to search "whales" on three search engines, you must run a search on each.

There are a number of standard search engines available, many with colorful names. Your ISP probably offers a choice. According to a recent article in *Family PC*, the most popular search engines include Yahoo, Lycos, InfoSeek and Excite. I start with Yahoo and InfoSeek and then go to the others if I need more information.

When you run the search, the computer displays a list of Web site names and brief descriptions. To check out a Web site, just click on its name. You get the information instantly. Speed and the large amount of information available are the two main advantages of the Internet. Convenience is another. It's available twenty-four hours a day, seven days a week. No more waiting for the library to be open or a magazine to come out on a newsstand.

When you find something useful, print the Web pages that contain the information you need. Keep these in your folder for that project.

The one disadvantage of Internet research is a concern over the quality of the information. Since it's so easy to host a Web site, anyone can do it, and at times it seems almost everyone has. Businesses have promotional agendas, and individuals may be unreliable, so the accuracy of information you find on the Internet can rightly be called into question. Evaluate it based on the content and the reputation of the Web site sponsor, and make your own judgment.

This problem of information uncertainty is not new. Writers have a long tradition of lifting information from secondary source material without verifying its accuracy firsthand. Errors in one article are often repeated in other pieces in which the original article was used as a reference. The Internet did not create this problem; it merely makes the sin easier to commit and more widespread.

GETTING OTHERS TO DO YOUR
RESEARCH AND WRITING FOR YOU

If you are writing a piece in which you wish to quote others or use their opinions, the Internet provides a timesaving alternative to conducting interviews, typing handwritten or taped notes and editing them into usable material.

Just go on Internet chat rooms and forums where people who know a lot about your topics hang out. Post a question and ask for comments. Mention that you're writing an article or book and may want to use their comments.

People will write back, often giving you great answers that are more articulate and better thought-out than what they'd say in a face-to-face or phone interview. Even better, these answers are all written out, so you can print them—or even just lift them from the E-mail and paste them directly into your notes or document. It's a great technique that saves time while actually enhancing the quality and quantity of your primary research. Try it.

Although the Internet is the best medium for this method, it isn't absolutely required. Once, when planning a book on careers for writers, I asked several writer friends to write me short letters telling me how they got into the business and giving tips for novices. When it came time to write the book, I got a lot of good material straight from these letters, without doing any interviewing or transcribing.

CALL BEFORE YOU GO

Before going to any meeting outside the office, I call the person I am meeting with to confirm. Some writers don't do this, fearing a confirmation call will give the client, editor, publisher, agent or interview subject an opportunity to postpone or cancel. But your time is the only thing you have to sell. Why waste it in unproductive travel or encounters?

Early in my career, I heard a commercial on the radio from a business selling billy goats for people to use to cut their lawns. Thinking this would make a nice feature for a newspaper I was freelancing for, I called the man and scheduled the interview.

After driving 75 miles to his place of business, I met him and asked to see the billy goats. "Here they are," he said proudly, waving his arm to indicate a roomful of shiny new power lawn mowers—which, I discovered upon inspection, were of a brand name called Billy Goat! Had I checked and clarified the situation before going there, I would have saved myself three hours, 150 miles of driving and embarrassment in explaining to my editor why no story on lawn-eating billy goats would be forthcoming.

QUICK TIPS FOR COPYEDITING AND PROOFREADING YOUR WORK BETTER AND FASTER

Best-selling novelist Sol Stein offers these quick editing tips:

- Cut most adjectives and adverbs.
- Cut clichés.
- Replace or cut similes and metaphors that don't work.

"Do you see any places where you might have padded the manuscript with unnecessary digressions, overly extensive patches of description, or anything else that strikes you as filler? You always strengthen text when you remove the padding," says Stein in his book *Stein on Writing.*

WORK WITH A COAUTHOR

Right now, I am teaming up with several coauthors on book and copywriting projects. One is a semicelebrity. Another is a millionaire entrepreneur and inventor. They provide the source material; I write the piece. Without these coauthors on my team, I would have a much harder time selling publishers on hiring me to handle the topics we are tackling together. Also, their reputations add credibility and, hopefully, will make readers want to buy our writings.

Another strategy is to coauthor with a fellow writer. I have done this on several occasions. You split the income, but you also split the work. So again, you can write more in less time. Another advantage of this arrangement: Since you can share the writing of article sections or book chapters with the coauthor, you avoid writing on topics you're not interested in.

When Gary Blake and I coauthored *Dream Jobs* for John Wiley, we had ten chapters—ten essays on careers in ten different industries. I wrote about the industries that interested me—

advertising, cable television, finance; Blake handled topics I was disinterested in—fashion, food, travel.

KEEP BUSY AND PRODUCTIVE

Isaac Asimov said he could never be stopped by writer's block because he had so many different projects he was working on simultaneously. If he got tired of writing an essay, he simply stopped and began work on a short story or novel instead. When he wound down on the novel, he'd move to a nonfiction book project or column.

DON'T OVERRESEARCH OR OVERWRITE

Robert Louis Stevenson once said, "The only art is to omit." While it's better to have somewhat more research and even somewhat more text than you need to make your space allocation or word count, going *too* overboard on excessive research and writing wastes your time.

Don't make things more complicated than they need to be. This includes the content, the concepts and the text of your writing. Don't overthink the piece. Keep things simple. If it's so complicated to you, the writer, that you barely understand what you have written, it will be unfathomable to most of your readers.

In a letter to Marilyn vos Savant, published in *Parade*, one correspondent gives this advice: "When promulgating your esoteric cogitations or articulating your superficial sentimentalities and amicable philosophical and psychological observations, beware of platitudinous ponderosity. Let your verbal evaporations have lucidity, intelligibility, and veracious vivacity without rodomontade or thespian bombast. Sedulously avoid all polysyllabic profundity, pompous propensity, and sophomoric vacuity."

Translation: Don't use big words. "When possible, use short, simple words that most people understand," writes John Daly in *Proof.* "At the same time, don't be afraid to use the exact word when that will do the trick, even if it's a bit longer."

VALUE YOUR TIME AND SPEND IT PRODUCTIVELY

Don't go to the library to look up a fact when you can call the research librarian and have her read it to you over the phone. Do interviews by phone instead of in person whenever possible to avoid travel and meeting time. My experience is that a twenty-minute telephone interview can yield information equivalent to a two-hour in-person meeting.

Another advantage of phone interviews is that you can type notes directly onto your PC. This eliminates the incredibly time-intensive activity of transcribing tape-recorded interviews—a task that can rapidly move a writing project from the black into the red. If you do tape-record, have someone else transcribe the tape for you.

If you interview people in person, consider replacing your tape recorder and notepad with a laptop or notebook computer. Denny Hatch, author of several novels and publisher of *Target Marketing* magazine, says taking interview notes with a laptop eliminates the time of transcribing tapes while resulting in more complete and accurate notes than scribbling with pad and pencil.

When interviewing sources, avoid promising to run copy by them for approval unless they insist on it. This review process will hold you up, slow your progress and create extra and unnecessary work. Have the subject review what you've written only if you feel it is beneficial to you. But don't make it your standard operating procedure.

I have never admired writers who spend more time talking about writing—going to conferences and readings, discussing literature at writers groups and book groups, daydreaming about being famous authors—than actually doing it. In addition to being a waste of time, it gives you the illusion that you are making more progress in your career than you actually are. "The wannabe writer has to commit," said the late Erma Bombeck in one of her syndicated newspaper columns. "Stop talking about clever titles and get the book written."

One writer who "gets the book written" is Ridley Pearson, author of the best-selling novel *Undercurrents*. Within 8½ years, he has produced nine screenplays and two books. He does as many as eight full drafts before he considers a novel good enough to send to his publisher.

WHEN YOU ARE "ON A ROLL," DON'T STOP

Keep going until the energy runs out. For example, I am typing this in my office at 8 P.M. on a Wednesday night. My wife called and asked me to come home an hour earlier to bring ingredients for dinner, but I said no, because I had a momentum going with this piece and didn't want to lose it. When she asked when I'd be home, I told her I didn't know; when I lost the momentum, I'd stop, turn off the PC and go home.

By the same token, don't wait for inspiration to start writing. Set regular hours and write during that time, even if you don't feel like it. "Inspiration doesn't pay anything," says Terry Whalin, author of more than forty books. "I'm an assignment writer. . . . I work under deadline. If someone says he needs his piece by four o'clock, I do it."

DO NOT ACCEPT THE FIRST OFFER EVERY EDITOR, PUBLISHER OR CLIENT MAKES

Negotiate for higher fees, bigger advances, larger royalties. When you are paid more, you'll feel better about your writing and do it with more enthusiasm.

At times, of course, you will take on quickie jobs for short pay. We all do. The key is to do them quickly and move on. Don't agonize for weeks over a book review for which you are being paid $10—it isn't economically feasible. Agonize instead over the annual report for which you are being paid $10,000.

PART TWO

WRITING MORE

Writers can earn more money by producing more work. Writing faster can contribute to this. But there are other ways to get more done, including making the best use of available time, working diligently, avoiding procrastination and not slacking off. Importantly, being prolific has to be a goal in itself; if you don't want to produce more, you probably won't.

CHAPTER 4

Do You Really Want to Be Prolific?

AS IS THE CASE IN ALL BRANCHES OF ART, SUCCESS DEPENDS IN A VERY LARGE
MEASURE UPON INDIVIDUAL INITIATIVE AND EXERTION, AND CANNOT BE
ACHIEVED EXCEPT BY DINT OF HARD WORK.

—ANNA PAVLOVA

The primary reason most writers are not prolific is they do
not really desire it. Isaac Asimov wanted to write a lot of
books, so he designed his life to increase his output (this included
focusing on topics on which he could produce books quickly
and avoiding travel so he could spend most of his time in his
study). Donald Hall, the poet, puts perfection before productivity
and so has revised at least one of his poems more than six hundred times! This chapter presents guidelines to help you assess
whether being prolific is important to you and whether you are
willing to do what is necessary to achieve superior productivity.
As author Derrick Welch says in his book *Defy Mediocrity*, "Ideas
without action are useless."

SET YOUR GOALS HIGH
Most writers who are ambitious look at other writers, see what
they produce and set their own goals slightly higher.

Unfortunately, this won't make you prolific. The majority of
writers have limited outputs, and therefore, even if they do 10
percent more, their outputs will still be small.

Do not use the average writer as a role model for productivity. I am amazed at the number of people I meet at writers
conferences who are full-time writers but have produced such

a small body of work. What do they do all day? How do they live?

When hearing of a famous literary novelist who was coming out with his first new novel in half a decade, Stephen King once commented, "Come on . . . it doesn't take five years to write a novel." We prolific writers want to get the job done, polish it and move on to the next piece. We care about writing and value quality, but we strive for excellence rather than perfection.

In his book *How to Write Fast,* David Fryxell gives the following examples of prolific, productive writers:

- Charles Harold St. John Hamilton, British author (1876– 1961), 75 million words, as much as 80,000 words a week
- South African novelist Kathleen Lindsay (1903–73), 904 novels
- Mystery writer John Creasy (1908–73), 564 books, got 743 rejection slips before getting published
- Georges Simenon (1903–89), Belgian mystery writer, Inspector Maigret series, over 500 books

Use these folks as your role models. Aspire to what they have achieved. Even if you reach only a tenth of your goal and achieve only a tenth of their output, you'll be two times more productive than 90 percent of the writers working around the world today.

I've found that prolific authors admire other prolific authors precisely because these writers are prolific. In his autobiography *It Came From Ohio!,* R.L. Stine, author of 250 books, comments: "I read an article about a writer in South America who has written over a thousand books! Sometimes he writes three books a day! My hero!"

Stine, incidentally, says he works six or seven days a week to write two books every month. Isaac Asimov worked seven days a week from 7:30 A.M. to 10:30 P.M., stopping only for business lunches, social engagements, telephone conversation and other activities he referred to as "interruptions."

Although you don't have to be a workaholic to be a prolific writer, it does help. Most writers who are more productive than their peers work more than just from nine to five. Claude Hopkins, one of the most successful advertising writers of all time, said he got twice as much accomplished as everybody else in his agency because he worked twice as hard and twice as long.

Thomas Edison, the prolific inventor, bragged about being a workaholic who only slept four or five hours a night. Frank Reick, the inventor of Tufoil motor oil additive, told me that while he was in the throes of pursuing his invention, he moved a cot into his lab so he could sleep there and not waste time going back and forth.

I am not telling you to be a workaholic or sacrifice the rest of your life. But in a sense, to be productive at anything, some sacrifices must be paid. When you get home from work, will you watch *Friends* and *Seinfeld* or work on a freelance assignment? My friend and colleague, writer Andrew Linick, pointed out to me once that everything we want—everything we want to do, learn, achieve or create—has a price. And that price is *time*. Prolific writers pay this price to be prolific. If you're not willing to pay it, there's a limit to what you can do.

Set realistic but ambitious goals. Do not be afraid to take on challenges and try new things. "In order to succeed at almost anything, it's necessary to risk failure at various times along the way," advises Dr. Joyce Brothers in her newspaper column in *Daily News*. Novelist John Creasy got 743 rejection slips, then went on to publish 564 books. In an article in the July 1997 issue of *The Writer*, freelancer Bill Vossler says, "I've published more than twenty-one hundred articles and I still get rejections, but I don't allow them to crush me and keep me from writing."

"If you stay committed, your dreams can come true," says Michael Blake, author of *Dances With Wolves*. "I left home at seventeen and had nothing but rejections for twenty-five years. I wrote more than twenty screenplays, but I never gave up." In 1889, the editor of *The San Francisco Examiner* sent Rudyard Kipling a rejection letter that said, "I'm sorry, Mr. Kipling, but you just don't know how to use the English language."

In freelance writing, age is not a barrier to success. Jenn Crowell got a six-figure advance for her first novel, *Necessary Madness*, when she was only seventeen. Ann Baer, on the other hand, published her first novel, *Down the Common*, at age eighty-two. But Baer is a youngster compared with Jessie Lee Brown Foreaux, who, at age ninety-eight, sold her first novel, *Any Given Day*, for an advance reported in the *Daily News* to be in the "strong" seven figures.

PROLIFIC WRITERS LIKE TO WRITE

May Sarton once said that while many people want to have written a book, not that many want to write one. I feel differently. And so do most of the prolific writers I know. We like to write! If we didn't, how could we put in the six to twelve hours a day or more needed to produce an unusually high output?

"My secret is that I love to write—the mechanical act of it," said Isaac Asimov in *Yours, Isaac Asimov*. "I am so ill-rounded that the ten things I love to do are: write, write, write, write, write, write, write, write, write, and write. Oh, I do other things. I even like to do other things. But when asked for the ten things I *love*, that's it."

Harlan Ellison, author of more than sixty books, said to me in an interview many years ago:

> I THINK I CAME OUT OF THE WOMB WRITING. THE FIRST THING I EVER SOLD WAS WHEN I WAS TEN YEARS OLD, A FIVE-PART SERIAL TO THE *CLEVELAND NEWS* YOUNG PEOPLE'S COLUMN, AND BEFORE THAT I WAS DOING MY OWN LITTLE NEWSPAPER IN THE NEIGHBORHOOD. I'VE ALWAYS WRITTEN. I NEVER *DECIDED* TO BE A WRITER, I WAS JUST . . . THERE'S A SCENE OUT OF A FILM CALLED *THE RED SHOES*, WHERE MOIRA SHEARER, WHO WAS A BRILLIANT BALLERINA, IS TALKING TO THE BALLET ENTREPRENEUR, A BALANCHINE KIND OF FIGURE. AND HE SAYS TO HER, "WHY MUST YOU DANCE?" SHE WANTS TO JOIN HIS COMPANY, AND SHE THINKS ABOUT IT A MOMENT AND THEN SHE SAYS TO HIM, "WHY MUST YOU BREATHE?" AND HE SAYS, "I MUST!" AND SHE SMILES AND WALKS AWAY. I DIDN'T CHOOSE TO BE A WRITER, THAT'S WHAT I AM—I'M A WRITER.

The vast majority of Americans dislike their work. "Everybody but a complete idiot or a college professor who has never hit a lick of work in their lives looks forward to quitting time, and the sooner it comes the better," a factory worker told Benjamin Hunnicutt, author of *Kellogg's Six-Hour Day*.

Perhaps the greatest advantage of the writing profession is that so many of us love our work. We want to write, and if we make enough money to freelance full-time, we can do it to the exclusion of other work tasks (meetings, project management, office politics) we do not derive satisfaction from. If you love your work, you are part of a fortunate, happy minority in today's society, and writers make up a large segment of that minority.

In an article in *The New York Times Book Review*, Paul Theroux says V.S. Pritchett once described writing as "a labor delightful because it is fanatical." Samuel Clemens commented, "Work and play are words used to describe the same thing under differing conditions," as reported in *The Sunday Record*.

Learn to like the work you do, or change to another occupation you do like," advises Dr. John A. Schindler in his book *How to Live 365 Days a Year* (which is condensed in Issue 18 of *Jerry Buchanan's Better Life Journal*). "Find your own creative discipline and the world will not be able to get you to stop long enough to get a good night's sleep."

Psychologist Mihaly Csikszentmihalyi has coined the term "flow" to describe the state of mind people are in when they love their work. According to an article in *American Way*, flow is "a state in which people are so involved in an activity that nothing else seems to matter; the experience is so enjoyable that people will do it even at great cost." If you've ever been so wrapped up in what you were writing that you didn't want to stop, you were probably in flow. The more you are in flow, the more you will enjoy work, and the more productive you will be.

To be a full-time freelancer, you must be productive if you want to make a living. In an article in *The Writer*, Bill Vossler says you should not quit your day job and become a full-time freelance writer unless you have sold at least ten articles for pay and have earned at least $300 each from two of those articles. "You must start selling to the middle-tier—$300 and up—magazines before you can support yourself," notes Vossler.

Most freelance writers earn their livings doing commercial work, often on assignment for a publisher or corporate client. We practice writing as a business or craft, rather than an art. Yet most successful writers just flat-out love the printed word. "Every word, not spoken but written, that led to others, filled his lungs with air and renewed his tie with the world," writes Peter Handke in *The Afternoon of a Writer*. Saul Bellow observed, "A writer is a reader who is moved to emulation." But in a letter to me, freelancer David Wood (who earns a six-figure income writing in New Hampshire) wrote, "the majority of neophytes aren't willing to work as hard as one must to succeed."

MONEY AND THE PROLIFIC WRITER

Do you need money? Most of us do. Unless writers are independently wealthy or have additional sources of income, they need to write to earn money to pay the rent or mortgage, health insurance premiums, utility bills, grocery costs, home maintenance expenses, doctor bills and video rental fees. But because most writers are semi-impoverished, they pretend to have an air of indifference about money. No wonder freelance writing consistently ranks among the lowest paying of the white-collar professions.

Prolific writers I have met tend to be money driven, or at least money conscious. They are not content with the meager income of the average writer. If they do not aspire to great wealth, they at least want to be comfortable. Vicki Cobb, the prolific author of more than sixty science books for young readers, once told me, "I like to write, but I want to make a lot of money!" Unless you're writing blockbuster movie scripts, best-selling novels or scripts for top TV shows, your pay per project will range from so-so to pretty good but never reach into the spectacular range. Therefore, to make a lot of money, you've got to write more (as well as sell more of what you write, for more money).

My definition of success: Doing what you want, when and where you want to do it, *and getting paid well for it—sometimes very, very well.* This is what you can achieve when you are productive and prolific and put "your nose to the grindstone" or your fingertips to the computer keys.

A wise person once remarked, "If you don't know where you are going, you are certainly never going to get there." Often his quotation is used by motivational writers and speakers addressing the topic of goal setting, but it also applies to freelance writing income.

How much money do you want? If you answered, "Enough," or, "A lot," you haven't clearly defined your income goal and hence are not working toward achieving a specific income. And without knowing where you are going, how will you get there?

As I mentioned previously, an important first step toward

increasing your income is to set a specific dollar goal. I would suggest you set an annual goal as well as a monthly goal. The annual goal helps you aim for an overall income figure; the monthly goal is simply to track your progress and make sure you are on course.

For example, let's say you want to earn $74,000 a year. That's a monthly income of $7,000. If you fall short for a few months, that's OK; it merely tells you that you must step up your income in the later months to stay on track. However, if after twelve months, your income adds up to less than $74,000, you have not met your goal.

And that's OK. The purpose of setting a goal is not necessarily to meet it but to provide a target toward which all your efforts are focused. Even if you do not earn the specific dollar figure, just having a goal and working toward it will have increased your earnings far beyond what you would have made just struggling along like everyone else. A goal gives you something to set your sights on, inspires hard work and is a catalyst for success.

Goals should be ambitious but realistic. As a self-employed writer, you can earn $50,000 or $150,000 or more, but it would be unrealistic to expect to make, say, $300,000 your first year or even in several years.

Advertising executive and founder of his own ad agency, Leo Burnett is credited with the following observation: "If you reach for the stars and fall, you will get the moon. But if you reach just for a tree branch and fall, you will end up in the mud." In other words, it's always better to set your goals a little higher, a little beyond your reach, rather than make them too easy. The goal should be difficult, because success requires hard work and a bit of ambition. If you set easy goals, you'll always achieve them, but you'll always achieve something easy. That applies to income as well as to output.

Another story (and I hope the author will forgive me, but I can't recall the source): Two salespeople decide one year that they will set sales goals. Each writes his goal on a sheet of paper. At the end of the year, they meet.

The first salesman opens his paper and says to the second salesman, "See, here is my goal: $50,000 in sales commissions per year. And I have done it. I achieved my goal!" He turns to his friend: "And how did you do?"

"Not as well," confesses the second salesman. "See, here is my goal, $1 million in sales—and I, unlike you, have achieved only half of *my* goal."

Here are some suggestions for making the most productive use of your time (that is, spending more time on billable tasks):

1. Work on client projects when you are freshest and most energetic. For me, this is in the earlier part of the day—from 7 A.M. until about 1 P.M.

2. If you are very busy this week, don't even leaf through the trade journals and magazines you get. Instead, throw them out.

3. Tell people who are calling you simply to be social or for free advice that you are too busy to talk and they should call you back in a month or so—or you will call them back.

4. When you get tired of working on a project, don't force yourself to continue (unless a deadline makes it necessary). Instead, put it aside and work on something else.

5. Try to conduct your activities from your office rather than making trips. Travel is an enormous time waster.

6. If you are busy working on a project and get a phone call from a client, tell the client, "I'm tied up right now and can't talk. May I call you back?" Then call back at a convenient time.

7. Try to eliminate unproductive activities that may be fun but don't add to your income. Years ago I gave up college teaching because it was taking away too much time from billable hours.

8. Try getting up earlier and putting in an extra hour every morning from Monday through Friday. That's five extra hours of writing time.

9. If you must work weekends, early Saturday morning is a good time. You can get in an extra three to five hours and still have the rest of the weekend free.

If you work on the basis of so many dollars per project, you have to figure out how many projects you can do in a week, then multiply by fifty to calculate your annual income.

Be realistic about how much you can do in a day. Example: One writer charges $300 for a radio commercial and tells me they are so simple he could probably do three or four per day. But like most people starting out, he is seriously underestimating the real work involved in getting a client, doing the research, writing the copy, sending it off, working with the ad manager on revisions, getting approval, invoicing and collecting the bill.

More likely, he could probably do two commercials on a good day, one on a not-so-good day, and some days he may have no work whatsoever. So, let's say five commercials a week. Multiplying five commercials times $300 a commercial gives $1,500 a week or $75,000 a year. Not bad.

If you are prolific, you can make a lot of money, even with smaller projects and small project fees. R.L. Stine once had a job writing the text for coloring books. Although he only got paid a flat fee of $500 per book, Stine says he was able to write two books a day. If you were to work five days a week at such a rate, you would be earning $250,000 a year!

If you deliberately choose to work on projects with a low per-hour payoff, you may get artistic satisfaction, but you are unlikely to get rich, much less make a living. I was amazed to read in James Van Hise's book *Masters of the Macabre II* that Stephen Spignesi, author of *The Complete Stephen King Encyclopedia*, spent more than eighty-five hundred hours researching and writing that 777-page book. If his advance was $10,000, that comes to $1.18 an hour! A server at McDonald's earns three times that.

SELF-ASSESSMENT TEST:
DO YOU WANT TO BE A PROLIFIC WRITER?

Respond to these statements honestly. Then score yourself and check your rating.

1. I am a perfectionist. I write and rewrite many times, because everything I do must be perfect.

   _____ True   _____ False

2. I consider myself an artist.

   _____ True   _____ False

3. The primary reward I seek from my writing is to receive lavish praise from critics and readers.

   _____ True   _____ False

4. It's very important to me to be well paid and make a lot of money from writing.

_____ True _____ False

5. I would rather write than do almost anything else.

_____ True _____ False

6. I would dislike any job I had except writing.

_____ True _____ False

7. I get a kick out of seeing my byline on lots of books and articles, and of getting samples of the many projects I write for my commercial clients.

_____ True _____ False

8. I find myself constantly keeping count of how many books, articles and other writings I have published to date. I keep a list of these things and check it often.

_____ True _____ False

9. The fact that I am so prolific is the thing people tend to notice most about me, and I like that very much.

_____ True _____ False

10. My ego is tied to my work. When I have too few projects to do or am waiting to find out from publishers, editors and clients whether I'm going to get a particular assignment, I get antsy.

_____ True _____ False

Scoring: On questions one to three, give yourself one point for every "false" answer, zero points for every "true" answer. On questions four to ten, give yourself one point for every "true" answer, zero points for every "false" answer. The more points you have, the closer your personality, attitude and beliefs are to those of most writers who are prolific.

If after answering the test questions, you feel you *do* have the personality of a prolific workaholic writer, don't fight it. The only way you are going to be really happy is if you are busy and productive. Use this book to learn how to increase your sales as well as your output.

On the other hand, if after taking the test, you feel you don't fit the profile of the prolific writer, stop and ask yourself, "Is being prolific really important to me? Is making a lot of money really important to me?" If you answer no, maybe you'll be happier slowing down, being less frantic and doing your writing at a more leisurely pace.

If you answer yes, how are you going to reconcile your desire to be prolific with the fact that you don't share the same attitudes toward writing as prolific writers do? You will either have to change some of your attitudes or habits or strike a balance between the desire to write a lot and make a lot of money and the desire to spend a large portion of your time on nonwriting activities.

If you decide to pursue a career as a prolific writer, be aware of the possibility for burnout. While being a prolific writer can be fulfilling, as human beings we have limits to our energy. If you work too hard, for too long without a break, you can become tired, fall out of "flow" and feel bored, de-energized, even depressed. The solution? Writer Dan Poynter recommends taking a week's vacation or getting involved in a totally new activity. Rest and relaxation can help recharge you when you feel burnout coming on. If you have young kids, take a week's vacation with them. If you have a significant other, travel to an exotic, romantic or exciting place. Or try a sport or an activity that always interested you but you never got around to.

CHAPTER 5

Work Habits of Prolific Writers

THE HARDER YOU WORK, THE LUCKIER YOU GET.

—GARY PLAYER

This chapter examines the work habits of some of the most prolific and productive writers—and shows you how you can adapt these habits to your own writing. Rob Gilbert, editor in chief of *Bits and Pieces*, says, "If you want to achieve a goal, find somebody who has already done it, study what they do, and model yourself after them." By taking up the habits of these highly prolific writers, you become more prolific, too.

STAY SEATED

Georges Simenon, author of the popular Inspector Maigret series of mystery novels, wrote over five hundred books. How did he do it?

Simenon said he limited his writing vocabulary to 2,000 words so he would not have to use a dictionary (there are more than 800,000 words in the English language, with 60,000 new words added since 1966). This allowed him to write continuously, without having to stop to open and search a dictionary for a word. The key to his success then, at least in part, was writing without interruption; he kept going and didn't let anything stop him while he was hot.

You've heard the term "seat of the pants" used to describe a method of working. Although it originally referred to a person who made decisions by instinct without a lot of planning or formal study, for writers the definition is different: You apply the bottom of your pants (your rear end) to the seat (your chair) and stay there until the work gets done.

This means getting into your chair, turning on your PC and *staying* there. No doing laundry. No walking the dog. No quick trips to the kitchen for a snack or to the den to watch the TV news. This sounds trivial but is in fact an important point. To get a lot of work done, workers must stay at their workstations. As a writer, your workstation is your desk and chair.

In an interview with the *Daily News*, novelist Elizabeth Richards, who earned $1.4 million for the publishing and film rights to her first novel, *Every Day*, said the best part of her job is "being able to work at home." Aside from the enjoyment, working at home or at an office near your home has the advantage of eliminating commuting, which can increase your productivity substantially. "I work in my apartment, and interruptions don't slow me down, since at the conclusion of the interruption I begin, full speed, at the point I left off," said Isaac Asimov in *Yours, Isaac Asimov.*

Many writers also say the solitude of working at home, away from a crowded office environment, helps them get more done than their corporately employed friends and neighbors do. "There comes a time when that which I write has to be written alone in silence, with no one looking over my shoulder, no one telling me a better way to write it," wrote Raymond Chandler in his essay, "A Qualified Farewell" in *The New York Times Book Review.* "It doesn't have to be great writing. It doesn't even have to be terribly good. It just has to be mine."

Another timesaving advantage of working at home is the ability to eliminate the bother and trouble of buying, wearing, laundering and dry-cleaning business clothes. It also eliminates the time-consuming task of making yourself well coifed each morning. *Worth* magazine reports that 90 percent of U.S. corporations have casual-dress days, up from 63 percent in 1992. Big deal. Virtually 100 percent of freelance writers I know have casual-dress day *every* day!

Yes, I realize that the hard-working, stay-at-home writer risks becoming an out-of-shape blob. According to the *UC Berkeley Wellness Letter*, a 130-pound person burns only forty-eight calories during thirty minutes of typing—less than she would use drawing, walking or playing the piano. Writing is sedentary work, so you must do other exercise to keep fit.

DESIGN YOUR OFFICE FOR
SEAT-OF-THE-PANTS OPERATION

When I say your key work habit as a prolific writer is to put your rear end in a chair and stay in it, I mean it literally. The more you are able to work continuously at your desk without interruption, the more you get done.

Therefore, I recommend you design your work space to minimize distractions and the need to get up. My office is on the quiet third floor of a small office building in northern New Jersey. At home, I would be constantly interrupted by my family, neighbors, salespeople and service personnel. Even on the busy first floor of this office building, there would be noise, delivery people knocking on the door and asking if I know where Mr. X's office is and other interruptions. But almost no one comes to the third floor. There is only one other office up here. My work space is quiet, and I can get a lot of work done.

All the materials I need—files, reference books, supplies, computer equipment, telephone, fax, copier—are right at hand. I can swivel in my chair or reach over to get what I need, without getting up and trekking across the room.

When you build your reference library, be generous yet selective. This means don't acquire a book unless it relates to the subjects you write on. By the same token, if you see a book you know would be useful, buy it right then and there. Don't hesitate because of the price; it's a small investment to save valuable time later to get information you need.

GET THE FIRST DRAFT DOWN ON DISK OR PAPER

Prolific writers Sidney Sheldon and Barbara Cartland dictate drafts then have their staffs transcribe their novels for editing. Copywriter Sig Rosenblum, who has written thousands of sales letters and direct-mail packages, dictates his first draft into a tape recorder.

I'm not suggesting you give up the keyboard for the tape recorder and dictate instead of type. But you can take your lead from Sheldon, Cartland and Rosenblum and learn to "dictate on paper" to boost your productivity.

By this, I mean you should get a rough first draft on paper fairly early in the writing process, tackling what many writers feel is the most difficult step. Once you've done this, you'll find you can relax because, in a sense, the piece is already "written." Now all you have to do is revise and polish.

Try this on your next project. You'll feel less pressured and more relaxed when you get a working draft "in the can" early; this relief of pressure actually allows you to work on the rest of the project more enthusiastically with less anxiety. You enjoy writing more, so you spend more time writing.

SET A PRODUCTION GOAL

Stephen King writes 1,500 words every day except his birthday, Christmas and the Fourth of July.

Ted Nicholas, author of the best-selling book *How to Form Your Own Corporation Without a Lawyer for Under $75*, recommends you write three double-spaced typewritten pages a day, six days a week. The pages do not have to be perfect, because you can edit and rewrite later.

"The important thing is to get the ideas down on paper," says Nicholas in the *Direct Marketing Success Letter, Special Edition*. "Make sure you complete three pages no matter what." Following this plan, you will have a finished book in three to four months.

If you don't like setting page or word goals, Nicholas recommends you write for two hours a day, six days a week. "Sometimes people are more productive using specific time as a daily goal. For many writers, blocks of time set aside is a better inducement for them in completing a book than anything else."

The writer who wants to meet deadlines and be successful sets a production goal and achieves it. The writer who truly wants to be prolific sets a production goal, meets it and then *keeps going* until he can do no more—or runs out of time—for the day. In an interview with *Dan's Paper*, writer Daniel Stern says he tells students in his writing courses "to write every day, to finish everything, even if it's bad, and to revise, revise, revise."

ENJOY THE WORK PROCESS

"I like my own writing—another secret to prolificity, since I can't wait till I write something so I can *read* it," said Isaac Asimov.

I don't know if liking to write can be taught, but motivational experts say we do have the ability to change our attitudes and behavior. Whatever your motivation, use it to enjoy not only being a writer, but the actual writing process itself. My motivation is avoiding boredom. Every day I come into my office and turn on the computer, I'm thankful I can make a good living writing and therefore don't have to do some nine-to-five job that would bore me.

Many prolific writers love writing so much, they never stop. English major Lee Falk, for example, created *The Phantom*, which was recently made into a feature film, in 1936. Six decades later, Falk, in his eighties, was still writing the comic strip, which appears daily.

"Enjoy your achievements as well as your plans," advised Max Ehrmann in his 1927 essay "Desiderata." "Keep interested in your own career, however humble; it is a real possession in the changing fortunes of time."

WORK DURING PEAK ENERGY TIMES IN A COMFORTABLE ENVIRONMENT

One proven way to increase your output is to write when you have the most energy and when conditions are best. If you're a morning person, take advantage of that energy by writing in the early hours, before the sun comes up. Poet Donald Hall and novelist Georges Simenon, both early risers, finished most of their pressing work each day by lunchtime.

My peak periods vary, but usually I follow Hall and Simenon and start early. You may be a night person. Do what works for you.

I believe a comfortable writing environment increases productivity, but space and solitude also help. Arrange to have an office large enough to hold your equipment and files. Do not have a TV in your office. Do have a radio or stereo if background music helps you work, as it does in my case.

Plenty of desk space and file cabinet storage also boost productivity. There's room to organize and store work materials so they're close at hand and easy to find. Having to search for a book or folder wastes time and can cause you to lose your pace when you're in a writing groove. I have two desks and two large tables in my office, so there is plenty of surface space for various writing projects.

Keep organized clipping files on all subject areas in which you write. Spend at least thirty minutes a day reading newspapers and magazines. Scan them for pertinent articles; clip and file information you can use in articles and books. Stay in this scanning mode; avoid the trap of getting caught up in miscellaneous reading, which can cut into your productive hours.

Always jot the source (magazine or newspaper, issue date and page number) on clippings. This saves time tracking sources later.

MAKE THE MOST USE OF THE TIME AVAILABLE TO YOU

Managing your time effectively is one of the greatest challenges facing the freelance writer and other self-employed professionals.

For most of us, our time is the only thing we sell. We don't have employees who earn money for us while they work, thus multiplying our income potential. We don't have products that can earn additional income independent of our creative efforts. We don't have vast estate holdings or big financial deals that bring in wealth while we laze in the sun. Nor do we hold patents on inventions that earn big royalties year after year.

We only make money when we work. Our time is all we have to sell. And since the supply is limited, it's important to manage time effectively and make every hour as profitable as possible. Although royalties can add to income, 99 percent of authors live on fees, not royalties.

The difficulty in managing our time as freelancers is caused by the fact that we rarely have just the "right amount" of work to do. Most freelancers feel they either don't have enough work or, if they are busy, have too much work and are overloaded.

For beginners, the problem is usually not having enough work. This section of chapter five is written to tell you (1) how to make the most of slow time so every hour is spent productively instead of wasted, and (2) what you can do to increase your business and start shrinking the frequency and length of those slow periods. Later, I'll talk about the opposite problem, giving you some time-management tips on what to do when you have too much work and feel too pressured.

People have a misconception about being busy vs. not being busy. They think that if you are not busy, you don't expend much effort and therefore have lots of leftover energy, while if you are busy, you come home exhausted from doing all that work.

Actually, the opposite is true. If you are not busy, time drags, the day seems endless and you drift through work in a malaise. Think back and remember the last time you were stuck in a boring class in college or high school, had to go to church or synagogue when you didn't feel like it or had to listen to a boring speech, lecture or conversation. You'd look at your watch and it'd say 10 A.M. You'd drift off, look at your watch an hour later, and it'd say 10:01 A.M.!

Actually, an hour *hadn't* passed; but when you were bored, the minutes *seemed* like hours! Being bored drains you, saps your energy; and not having enough work to fill one's day can be terribly demoralizing to the self-employed professional working at home. Don't worry—I'm going to help you avoid it.

As for the opposite situation—being too busy—although this may physically tire you, mentally you will feel happy, fulfilled, even energized. At the beginning of the day, you'll plunge into your tasks, knowing you are a productive individual with plenty of projects to attend to. At the end of the day, you'll turn off your PC, put your feet up and reflect on your success, happy that you achieved much during the day yet still have a full schedule of more high-paying work to keep you busy.

USE TIME PRODUCTIVELY

Let's say you are just starting out in this business and do not have enough work to keep busy eight hours a day, five days a week. This is only natural. Even years from now, you may have weeks or even months when things are slow. The key is to keep busy and productive during these hours so they are not wasted. The temptation is to plop into bed for a nap or watch television. Don't do it! Always consider working hours *as* working hours, and make a commitment to do work during them.

How can you spend these hours productively if you have only one or two small assignments? The answer: time fillers. These are activities that you don't do as normal parts of your routine, but you do when you have extra time on your hands. The important thing about a time filler is that it earns you extra income, enhances your professional growth in some way or has some other productive goal. Its purpose is to *avoid* wasting spare time and instead to use it productively.

Here are time fillers you can use to turn your "dead time" into productive, profitable time:

1. **Write magazine articles.** If you have spare time, says successful direct-mail writer Milt Pierce, write a magazine article. Writing articles keeps your writing muscles in shape, earns income, gets your name around and provides you with writing credentials that impress clients. Reprints of articles can even be used in promotional mailings aimed at getting new clients.

   Your own experience is often the best source for articles. Years ago, I had the unpleasant experience of having two of my books go out of print because the publisher went out of business. This gave me the idea for an article on the subject for *Writer's Digest*, and I proposed a short article on "What to do when your book goes out of print." One week later I got the go-ahead to do the article. It was a nice change of pace from my usual work; and in the process, I earned a fast $350.

2. **Work on a book.** Spend your spare hours writing sample chapters or a proposal for a book, fiction or nonfiction. If you can sell the book to a publisher, writing the book is an ideal project for filling empty time between client assignments. For the fifteen years I have freelanced, I have almost always had at least one book contract in my files. This way, I had the psychological cushion of knowing that no matter what happened in my business, I always had a book to work on and thus could always (truthfully) say I was busy. A book is a great time filler: fun, profitable, prestige building and long-range—it can keep you busy for nine months or more.

3. **Do pro bono work.** Is there a favorite charitable cause that could use your writing talents? Perhaps a local animal shelter, senior citizens group, library fund-raising drive or community theater. If your schedule is not filled to overflowing with commercial assignments, volunteer to contribute your services to a worthy cause for low pay or no pay. In addition to sharpening your skills and making you feel good about yourself, you will be helping others and making useful contacts with people who may be in a position to hire you on a paying basis.

4. **Take a part-time job.** Many advertising agencies, publishers, and PR firms hire freelance writers on a part-time basis. The writer works, almost like an employee, in the agency's offices one or two days per week according to a regular schedule. Although the pay may not match your regular fees, it can be quite good and it does give you a steady weekly paycheck. This type of activity eliminates the angst that comes from being without work, and instead of having to find enough freelance work to fill five days a week, now you only have to fill three or four days. Try it!

5. **Become a publisher.** Many of my freelance friends, especially those with desktop publishing systems, are constantly toying with the idea of publishing their own books or other information products, such as reports, newsletters or cassette programs.

   This makes good sense. If you are a writer, you are probably an expert in one or more fields. (For example, two of my fields of expertise are direct mail/direct marketing and how to make money as a freelance commercial writer.) A self-published book provides a vehicle through which you can sell your expertise without actually having to render a service to a client. As a result, you escape from being restricted to selling your own time and you actually have a "product" that can make you money even when you're not working. In my "product line," I have seven reports, half a dozen books (not self-published; I sell books I've published with major publishing houses), several audiocassettes and even a video.

6. **Teach.** In the 1980s, I taught adult education evening classes in writing at New York University as well as several other adult education programs. Although the pay is meager, any extra dollars in your pocket are welcome, especially at the beginning of your career.

   Teaching a class offers a number of other advantages. First, writers are often too solitary for their own good, and teaching gets you into the world, out among people. Second, it gives you exposure and enhances your reputation. (I have gotten several clients who called me after seeing my course described in the New York University course bulletin.) Third, you learn a lot about a subject by preparing to teach a course in it. And fourth, the material gathered for a course can be recycled into an article, book, report, audiotape, lecture, etc.

If you want to teach, write to college, university and high school adult education programs in your area and request their night school/continuing education catalogs. Then write to the program directors proposing courses on topics that would fit their current programs but which they do not now offer. This is how I got a teaching assignment at New York University.

7. **Create a seminar.** Sponsoring your own seminar is like "self-publishing" your own course and is an option to consider when you can't get a local college to offer your course or when you want more control and a greater share of the profits. As a part-time venture, you can create and market your own seminar, offering it either as a public or private seminar.

D. Michael Denny, a highly conceptual New Jersey advertising writer, developed and now markets a course in "Conceptual writing for marketing communications" to advertising and marketing departments at large corporations, earning substantial fees for each session. Gary Blake, a former freelance magazine writer, does the same thing with highly profitable seminars on business writing for corporate managers.

These are private seminars sold to corporations and held in their facilities. You can also rent your own room in a hotel, send out invitations and hold a public seminar on your topic. Several times I have given a self-sponsored seminar in "How to become a published author" and earned profits of approximately $1,200–$1,500 for the one-day seminar (held on Saturdays).

8. **Learn a new piece of software.** Every time you master a new piece of software, you enhance your productivity for years to come and substantially increase your efficiency and overall profits. Yet most of us self-employed professionals are too busy to take time out to learn new software. Unlike our corporate counterparts, who are all too happy to get out of work for a few days or a week and learn new programs at company-paid training, most of us freelancers can't afford to take time off from business for education.

So when you have a slow period, take advantage of time to further computerize your business. Some of the software you should be looking into includes database (for maintaining client lists), word processing (if you are not already using it, you should be), telecommunications (learn how to use that modem!), online information services (becoming familiar with one or two of these can save hours of research time), spelling checkers, spreadsheets, graphics, desktop publishing and accounting.

9. **Organize your files.** Not busy today? Go out, get some cardboard boxes or lawn and leaf bags. Now go through your files and your office and throw away all the old files, papers, books, back issues of unread magazines and other junk cluttering your space—the junk we all save but don't need.

Reason to do this: Most of us, whether we work at home or rent outside offices, have limited space. And you will soon fill that space if you don't periodically purge yourself of the flotsam and jetsam of life.

Warning: The one thing you should hesitate to throw away are files of past clients or good prospects. Invariably, the day after I throw away an old file that has been sitting around for years gathering dust, that client will call with an assignment (after not contacting me for years) and say, "Oh, by the way, do you still have our material on file?" It never fails.

10. **Organize your office.** I know mine needs it! Too many notes and papers are pinned to my bulletin board, and I never seem to have enough shelf space. Use your spare time to neaten and organize your clutter or physically change or add to your office to make it more efficient. I paid a contractor more than $12,000 to finish two rooms in my basement so I could use them for storing books, papers and files that are old and no longer fit in my primary office. And you can never go wrong buying an extra four-drawer file cabinet or big bookcase to neaten the overflow of books and papers when your office gets too crowded.

Making your work space better always pays off in increased efficiency. Even if you have only a couple of spare hours, you can always clean out and reorganize a desk drawer or two, right?

11. **Spend more time on each project.** Let's say you could normally handle four projects per month, but this month you only have one. One good way to spend your extra time is on doing a better-than-usual job on the project you do have. You'll enjoy having the time to truly do as thorough a job as possible, and you'll probably be rewarded with more assignments. So if job B and job C haven't come through yet, dedicate yourself to job A and it will pay off.

12. **Read.** One of my greatest frustrations with my chosen career of writer/information producer/consultant is that there is so much to learn, so much to read, and never enough time to read it.

    My wife (also a writer) and I frequently comment to each other that we could easily spend each day reading the material that crosses our desks, leaving no time for client work. But since the clients come first, the reading is pushed aside for later or often neglected altogether. Sometimes I am truly saddened by all the good articles and books I want to read and that deserve to be read but which I will never have time to read.

    Slow times should not be wasted in idle daydreaming but are an ideal period of self-education. Read books on business, books on advertising, books on marketing, books on communication, books on whatever topic you deal with in your practice. I am particularly fond of business books, how-to books on marketing and advertising, books on succeeding as a self-employed writer/consultant and books on writing—and can never keep up with the reading. For the writer, self-education does not end with school but is a lifelong process. If only there were more hours in the day!

13. **Take a course.** Slow times are also good times to take a course in any subject that interests you or would add to your professional growth. Although the tendency is to take only business and writing courses, don't forget to treat yourself to something that's purely fun and appeals to your self-interest, for example, short story writing, oil painting or Greek history.

14. **Be social with other writers.** I know I seldom see other writers or go to writers luncheons or other business club activities because I simply don't have the time. But this type

of networking is worthwhile: It can stimulate your thinking, expose you to new ideas, broaden your network of contacts and even result in referrals and new business. So if you have the time, join a local advertising or marketing or writers club and go to the meetings. Get to know fellow writers and communications specialists in your area. Once they get to know you, your phone may start ringing more frequently than it does now.

15. **Do something nice for yourself.** I remember that when I quit my job in 1982 and began my freelance writing practice, I promised myself that the first thing I would do is take a week off and just spend it doing things in Manhattan. Like many New Yorkers, I spent so much time working in the city I never really got to see it as a tourist might.

   Fortunately or unfortunately, depending on your viewpoint, I was busy enough that the week off to see Manhattan never took place, and now that I have moved away from the city and am even busier, it never will. That's too bad. I'm truly sorry I never did it. So if you have the time to do something for yourself, do it. My desire now is to spend a month in a log cabin at a lake banging out a novel on a laptop PC. Now if only I can find the time. . . .

16. **Become an expert in a specific field.** All of us freelance commercial writers write about fields in which we have some degree of knowledge (even though that knowledge may be only what the client has told us). Wouldn't it be nice to learn about these fields and dazzle the clients with your knowledge?

   When you have the extra time, go to the library and do some reading and research. Build a good clipping file of information. Build a small library of books on the topic. Spend spare time becoming an expert in a field, then sell this expertise as part of the package you offer clients in that field. It will pay off.

17. **Do marketing you never have time to do.** I constantly come up with marketing ideas that I think would bring me more business but that I don't implement because I don't have the time. Slow periods provide a good time for putting that extra effort into your ongoing program of self-promotion, image building and marketing of your freelance ser-

vices. Now is the time to send out that press release, write that article or mail those sales letters you've been meaning to send out. Do it!

MINIMIZE YOUR "DOWNTIME"

Many freelance writers suffer from a "crisis-lull-crisis" rhythm in their businesses: They get very, very, very busy, finish work in a burst of concentrated and frantic activity, and when they are through with their assignments, find they have nothing else on the horizon. Nothing!

To get more business, they dive into a period of active self-promotion, making phone calls, writing letters and doing all the other marketing activities discussed in part four of this book.

Weeks or months later, this activity begins to pay off. New prospects hire the writers, who get busy again. So busy, in fact, that they stop all self-marketing activities and just do the work they have. So when they finish in a few weeks, they naturally have no prospects or potential projects lined up and have to go out and frantically scramble to get new assignments.

You can avoid this unpleasant situation—and keep constantly busy—only through constant self-promotion and application of the marketing techniques for promoting freelance writing practices. The trick is to maintain active, ongoing marketing *even when you are busy and your schedule is filled with projects.*

This is the secret. If you stop marketing, you will eventually find yourself with no prospects and no work, no matter how busy you are today. If you market continuously, you will always have a steady stream of fresh sales leads, prospective clients and new projects to bid on. This is the simple technique I promised to reveal that can prevent slow periods and virtually ensure a steady stream of work.

Not everyone sees the sense in this. Many of the members of my writers club have privately told me, "You are crazy to waste money advertising and writing articles and giving talks when you are already booked up with work." When they say this, I only smile.

Do my techniques work? I can't say that I'll never have a slow period or hit a slump again. No one can guarantee that. But I have been continuously busy and turning away work every month for the past two years. How many other writers can say that?

LEARN TO HANDLE PRESSURE AND JUGGLE MULTIPLE PROJECTS

Know anyone who's just too busy? If you are a beginning writer, your reaction is, "That's a nice problem to have." And in a way, it is. But it is still a problem. If you've been in this business for a spell, you know how difficult it can be to cope with an overload of work. Here are some suggestions for doing so:

1. **Learn to say no.** It's scary to turn down work. But when you're truly too busy, it's the best thing to do. After all, if you take on more than you can handle and miss a deadline or do shoddy work in order to *make* the deadline, that will do far more harm to your client relationship and reputation than saying no.

   I rarely say no to a current client, unless the deadline is so tight I cannot possibly make it. If that's the case, I ask if there's any reason why the deadline can't be a few days longer, and I usually get it. (Most deadlines are artificial and have no logic behind them.) If the client cannot be flexible, I politely explain that the deadline is too short, thank her for the offer of the job, apologize for not being able to take it on and suggest she give it to one of her other resources (other freelancer, in-house writer, ad agency, production studio).

   However, I *frequently* say no to new prospects who call me during a busy period. When they start to describe their projects or ask about my service, I stop them and say, "I'd be delighted to talk with you about this project. But I don't want to waste your time, so I must tell you now that I am booked through the end of September (or whenever). If the project is not a rush or you can delay it until then, I'd be happy to work with you. If not, I'll have to pass."

   Amazingly, the usual reaction is not anger or hostility (although a few callers get mad); instead, most are impressed, even amazed. ("You mean you are booked through *September*? Boy, you must be good!" one caller said today.) In fact, turning down work because you are booked frequently creates the immediate impression that you are in demand and thus tops in your field and, along with this, creates an even stronger desire to work with you. Many people you turn down initially will call you back at the month you specify and ask, almost reverently, always respectfully, "You said call back in September. I have a project. Can you work with me now?" Try it. It works!

2. **Set the parameters.** An alternative to turning down work cold is to set the schedule and deadline according to your convenience, not the client's. "Well, I am booked fairly solidly," you tell the prospect. "I can squeeze you in; however, it will take seven weeks (or whatever) instead of the usual three to complete your project, because of my schedule. If you can wait this long, I'll be happy to help you. If not, I will have to pass on the assignment."

Again, many prospects will turn to someone who can accommodate their original deadlines. However, many others will say yes to your request and hire you on your terms.

3. **Get up an hour earlier.** I find that mornings are my most productive time. I work best from 7 A.M., when I usually start, to 1 or 2 P.M.; after that, I slow down. If I am extremely busy, I try to start at 6 A.M. instead of 7 A.M., and find that I get an amazing amount of work done during that first extra hour. Also, it makes me less panicky for the rest of the day, because I have accomplished so much so early.

4. **Work an hour later or work one or two hours in the evenings.** If you usually knock off at 5 P.M., go to 6 P.M. Or if you generally watch television from 8 P.M. to 10 P.M., work an extra hour and a half from 10 P.M. to 11:30 P.M. I prefer the extra morning hour for client projects; evening writing is for my own self-sponsored projects, such as books, articles or self-publishing.

5. **Put in half a day Saturday morning or Saturday afternoon.** Sometimes, I have to work all weekend, although I prefer not to and don't think it's mentally healthy for me to do so. If you have to work weekends, Saturday morning— say from eight to noon—is the best time. You get that early morning energy and get the work out of the way so you can relax and enjoy the rest of the weekend. If you are not a morning person, try Saturday afternoon. If you put the work off until Sunday, you'll probably just spend all Saturday worrying about it or feeling guilty about it, so don't. Get it done first thing and then forget about it.

6. **Hire a temp.** If you are under a crunch, consider getting temporary secretarial help for such tasks as proofreading, editing, research, retyping of manuscripts and trips to the post office. Spend the money to get rid of unnecessary administrative burdens and free yourself to concentrate on the important writing tasks in front of you.

7. **Break complex tasks into smaller, bite-size segments.** Rush jobs are intimidating. If you have two weeks to write a major brochure and you put it off until the last three or four days, the task looms large and panic can set in.

   The solution is to break the project into subprojects, assign a certain amount of the task to each day remaining and then write this on a sheet of paper and post it on the wall or bulletin board in front of your desk.

8. **Ask for more time.** When you are just starting out, you naturally want to please clients and thus you agree to any deadlines they suggest. In fact, you encourage tight deadlines because you believe that doing the work fast is a sign of doing your job right and pleasing the clients.

   As you get older and more experienced, you learn two important truths: First, most deadlines are artificial and can be comfortably extended with no negative effect on the client's marketing efforts whatsoever; and second, it's more important to take the time to do the job right than to try and impress a naive client by doing it fast. What matters is not that the copy was written fast but that it works—sells the product, educates the reader or does whatever it is supposed to do. So if you need extra time, ask for it. This is real service to the client. Doing rush jobs is not.

9. **Get a fax machine.** Before the fax machine, if I had a project due Wednesday, I pretty much had to be done with it on Tuesday at 3 P.M. so it could be printed and ready for Federal Express pickup by 5 P.M. Now, with a fax, the job due Wednesday can be finished Wednesday at 4 P.M. and on the client's desk at 4:15 P.M.—giving me an extra day on every project.

10. **Get E-mail.** Learn to browse the World Wide Web and send E-mail over the Internet. You'll save time and energy, and get more done. (See chapter seven for more information.)

CHAPTER 6

Surefire Techniques for Increasing Your Output and Sales by 25 Percent or More

WORK IS MUCH MORE FUN THAN FUN.

—NOEL COWARD

Not every writer wants to be Isaac Asimov or Georges Simenon. This chapter focuses on helping the average writer achieve realistic incremental productivity increases without rearranging his life in the service of maximum productivity. By following these tips, almost every writer can increase output 10 to 25 percent within a few short weeks.

REDUCE THE "AGONY" FACTOR IN YOUR WRITING

Eliminate self-doubt. It's OK to be critical while editing, but don't be critical of your writing *while* you are writing it. Know that if you have something to say or you can say it in an amusing fashion, people will read and enjoy what you write.

Karen McIntyre, a writer for Ogilvy and Mather, says, "Don't be afraid to write bad first drafts. Separate writing from editing." Joe Vitale, a successful Houston-based freelance writer, has outlined a seven-step process for writing and editing:

1. First determine what you want to write about. Your professor wants a paper on the death instinct in ducks? OK. State that as your goal.
2. Research the topic. Research may be as simple as listing random thoughts on the idea to reading and studying hundreds of books. Do what you think is needed.
3. Write a hot first draft nonstop. Write without pausing and

do your best to get a full rough draft. Don't balk if you're writing a book. A lot of famous books were written in weeks. Vitale's first book was written in two weeks, and his one-act play was written in two days.

"I was an English major and the beginning of every paper was always the worst part," says ad agency writer Gwen O'Connor. "I found that stream of conscience writing works really well. It doesn't matter what you put down and it definitely clears your head to start writing."

4. Have a cup of coffee. Take a minibreak of about twenty minutes. Take a shower. Do something else for a while as you consider what you have just written and reflect on what you'd like to add or change.

   Copywriter Deb Slogik says, "When I get blocked I just get up and walk away from the work for at least half an hour. I'll read, listen to music, talk on the phone, take a bath, whatever it takes to shift my focus from what I was writing to something else. If I don't force it, and come back after a while, my head seems a little clearer and I'm able to focus."

   Another writer, Andrew Bayroff, comments, "Whenever I have a block, I simply remove myself from the piece for a period of time, then come back to it: an hour, a day, or a week later, whichever will do away with the block."

5. Write another rough draft. You might build on the work you created in step three, or you might write something new.

6. You deserve a break. Go shopping or tile your bathroom. Take at least three days and ideally three weeks to let your inner writer work on your piece. If you have a deadline and can't take a break, take a few minutes or an hour if you can.

7. Rewrite your material. Put it all in logical form. Cut up the paragraphs and reorder them. Check your spelling. Add the facts you may have left out of the drafts. Most of all, either read the work to yourself or, best of all, get someone to read it to you. Jack London often read parts of his novels-in-progress to the winos and wanderers who fed off him. Anyone will do.

"Get better organized," writes Henry Pratt in an article in *The Writer*. He tracks his writing projects with a simple log, indicating at a glance for each article the title, the magazine or newspaper he submitted it to, the date sent and what editorial action was taken. Other advice from Pratt:

- Keep necessary materials close at hand.
- Develop a work plan.
- Make to-do lists.
- Handle each piece of paper only once.
- Expand your vocabulary and spelling skills.
- Get up a little earlier.
- During writing time, write.
- Make an outline.
- Revise effectively.

INTERVIEW WITH TERRY WHALIN

Terry Whalin, a specialist in Christian and inspirational writing, is one of the most productive writers I know. I asked Terry to share his productivity secrets. A transcript of our interview (conducted by E-mail over CompuServe) follows:

Q: Why are you so much more productive than most writers— is it just long hours? secret techniques? natural speed?

A: For a guy who earned a C in typing, I'm a quick typist. Ever since taking the class as a sophomore in high school, I've been typing every day. As a college freshman, I learned to write at the typewriter or now the computer. Composing at the typewriter takes a bit of practice but certainly cuts down on the writing time. You think and type. It's a skill every writer should have. I've not tested myself on my typing speed but everyone who watches me type thinks it's fast.

The ability to focus on a single task and bring it to completion is another productive skill that I possess. Many people are easily distracted or try to accomplish too many things in a given period of time. Naturally, I'm able to focus on a single task then bring it to completion. It's a much-needed skill for a writer.

I've always had the ability to write my initial draft quickly. I put my ideas on paper then return to them later and give them a heavy edit. Some people are stalled with looking for the perfect word. I move ahead and write.

Naturally, I've got a thesaurus in my mind. It's another

ability that I possess and is extremely useful for my writing. Some people use a thesaurus constantly in their writing. I have one but hardly ever use it. Alternative words and wording come to me naturally.

You suggested long hours. I do commit long hours to my craft but I try to continually balance between time with my family and some relaxation time. Even in my time of relaxation, I'm learning about my writing and analyzing other people's stories and writing. For example, I read a writing book per month and have done so for about the last ten to fifteen years. I'm committed to continually growing in my ability and information about the craft of writing.

When I write a personality profile or an interview article, I usually try to write the article soon after the interview. Then the thoughts and quotations are fresh. I create the article mostly from my notes and memory, then listen to my tape recording. My feeling is that transcribing tapes is a huge waste of time for a writer. I always return to my tape, listen to it, then adjust my quotations accordingly. To transcribe the tape ahead of time, puts the words firmly on the paper in cement.

I organize my writing with a simple outline, then write from this outline. The simple words of an outline maintain my flow and focus for the article. I'm not completely tied to the outline because sometimes the article changes as I write, but at least I have a solid beginning, middle and an ending—something that some writers struggle to accomplish with a magazine piece.

One of the ways I'm always productive is that I'm constantly searching for new projects and new ideas. I'm continually reading and thinking about ideas for magazine articles or books. I'm in regular dialogue either in writing or on the phone with editors about ideas. I don't rest on my laurels when I complete a project but turn to the next one. I learned this lesson the hard way with my freelance business. Shortly after I started it several years ago, I signed three book contracts and received the corresponding advances. I immediately set to work on these projects and completed them—one, two and three. While immersed in the writing, I did no marketing—other than for a few low-paying magazine articles. After completing the last book, I had nothing to turn to for the next project. Talk about scary! I've made a pledge never to let this happen again. Currently I'm holding four uncompleted book contracts and marketing for additional ones. I want to have a steady stream of work and be able to turn down projects. In fact, I turned one down last week.

Another tip related to writing is to celebrate the diversity of writing. You may not be a writer for mysteries but you can write great children's books. I'd encourage you to constantly experiment with different types of writing. Select the ones where you are successful but be looking for new ones. The ability to write different types of pieces brings some diversity to your day and the tasks. Some days I'm writing children's books but other days it's a magazine article and yet other days, I'm writing a self-help book. It is never boring.

Q: What advice would you give a writer who wants to emulate your productivity and be faster and more prolific?

A: Join a newspaper staff and learn how to meet deadlines. The longer I'm in this business, the more I understand it is a rare person who can write to deadline and specifications. Typically if you ask an author to write a 2,000-word piece, they will send you 3,000 and figure, "The editor can cut what he wants." Instead they create more work for this particular editor. Maybe the editor asked for 2,000 words with the finished product goal of 1,500. You doubled the editor's work. Also when I was a magazine editor and set deadlines for our assigned articles, we always planned for delays from the authors. Usually we needed that extra time planned into our schedule—the author called and requested extra time. It is a rare person who can meet the deadline.

You will establish yourself better in the writing field when you meet a deadline with quality material. One of the easiest means to learn this skill is through newspaper journalism. Throughout high school, I wrote for my school newspaper. Then in college, I joined the staff of one of the largest college dailies in the country, *The Indiana Daily Student.* . . . The feedback was immediate and it called for immediate production. There wasn't time for writer's block, sharpening pencils or making coffee or any of the thousands of other time wasters that writers use. Instead, I had to sit down and write my story. It taught me quick organization, how to work from a simple outline and how to write whenever it was needed. From interviewing hundreds of authors and then writing their profiles, I've learned that the few authors who regularly meet their book deadlines were trained in newspaper writing. Then when an editor gives you a few weeks for magazine deadlines or several months for a book deadline, it looks entirely possible and without the stress of day to day newspaper writing.

If you can't join the staff of a newspaper or gain such training, set reasonable goals and write every day—volumes of material. Whether they are published or not, every writer I know has reams of unpublished material in their files. I have stories where I've written two or three chapters and a proposal, then marketed but it never found a publisher. I don't look at these chapters as wasted but as a learning process. I see so many writers who produce one article or two articles or five articles, then expect these to sell before writing anything else. This is an unrealistic expectation. Write every day and write volumes of material.

Always work at growing and improving your craft. Never figure that you've arrived and there is nothing else to learn. Despite a B.A. in journalism from one of the top journalism schools in the nation, I read a book about writing each month. In each book, I may only find a kernel of an idea but it is usually there. I read about writing different genres, styles of writing, fiction, nonfiction, magazine articles, books, greeting cards, etc. The possibilities are endless. I suggest joining the Writer's Digest Book Club and increasing your writing book library or checking them out of the public library. Just continue to work at improvement.

Take workshops and learn from the experience. I asked one of my author friends several years ago if he ever took workshops. He puffed out his chest and said, "I'd be happy to go if they want me to teach." That wasn't my question but it showed me that this undisciplined yet proud writer was unwilling to continue to grow in his skills.

Don't assume you know it all. While I was listening to a

talk at a conference in Southern California several years ago, I turned to another person and asked, "Have you ever taken a class with the speaker?" This woman pulled herself to a greater height and said, "No, I'm a professional writer!" At that point in time, I had published in about twenty different publications and was an editor of another publication plus had written several books. I too was a professional writer, and sadly this woman's attitude is too common.

I've seen this attitude repeatedly when an author's material is edited or possibly when an editor requests a rewrite. I suggest that you rewrite rather than mounting any objection. The professional writers are always willing to learn, grow, and rewrite. The people with a single book manuscript or a single magazine article are offended. Don't fall into this trap with your writing. I've seen many novelists work and rework their single novel idea because it does not find a publisher. Maybe you need to move on to a fresh story and then return to the old one several years down the road. The time invested is never wasted. The attitude that you've arrived on some great pinnacle of success only turns people off.

Q: Is there anything about the markets you write for that enables greater productivity?

A: Be an expert in your field. Find that field first (there are many to choose from) then write what you know. For example, I don't write in the medical or science area. I've done it sometimes in the past but it's a stretch for me.

Also be constantly looking for ways to gain extra mileage from your writing. For example, I've been writing about people for the last ten years through personality profiles. Some of these small magazine interviews have turned into full-blown book projects. It's a simple means to increase productivity.

Q: What do you see as the rewards of your productivity and great output?

A: I enjoy the opportunity to help people through my writing. Maybe it's a message that they want to get out to the public through books. Maybe I've discovered a different twist for a particular person which the general public has yet to see.

Also writing is an opportunity to make a difference in our world. Maybe I'm an idealist but I've seen the printed page change lives for centuries. For example, the world's best-selling book, The Bible, is still changing lives—every day around the globe. You and I have the opportunity to be a part of that influence of the printed page with our words and our writing. I count it as a great privilege and something I never want to take for granted.

As a freelance writer, I enjoy the flexible work schedule. I certainly put in the hours for my writing and work, but I balance with exercise and some fun mixed into my day. I could not have this type of flexibility if I were editing for a magazine or working as a book editor for a publishing house. I enjoy setting my own schedule and yet I'm disciplined enough so it works for me.

Q: How do you sell so many books? Do you have an agent? an in with publishers?

A: I spend a portion of my time each week in marketing. It began small. People look down on small book reviews. I'm still writing them for a trade magazine—every month as I have for fifteen years. In the early days of my freelance writing, I wrote a lot of book reviews and roundup articles on products. It taught me a great deal about what was in the marketplace but also put me in touch with editors and publishers—relationships that I still maintain today. Money wasn't the issue at first in my writing; relationships were. These personal relationships with editors—if cultivated and maintained—will bear fruit in terms of contracts, extra work, and book sales. The trade-off with relationships is that your work must be excellent.

To increase my financial ability in the marketplace, I've recently begun working with a New York agent. This agent's experience with the highest areas of publishing have given me additional earning power as well as another sounding board for my ideas and book proposals. It's taken my writing in an exciting and new direction. Yet too many writers want to immediately jump to an agent and writing books. My advice is to apprenticeship in magazine writing and not be too quick to jump into books. I'm still writing magazine articles. In fact, I've found that my magazine pieces will reach millions of readers where my books may only reach several thousand. The exposure is worth the time and investment for the magazine pieces. Also these magazine pieces can lead you to the people who need books written. You place yourself in the flow of ideas and people connections.

TONY SEIDEMAN'S PRODUCTIVITY AND SELLING TIPS

Tony Seideman is a full-time freelancer who specializes in writing primarily for trade publications. He describes the following list from a personal letter to me as "a few scraps of wisdom I've picked up in my years as a freelancer. I've got a lot of opinions, some of which go very much against conventional wisdom. But I've worked for more than sixty publications, and have about a 60 percent to 75 percent success rate in my mailings, so I'm doing something right":

1. **Never submit to the slush pile.** "I rarely submit to consumer publications. Why? Because their editors—chief, managing or associate—won't talk to me—and if an editor can't spare the time to spend a moment with me, I don't want to waste my time and energy sending a proposal to them. Putting together a good proposal takes at least an hour or two of my time, three dollars in Xeroxes and three in postage. There's no way I'm going to put that kind of effort into a blind mailing."

2. **Call, mail, call, call, call.** "I have a very specific rhythm I follow. I always call first, get an idea if a publication is looking for my material, get a sense of what kind of material they're looking for, and then do a package tailored directly to the needs of the publication. This approach has enabled me to get into publications ranging from *Gourmet Retailer* to *Professional Boatbuilder*."

3. **Talk to the person who does the work.** "I always call publications. But I almost never call the editor in chief first. Instead, I usually start with the managing editor, since they're the ones who do the most work. Editors in chief are too busy; people lower down the masthead usually don't have the power to make decisions. The lowest I'll go is

associate editor. Sending stuff to assistant editors is the same as putting it on the slush pile."

4. **Go to the trades.** "If you look at my material, you know that I've overwhelmingly spent my time working for trades. There's a good reason for that. Trade publications are hungry for people who can write articles at a reasonable price. Although they don't pay as much per article as consumer magazines, the pay per hour they offer is often far better. That's because most trade publications are so understaffed they don't have the time to demand the multiple, nit-picking, agonizing rewrites that consumer magazine editors do. Also, it's possible to get by with one or two sources for many trade stories; while consumer magazine editors will demand many more."

5. **Target, target, target.** "In all markets, the name of the game today is specializing. I'm a generalized specialist; give me a niche, and I'll make my home in it. But the hook I usually use to get in the door is my ability to write about automation for retailers and small businesses. What really gets editors excited, however, is when you show you understand the direct and specific needs of their readership. So talk about in-depth knowledge of marketing and promotion—but relate it all directly to the readers of the editor's publication. I'm also lucky enough to have clips that cover a wide range of areas, from boatbuilding to multimedia. I shape the selection of clips to match the needs of the publication I'm soliciting."

6. **Put together a professional package.** "I know I don't need to tell you this, but it bears repeating. I'm not looking to sell editors one story. I'm looking to sell them services they may end up paying tens of thousands of dollars a year for. I try to send them promotional materials of a quality to match what I'd like to see if I was buying something that valuable. Currently I use two-sided folders that are a bright but not tacky blue in color. On the left side I put my cover letter and queries. On the right side I put my clips—color Xerox on top. It's expensive, but it also gives me a huge edge over the competition."

7. **Don't get assignments—build relationships.** "One of the most important strategies any writer can adopt is to

avoid selling stories one at a time. The key is to establish relationships and then build on them. That's why I always send three or four story ideas with each of my proposals, and note in phone conversations with editors that I'm available on an ongoing basis. And I always call after I finish, ask what's next, and send new ideas promptly."

8. **Ideas are free—don't worry about losing them.** "Many journalists are very proprietary about the ideas they create. I'm not. I put together lots of them and send out more. Yes, I'm not thrilled if editors turn them over to someone else—which they've done. But I can always think up more, and demonstrating creativity is a good way to create and reinforce relationships."

9. **Proposals are a starting point.** "Time and again, I've sent editors carefully crafted ideas—and then they abandon all of them and assign me what they wanted written. I don't mind that at all. Usually, I can spin the stories to make them say what I want to anyway. And I'm in this for a living, not to gratify my ego."

10. **Editors are always right.** "What I want to write isn't important. What's critical is what the editors want me to write. No matter how great I think an idea is, if the editor doesn't want it, it's foolish for me to try and force them to take it. Editors know their magazines better than I ever could. So what they say, goes. In fact, listening to editors—and writing for their specific audiences—is one of the most important skills any freelancer can develop."

11. **Learn to say no.** "This is one area where I'm still sadly lacking. But there are stories that simply aren't worth doing. Trade publications don't pay much, and most don't ask for a lot in return. Those that do ask for a lot aren't worth writing for. Period."

12. **Persist, persist, persist.** "If an editor seems to be saying yes, I'll pursue them relentlessly, calling every couple of days until they either tell me to go away or assign me a story. I've had situations where eighteen months passed between the time I sent in a proposal and turned in my first assignment—but the piece was a $2,000 one, for a very reasonable amount of work."

CHAPTER 7

Using Technology to Boost Your Productivity:
Computers, Software, Office Equipment and Online Services

REMEMBER, NOTHING THAT'S GOOD WORKS BY ITSELF,
JUST TO PLEASE YOU; YOU'VE GOT TO *MAKE* THE DAMN THING WORK.
—THOMAS ALVA EDISON

This chapter gives you a quick nuts-and-bolts discussion on equipment you must have—and equipment you should have—to be a productive, prolific writer. It covers recommendations on Internet connections, online services, computers, modems, CD-ROM drives, fax machines, telephone systems, photocopiers, scanners and voice mail systems. Also included are my recommendations on software for word processing, desktop publishing, spreadsheets, graphics, virus protection, accounting, contact management and grammar and spelling checkers.

Ever since the typewriter was commercially introduced in 1873, advances in writing technology have enormously increased the speed and efficiency with which the written word can be produced. This is a good thing for writers, since writers' advances and fees have not simultaneously kept pace with inflation.

The first word processor was introduced in 1965. It consisted of a magnetic tape storage system linked to an electric IBM typewriter. The first personal computers were introduced in France in 1973.

Many writers resist technology, especially those of us who grew up in the business pounding on IBM Selectrics. But the fact is, technology can dramatically increase your productivity; and the more you embrace it, the more you'll produce.

DO YOU NEED A COMPUTER?

In today's market, yes. Get the best computer system and software money can buy. If you can't afford to buy, lease: The low monthly payments make computers affordable, and you can lease software as well as hardware. If your local computer seller does not offer financing in-house, have him arrange it for you by calling Studebaker-Worthington Leasing Corporation, (800) 645-7242.

Ask the computer salesperson to recommend a system configuration in terms of processor, memory and hard disk storage. Then get twice that—or at least as much above the recommendation as you can afford.

Reason? Whatever you buy today will cease being state of the art as soon as you learn to use it, so you can never have too much computer. Example: When I got my new system, I was thrilled to be buying "top of the line"—a 486 machine. The instant it was delivered I read about Pentium in the newspaper and realized I was already a generation behind. Now they're talking about a P6 chip that will soon render Pentium obsolete!

As of this writing, top-of-the-line PC for small business or freelance is a Pentium II chip operating at 233 MHz.

According to the *Daily News,* the U.S. market for PCs expanded 13.6 percent in 1996, and the worldwide PC market is expected to show double-digit annual growth for the rest of the decade. By the year 2000, Dataquest expects worldwide PC shipments to reach more than 131.7 million units, for revenues of $264.3 billion. By the year 2001, more than 282 million PCs will be connected to the Internet.

"Not to be at least semi-computer-literate today, or to keep putting off acknowledging that computers are the moneymaking tool of the century, is to keep your head in the sand while the rest of the world passes you by," writes Sheldon Schwartz in *Spare Time Opportunities.*

Equip your computer system with as many productivity-boosting tools as possible. Hardware should include a high-speed fax/modem (56 kbps or ISDN), floppy disk drive, 100 MB zip drive, 16X CD-ROM drive, PS/2 keyboard, three-button mouse, Windows 95, 2 MB PCI video card with plenty of hard disk storage, tape backup and laser printer (at least an HP LaserJet 4L or better). You'll love the speed with which laser printers print manuscript. No more wasting time waiting for your dot matrix or daisy-wheel clunker to crank out pages.

As for hard disk storage, here's my rule of thumb: A working writer can never have too many megabytes. Current state of the art is 6.4 GB (gigabytes). Get at least 100 to 200 MB or more. My wife uses a PC with 1.2 GB of hard disk space.

Scanners save time transforming hard copy research material into editable PC files you can incorporate directly into your document without rekeying. The HP ScanJet 3P scanner or an equivalent machine is perfect for the small office; cost without options such as feed trays is around $500.

Another useful piece of equipment is a photocopier. You can get a decent small-office copier new for around $1,000–$1,500. Home copier models, acceptable for office use, are available for under $700. I have had a Toshiba BD3110 for years and am very satisfied.

As far as software, I recommend Microsoft Windows, Microsoft Word or WordPerfect, and a contact management program such as ACT or TELEMAGIC for maintaining a database of editorial contacts and generating personalized query letters using mail merge capability. My preference for Word or WordPerfect is based on the observation that many book and magazine publishers like getting copy on disk in these formats. Most don't yet require it; but in the future, they may.

According to a survey of magazine editors conducted by *Folio* magazine, Word is the most popular software among editors, with 59 percent using it, followed by almost 30 percent using Word-Perfect. As a Word user, I'm pleased with the program, which comes with a built-in spelling checker and grammar checker. I don't use the grammar checker. I do use the spelling checker, but only as a backup to my own proofreading. As you probably know, spelling checkers don't catch every typo, and it's a mistake to rely on them alone without doing your own proofing.

You can buy Word alone or as part of Microsoft Office Suite. I recommend doing the latter. Word is integrated in the suite with two other excellent Microsoft programs, Excel, a top-notch spreadsheet, which most writers I know don't use much, and PowerPoint, a program for making slides and presentations.

Microsoft Office Suite does not include a desktop publishing program, although Word has rudimentary desktop publishing capabilities. For desktop publishing, use Aldus PageMaker or QuarkXPress.

You need a virus protection program. I recommend installation of McAfee VirusScan. A big advantage is you can get free upgrades to combat the latest viruses, and these upgrades can be downloaded over your modem. Another popular anti-virus program is Norton Anti-Virus.

Many small businesses use Quicken to handle bookkeeping and accounting. I own QuickBooks Pro, which is a little more powerful, a little more expensive and a little more complicated.

Use one of the commercial online services, such as America Online or CompuServe. CompuServe's toll-free number is (800) 848-8990. America Online's is (800) 827-6364. Although America Online bought CompuServe in 1997, the two continue to function as separate entities.

In addition to speeding research, being online will save you time in submitting your work to publishers, editors and clients. Instead of having to print and mail a manuscript and transfer files to a floppy disk, you simply hit a button and instantly "download" your copy to your editor's E-mail address. I have submitted book chapters, commercial assignments and book proposals in this fashion, and I love it. You can literally send a book proposal in fifteen seconds! You also save money by eliminating postage: It cost me only $.14 in transaction charges to E-mail a book chapter to one of my editors today.

Keep a log of all outstanding book proposals and queries. A good practice: As soon as a query comes back rejected, send it out immediately to another magazine. This is easy when you keep query letters on disk.

Get on the Internet. Going to the library is a time-consuming process. Research can be done much more rapidly using your personal computer and a modem.

Modems are inexpensive, so invest in the fastest modem the computer store can sell you—which as of this writing is either a 56 kbps or an ISDN modem. Slower modems take longer and increase your phone bill.

FAXES AND TELEPHONES

Faxes and E-mails have replaced regular mail and express package delivery as the standard method of transmitting copy between writer and client. According to one industry newsletter, between 200 and 300 billion pages of documents are faxed worldwide each year. Get a plain paper fax—laser or ink jet. Avoid faxes that use thermal paper, since this paper is difficult to handle and store and faxes printed on it fade over time. Buy the highest-speed fax you can afford. In addition to my regular fax machine, I have a fax/modem, but I haven't had time to learn how to use it yet. In 1996, I bought a new HP Fax 700 for around $600 and am very satisfied. It's an ink jet machine, and the copy qualities are excellent.

Get a quality phone set from any reliable manufacturer. AT&T phones are excellent. So are Northern Telecom and CIDCO.

If you are getting a new phone or upgrading your phone system, consider getting equipment offering the following features:

1. **Push-button dialing.** Rotary phones are obsolete. If you have one, get rid of it. You are wasting too much time dialing. And rotary phones can't navigate through the menus of many of your prospects' voice mail systems.

2. **LED display.** This is used to display the status of various features and functions. When you have Caller ID, the display can identify the source of incoming calls. Some regional telephone companies offer Caller ID, which shows you the name of the caller or her company as well as the phone number. You can decide whether to take the call or have Call Forward or voice mail handle it.

3. **Caller ID.** Calling number ID presentation is especially valuable to writers and others who screen calls. It is also useful for help desks, support lines, customer service departments and other departments who can respond more professionally when they know in advance who is calling. Calling number ID works with Call Forward, Call Waiting and Three-Way Calling.

4. **Memory dial.** You can store important phone numbers in memory and dial them at the push of a button. This can significantly cut down dialing time when calling your most important prospects and customers.

5. **ISDN compatibility.** ISDN, short for Integrated Services Digital Network, is an internationally accepted standard for high-speed data communication. ISDN lines transmit data at

higher rates than regular telephone lines. You'll save time and reduce phone bills when communicating with customers by modem, E-mail, online services, fax and the Internet.

6. **ISDN line.** To take advantage of ISDN, you need an ISDN phone line as well as an ISDN phone. The main advantage of ISDN for freelance writers is much faster Internet access, especially to sites with heavy graphics. As I write this, Bell Atlantic tells me it will charge me $37 a month to convert one of my phone lines to ISDN plus $.02 per minute for transactions.

7. **Multiple lines.** Your customers should never get a busy signal when they call you. One solution is to use voice mail. For a small monthly fee, you can get voice mail service. When you are on the phone, calls can be forwarded to a voice mail box which takes the caller's message. An alternative is to have more than one phone line. You can get a phone that can handle two different phone lines (with two different numbers even) for under $150. You'll probably want separate lines anyway for your phone, fax and modem.

8. **Conference calling.** Some prospects may want to include other people on the call. If they have a speaker phone, they can gather around it in a conference room. If they don't, you can use the conference calling feature (called Three-Way Calling by some telephone companies) to call multiple parties and link them in a conference call.

9. **Redial.** When you get a busy signal or have another problem when dialing, just hit the redial button. The phone will automatically redial the number for you, saving you time and effort.

10. **Extra function keys.** Get a phone with some extra function keys so there are some keys that do nothing. This allows you to add new services and features as they become available without upgrading or replacing your existing telephone equipment.

11. **Extra-long cord.** If you like to get up, stretch your legs and walk around while you talk on the phone, get an extra-long phone cord—at least six feet. A short cord, if bent and twisted, may also cause a crackling or interruption on the phone line.

12. **Headset.** I don't like them, but many swear by them. The advantage is that they leave your hands free to make notes, pull files and use your computer while you talk.

13. **Speaker phones.** Use the speaker phone only when you need to have a group of people participate in a call. Don't use your speaker phone for regular one-on-one calls; the voice quality is inferior to a regular phone handset.

14. **Voice mail.** For a nominal charge, you can get voice mail provided by your local telephone carrier. Instead of a telephone answering machine in your office taking calls, messages go into a voice mail system in the phone company's central office; you retrieve messages using a special code. Voice mail eliminates the need to maintain and occasionally replace an answering machine. Unlike phone answering machines, voice mail keeps working even when the power goes off, preventing missed calls.

15. **Voice-activated dialing.** Speech recognition enables callers to dial numbers by saying the number, dial specific parties by speaking the person's name and automatically identify themselves to the network by voice, without having to remember or punch in a personal identification number. It saves time when dialing and eliminates the need to carry an ID card or telephone directory.

16. **Message waiting indicator.** Users are automatically alerted when they have messages waiting for them in voice mail. Notification can take place via a message on the phone's LED display or an audible tone. The need for users to call in to see whether they have voice mail messages is eliminated.

17. **Single-Number Reach.** If you have multiple phones—several business phones, a cellular phone, home phone—callers can reach you by calling a single number. This eliminates the need for callers to remember multiple numbers when they want to track you down.

18. **Call transfer.** This allows you to transfer calls to other people within your office and is ideal if you work with other tellesellers. Use it to transfer calls meant for others in your company, eliminating the need to ask the caller to call back.

19. **Do Not Disturb.** You can set your phone to automatically route calls to another phone (such as your assistant's or

secretary's) or to your voice mail box if you want to work undisturbed.

20. **Selective Call Acceptance.** A variation of Do Not Disturb, this feature allows certain calls to get through your Do Not Disturb screen, based on the caller's phone number or ID. Therefore you can avoid calls you do not want to get while enabling important prospects to reach you at all times.

21. **Voice message retrieval.** This lets you retrieve your voice mail messages from phones other than your own. It's useful for writers who sometimes attend meetings outside of the office.

22. **Call Forward.** Call Forward means the phone forwards (sends) the call to another phone. You can have calls forwarded immediately, when the caller receives a busy signal or when the phone rings but is not answered.

23. **Call Waiting.** This feature allows a single phone on one phone line to simultaneously receive multiple calls. When the user is on the phone and another party dials that number, the user hears a beep tone. The tone lets her know someone else is calling. The user can ignore the call and let the phone ring (or combine call waiting with another service to have the second call picked up and answered by voice mail). Or, by pressing a key, she can put the first call on hold and take the second call. The user can toggle back and forth between the two calls at will.

Which features are available in your area code depends on what your phone company is currently offering. Call for details.

CHAPTER 8

Outsourcing:
Hiring Others to Work for You

GETTING RESULTS THROUGH PEOPLE IS A SKILL
THAT CANNOT BE LEARNED IN THE CLASSROOM.
—J. PAUL GETTY

Writers are basically selling their time, yet many writers fritter their valuable time away handling the most mundane tasks. A better strategy is to hire others to do nonwriting tasks for you and concentrate on writing, selling, marketing and customer service. This chapter gives the nuts and bolts of hiring temporary, part-time and full-time help including both staff and independent contractors. I will show readers how I have increased my net profits by outsourcing a large number of nonwriting activities to outside firms. These activities include faxing, typing, filing, library research, bookkeeping, tax preparation, photocopying, going to the post office and selling and marketing.

THE GROWING POPULARITY OF OUTSOURCING
Manpower, the world's biggest staffing agency, now employs 1.5 million people. According to the National Association of Temporary and Staffing Services (NATSS) 21 percent of temp workers in the United States can be classified as "professional and technical." A Coopers and Lybrand survey shows that in 1996, 81 percent of America's fastest-growing companies hired temporary, part-time or contract employees. In 1996, NASA outsourced operation of the space shuttle to a consortium of private contractors. And Dun and Bradstreet Information Services reports

that 40 percent of small businesses outsource at least one function.

One factor contributing to the growth of outsourcing is ongoing corporate downsizing. Last year, AT&T announced the layoff of 40,000 employees. IBM recently offered early retirement or layoff to 60,000 people, and after the Burroughs/Sperry merger, Unisys fired 50,000.

More and more Americans are becoming self-employed. These include writers as well as the word processors, clerks, programmers and others who provide professional and clerical services. In 1992, *The Wall Street Journal* reported that about 10 million Americans worked in their own unincorporated businesses. *Occupational Outlook Quarterly* estimates that more than 15 million workers are self-employed, with 3 million owning incorporated businesses. During the past decade, more than 700,000 workers made the transition from corporate employment to self-employment.

An article in *The Record* reports that the use of part-time workers is growing. Part-timers made up 16 percent of the national workforce two decades ago; today 18.5 percent of workers—22 million people—work part-time, according to the Bureau of Labor Statistics.

WHY CONSIDER OUTSOURCING?

Many beginning writers are puzzled by the notion of hiring help. Following are some of their reasons:

- They think they're too small to need or afford help.
- They see themselves as "freelancers," not small businesses.
- They don't have enough work to keep an assistant busy.
- They don't make enough money to be able to afford to pay someone else to do some of their work.

But as you become busier, you realize the amount of work you can do, and, therefore, the amount of income you can generate, is limited by your own energy and the number of hours you can work in a day. One way around this is to spend more of your time on billable work, especially work that earns a high hourly rate. To do this, you have to free some time by *not* doing work that is not billable or is billed at a low rate. This is where hiring help comes in.

You make money by thinking, writing and servicing editors, publishers and clients. Everything else—learning how to use a particular computer program, scanning source materials, going to the library, buying supplies—is a waste of time that could be spent on revenue-generating activities. Some or all of these nonessential activities can be outsourced to others.

WHAT TO OUTSOURCE

Writers outsource all different kinds of tasks, including the following:

- research
- filing
- typing
- proofreading
- sales and marketing (through agents)
- bookkeeping and accounting
- writing (by subcontracting to other writers)
- computer work (e.g., building a Web site, installing new software and hardware)

You can outsource all or some of these tasks. It's up to you. My policy is to do all the writing myself and outsource the administrative, clerical and secretarial work to subcontractors (which I'll discuss in a minute).

Obviously, to make a profit, you have to pay the subcontractor less money than it would cost you to do the work yourself. This means either the subcontractor charges less per hour for her services than you do or she charges less for the task because, given her high degree of proficiency, she can do it in a much shorter time frame than you can. I don't do filing, for example, since I can pay someone to do it for a fraction of the money I'd make spending the time on writing projects. My attorney is more expensive and earns fees equivalent to mine, but I still use him on contracts and for other needs. Not only does he do a much better job than I would, but he can do in one hour (and bill me for one hour) what would take me half a day or more.

FREELANCE VS. STAFF

Let's say you are interested in getting help around your writing office. A major decision is whether to hire an employee or outsource.

When you hire employees, they generally work on your premises using your office space, equipment and supplies. You pay them salaries and often provide benefits, such as sick days, vacation and health insurance.

When you outsource, you contract with an individual or small firm that provides the services you need on a fee basis. This fee can be a project fee but is usually an hourly fee. The independent contractors typically work on their premises, using their office space, equipment and supplies. You pay their invoices like you would pay a bill for any product or service you buy.

I have had both staff employees and subcontractors and prefer the latter to the former by a wide margin. Here's why:

1. Subcontractors and other part-time workers can perform as well as full-timers but, on average, earn 40 percent less. Only 12 percent get a pension, and only 15 percent get health care benefits. Therefore, they are cheaper to employ.

2. There is no long-term commitment and no recurring overhead. You pay the subcontractor only when you give her work to do. An employee gets paid as long as he shows up, whether he has work to do or not. When you don't need the subcontractor, she works for her other clients (or takes time off) and you don't pay her.

3. Subcontractors are independent and responsible for their own welfare. Employees may depend on you for guidance, career satisfaction and other needs—responsibilities you may not want to deal with.

4. Using subcontractors is less complex from an accounting and paperwork point of view than having employees. Employees require Social Security tax, FICA, workmen's compensation and other complexities. Independent contractors are paid as vendors. Note: The Internal Revenue Service requires that people who are paid as independent contractors (not employees) work on their premises, not yours, and have other clients. Consult your accountant or tax attorney.

5. Subcontractors are more motivated because they are sellers and you are the buyer. They have a customer-service orientation, which is a welcome change from the attitude of resentment or indifference many employees seem to have toward the boss.

6. Subcontractors provide their own equipment and office space, buy their own furniture and pay their own utility bills. Often the subcontractors will have better equipment than you do, and as their client, you get the benefits of this equipment without buying it. So subcontracting can actually reduce your overhead and capital costs, while hiring employees increases those costs since you have to supply the employees with a fully equipped work space.

WHERE TO FIND HELP

When my longtime staff secretary quit because of a personal situation, I wondered where I would find another assistant. A colleague suggested that instead of hiring a full-time secretary, I find a typing/word processing/secretarial service to handle my needs.

I looked in the local paper and yellow pages and called several services. I explained I was a busy writer looking for substantial secretarial support and asked each service provider—most of whom were individuals working from their homes—whether he would be interested in having a client who would provide a substantial amount of business on a regular basis.

Every word processing and secretarial service I talked to became excited at the prospect of having such a client! Apparently, the word processing and typing business is sporadic and project oriented; having a regular client on retainer was unusual and a welcome change that would bring greater income and financial security.

I interviewed several word processing services and chose one person. I explained that I would buy thirty hours of her time a week, by the week, and pay for a month's worth of service in advance at the beginning of each month. In return, I wanted the best rate she could offer me and a high level of service.

This person, who is now my assistant, works for me from her home in a town eight miles away. It's close enough that she can easily come over to do some work here or pick up materials if required, but mostly we work by fax and E-mail. In fact, her small word processing business has a part-time messenger to serve me and her other clients, and I only see her a few times a year.

This "virtual office" approach has many advantages and few drawbacks. In addition to the six advantages of outsourcing already discussed, I can work in privacy without having my assistant physically present (privacy and solitude are, to me, productivity boosters).

The only drawback is my subcontractor isn't here every day to run certain errands, but I found a solution: I hired my former secretary as a second subcontractor. She works for me after her regular job, from 4:30 P.M. to 7:30 P.M., and can therefore go to the post office and bank and do other errands. I also have an independent sales rep who negotiates deals for me with corporate clients, a literary agent who does the same with publishers, an accountant who does my taxes and a freelance bookkeeper who handles accounts payable and receivable. Obviously I am a big fan of outsourcing. It works for me, and I recommend you try it.

I found my sales rep when I went to a trade show and attended a workshop on self-promotion for freelancers. I was so impressed that, after the seminar, I called her and ask if she would represent me, so I could outsource all of my personal selling to her. She agreed and it has worked beautifully ever since. She is compensated similarly to the way literary agents are compensated (see part four), based on a percentage of my gross sales.

Start small. Hire a part-time secretary or word processor to work for you one day a week. If you can keep her busy, like having the help and feel it frees you to increase your writing output and income, you can always buy more of the person's time or, if she is too busy, hire a second helper.

One caveat: Since most of your fellow writers don't use subcontractors, you may not be able to find someone through referral. Call people who advertise word processing, typing or secretarial assistance in the local paper or yellow pages. Interview them face-to-face before hiring someone. Start on a trial basis, and don't promise anything more regular until both of you are satisfied the relationship is working well.

Another source of help is college students, who can be hired as part-time assistants or summer interns. The problem is that after the summer, or when they graduate, they're gone. The value of an assistant increases as he learns your procedures and business over time; this advantage does not exist when you hire college students and other transients who don't stick around. A professional word processor or secretary running his own services business, on the other hand, wants to make that business grow and is looking for long-term client relationships.

PART THREE

INCREASING YOUR SALES

Writing faster and more can add to your writing income, but you'll do even better if you sell most of what you write. This section shows how to increase your sales, sell a higher percentage of the things you write or want to write and minimize speculative work and rejection, which eat away at your time and income.

CHAPTER 9

Queries and Proposals That Lock In the Assignment

EVERYONE LIVES BY SELLING SOMETHING.

—ROBERT LOUIS STEVENSON

Writers spend a lot of uncompensated time proposing ideas, pursuing clients and editors and selling themselves and their work. If the "closing rate" (percentage of clients and editors who give you the go-ahead) is low, you will waste a lot of time, and therefore be less productive and profitable. This chapter shows how to write pitch letters, query letters and proposals that sell 80 percent or more of your work to maximize your income and minimize time wasted. It includes samples of successful letters and a proposal you can use as models.

How you market your writing affects your productivity and income. Knowing how to market will help you make more sales more quickly. And knowing what to sell—and whom to sell it to—can bring you assignments with a favorable revenue-to-work ratio.

Learn the proven formulas for writing query letters and book proposals. Study the query letters and book proposals of successful authors, and copy their models. Once you familiarize yourself with these formats, you'll be able to quickly generate project ideas and present them to the appropriate editors and publishers. Two books I highly recommend are Lisa Collier Cool's *How to Write Irresistible Query Letters* and Michael Larsen's *How to Write a Book Proposal*.

QUERY FIRST

Write on assignment, not on speculation. Send queries and proposals first; get go-aheads; then write to fill the orders. I know from experience that I write much faster and more confidently when I know what I'm writing is already sold and will be published. With on-spec projects, I dillydally, making little progress, because no deadline looms and no one is waiting for my manuscript.

Always have a deadline. Usually the book publisher or magazine editor will assign one to you. If not, set one yourself. Make the deadline a specific date—not "in a week or two." To make it more real, share it with your editor or publisher. Jobs without definite deadlines seem to go on indefinitely and at a snail's pace. Work expands to fill the time available. The most money I've ever made writing has been on projects for which deadlines were tight and I had to work quickly.

Have multiple markets so you can sell all of the different types of materials you write. Traditional publishers are not your only option. Many authors self-publish certain works they feel are not appropriate for traditional outlets. This allows them to write more freely, without apprehension about which publisher will accept the piece.

For example, Joe Vitale, a Houston author with many published books and articles, got the urge to write a short piece on how to write faster and more productively. In four hours, on a Sunday afternoon, he wrote a 2,500-word essay, "Turbocharge Your Writing." Published as a 22-page pamphlet, "Turbocharge" has sold more than seventy-five hundred copies (cover price: $5.95)—a handsome profit for the author by any standard.

Study *Writer's Market*, but don't be afraid to send queries as the impulse strikes or opportunities arise. I have made numerous sales by contacting magazine editors, book publishers and corporate clients whose names I came across in my leisure reading rather than through deliberate research.

If you see a new magazine that appeals to you, write a query to the editor. If you see a book you like, contact the publisher. If you get a promotion from a local business, contact the owner and ask if he needs additional materials written.

Example: In a toy store, I saw a series of science books for young children, liked the books, wanted to write for the series. I jotted down the name of the publisher and series editor, then wrote a letter proposing additional titles in the series.

She didn't need more books for that series, but was starting another, and invited me to write a volume. I turned it down because the terms were not acceptable, but the offer was mine, if I wanted it.

(On reflection, I wish I had taken it. In fact, I have lingering regrets over all the book projects I've turned down. This is an occupational hazard of the writer who is also a book lover and addicted to being prolific.)

Proposing an additional title for an ongoing series of books is an effective strategy for making a quick sale. If the series is successful and the publisher is looking to continue it, she will be receptive to new ideas that fit well into the series. Also, she'll probably accept a short description and table of contents in lieu of a full book proposal, saving you an enormous amount of research and writing time. Four of my published books were sold in this manner.

Writing magazines and seminars teach us, "Come up with ideas and pitch them to editors and publishers." But I've had success with the opposite tactic: asking editors and publishers what *they* want and writing it for them.

This strategy is especially effective when receiving a turndown for one of your own ideas. Instead of just grumbling or walking away, ask the editor, "Well, what *are* you looking for?" Many will answer with specifics, virtually handing you a writing assignment.

Another common writer's mistake is the relentless pursuit of new markets to the exclusion of current customers. New markets are fine, but don't neglect your best prospect: the editor who has already bought something from you. It's easier to make repeat sales to the same customers than to make first sales to new customers. This is true in freelance writing and virtually every other business.

Come up with ideas aimed at the magazines and book publishers for whom you've already written. If they like your ideas, you get quick sales, since they already know and feel comfortable with you and your work. A new publisher or editor, on the other hand, not only has to be sold on the idea, she has to be sold on you, as well—which takes longer and delays the assignment of new work.

Write for those magazines you actually read. You have a better grasp of their editorial requirements and also know what they've done recently. Your queries will sound more authoritative and hit the mark more often. Make magazine reading a hobby, and you will gain more intimate knowledge of potential markets. This will enable you to write queries more quickly, and your acceptance rate will be greater.

Use an agent. Agents do the marketing for you, saving you time, freeing you to write. In most cases, literary agents handle books only, not articles or stories. So as far as short stories, essays, poems and articles, you're on your own.

I use an agent to handle all book deals. Even when the publisher comes to me directly (this can happen once you become an established book author, but at first you'll have to approach the publishers), I turn the project over to my agent for negotiation: She'll do a better job, and I don't have the time or inclination to do it myself. While she is negotiating the contract, I am writing the proposal for the next book. Use of a good agent frees you from having to negotiate advances, royalties and deadlines so you can do more work.

I also use several agents who market me as a writer to corporate and business clients. Each gets a commission on every sale he or she makes. The main reason to use them is they handle a task I dislike—fee negotiation—and leave me free to handle more assignments.

QUERY LETTERS THAT SELL

A query letter is, in essence, a sales letter. The American Society of Journalists and Authors sends a tip sheet to members that states, "A query letter is what an author uses to sell an idea for an article to an editor. A typical query letter begins with a hook to grab the editor's interest and continues by describing the idea. The query letter should also include the writer's unique qualifications for the assignment."

Let's review a few basic facts before I present the sample query letters.

1. **Editors look for *professionalism in query letters.*** This means no typos, no misspellings. You address the letter to a specific editor by name. And you spell his name right.
2. **Editors look for familiarity with their magazines.** Don't suggest an article on hunting elk to the newsletter for the

ASPCA (American Society for the Prevention of Cruelty to Animals). Sounds obvious, but such things happen every day; for example, writers proposing how-to articles to magazines that don't do how-to. Study the market before you query.

3. **Editors look for good writing.** If you can, write the first paragraph or two of your query so it could be used, as is, as the lead for your article. This shows the editor that you know how to begin a piece and get the reader's attention.

4. **Editors hate lazy writers**—those who want to see their bylines in magazines but refuse to do research to get their facts straight. Put a lot of hard nuts-and-bolts information—facts, figures, statistics—in your letter to show the editor you know your subject. Most query letters (and articles) are too light on content.

5. **Credentials impress editors.** Tell the editors why they should hire you to write the article. If you are an expert in the subject, say so. If not, describe your sources. Tell which experts you will interview, which studies you will cite, which references you will consult. Also, list your previous publishing credentials if you have any—especially books and articles in well-known magazines.

6. **Editors hate to take risks.** The more fully developed your idea, the better. If you spell out everything—your topic, your approach, an outline, your sources—the editor knows what he will get when he gives you the go-ahead to write the piece. The more complete your query, the better your chance for a sale.

Freelance writer Constance Hallinan Lagan advises that when a magazine says "query only" in its guidelines, you should send a query letter, not the completed article. And always enclose a self-addressed, stamped envelope (SASE).

On the following pages are sample query letters. All were successful and resulted in an assignment to write an article.

Sample Query Letter: A Travel Article for Newspapers

Writer Carol Andrus had enormous success with this simple, direct query letter. It sold one article on India to sixty-five newspapers throughout the United States, Canada, Australia, New Zealand and even India.

Mr. Larry Townsend
Travel Editor
The Chicago Tribune
1801 Michigan Avenue
Chicago, IL 30344

Dear Mr. Townsend:

Three summers ago, I decided to explore India by myself.

The prospect of being all alone on the other side of Planet Earth unnerved me, so I devised a method to have a ready-made roster of "friends" and "family" waiting for me.

The results were truly astounding! I have just now returned from my *second* trip to India, where I was the guest of honor at two weddings . . . just two of the many friendships that I made that unforgettable summer.

I have an article on this "experiment in travel." It's a good read, has lots of human interest and offers generic travel advice. It's just over 2,000 words, and photos are available.

If this sounds interesting, drop the enclosed SASE in the mail.

Very truly yours,

Carol Andrus

Sample Query Letter: Multiple Article Ideas

Although writers usually present one idea per query, Tony Seideman and others have been successful using queries to pitch multiple ideas (usually no more than two or three) to an editor simultaneously, then letting the editor pick which one he wants to develop into a story. The query gives the writer's qualifications; the article ideas are summarized on separate sheets. Seideman said he eventually talked with the editor and sold him one idea immediately while setting the groundwork for a longer-term relationship.

Mr. Paul A. Holmes
Editor
Inside PR
235 W. Forty-eighth Street, #34B
New York, NY 10036

Dear Paul:

PR people are among the world's most overworked, undercredited professionals. I know. I've been causing them grief for almost twenty years as a writer for publications ranging from *Rolling Stone* and *Family Circle* to *Multimedia World* and *Computer Entertainment News*.

As a longtime journalist, I understand how important PR people are to the newsgathering process. I also respect them for putting up with one of the most stressful careers in existence. And I'd like to work with you to do stories that would help make their lives easier. For more than fifteen years, I've made the complex comprehensible, specializing in telling business people about the tools, techniques and strategies they can use to win in an increasingly challenging marketplace.

Topics where I have exceptional expertise include

- Business history and achievement
- Multimedia and the Internet
- Electronic commerce and telecommunications
- Cable and broadcast television and the print media
- High-tech databases and direct mail
- Customer service and satisfaction

Enclosed are copies of my work that deal with the tools PR people can use and some reputations I've helped manage. If you'd like, I'll be glad to send some story ideas once I get a better idea of what you're looking for. Thanks again for your interest. I'll call next week to see how we can work together further.

Sincerely,

Tony Seideman

Sample Query Letter: Article Outline Attached

If the article requires more description than can comfortably fit
in a brief query letter, consider summarizing the key article points
or discussing the details in an outline written on a separate sheet
and enclosed with the query letter. That's what I did to sell a
how-to article on technical writing to a trade journal for chemical
engineers. This query sold because it took a general topic (technical writing) and slanted it toward the specific audience reading
the magazine (chemical engineers).

Mr. Kenneth J. McNaughton
Associate Editor
Chemical Engineering
McGraw-Hill Building
1221 Avenue of the Americas
New York, NY 10020

Dear Mr. McNaughton:

When a chemical engineer can't write a coherent report, the true value
of his investigation or study may be distorted or unrecognized. His
productivity vanishes. And his chances for career advancement diminish.

As an associate editor of *Chemical Engineering*, you know that many
chemical engineers could use some help in improving their technical
writing skills. I'd like to provide that help by writing an article that gives
your reader "Ten Tips for Better Business Writing."

An outline of the article is attached. This 2,000-word piece would provide
ten helpful tips—each less than 200 words—to help chemical engineers
write better letters, reports, proposals and articles.

Tip number three, for example, instructs writers to be more concise. Too
many engineers would write about an "accumulation of particulate
matter about the peripheral interior surface of the vessel" when they're
describing solids buildup. And how many managers would use the phrase
"until such time as" when they simply mean "until"?

My book *Technical Writing: Structure, Standards, and Style* will be
published by the McGraw-Hill Book Company in November. While the

book speaks to a wide range of technical disciplines, my article will draw its examples from the chemical engineering literature.

I hold a B.S. in chemical engineering from the University of Rochester and am a member of the American Institute of Chemical Engineers. Until this past January, I was manager of marketing communications for Koch Engineering, a manufacturer of chemical process equipment. Now, I'm an independent copywriter specializing in industrial advertising.

Ken, I'd like to write "Ten Tips for Better Technical Writing" for your "You and Your Job" section.

How does this sound?

Sincerely,

Bob Bly

Article Outline

Ten Tips for Better Technical Writing
by Robert W. Bly

1. *Know your readers.*
   Are you writing for engineers? managers? laymen?

2. *Write in a clear, conversational style.*
   Write to express—not to impress.

3. *Be concise.*
   Avoid wordiness. Omit words that do not add to your meaning.

4. *Be consistent . . .*
   . . . especially in the use of numbers, symbols and abbreviations.

5. *Use jargon sparingly.*
Use technical terms only when there are no simpler words that can better communicate your thoughts.

6. *Avoid big words.*
Do not write "utilize" when "use" will do just as well.

7. *Prefer the specific to the general.*
Technical readers are interested in solid technical information and *not* in generalities. Be specific.

8. *Break the writing up into short sections.*
Short sections, paragraphs and sentences are easier to read than long ones.

9. *Use visuals.*
Graphs, tables, photos and drawings can help get your message across.

10. *Use the active voice.*
Write "John performed the experiment," not "The experiment was performed by John." The active voice adds vigor to writing.

Sample Query Letter: *Writer's Digest*

If you've ever wanted to write an article for *Writer's Digest*, take a look at this query letter. It sold an article that became a cover story and was reprinted several times in *Writer's Digest* special issues.

Mr. William Brohaugh
Editor
Writer's Digest
1507 Dana Avenue
Cincinnati, Ohio 45207

Dear Mr. Brohaugh:

John Frances Tighe, a soft-spoken, bearded gentleman, modestly refers to himself as "the world's second-most successful freelance direct-mail copywriter."

John's fee for writing a direct-mail package? $15,000.

But that's peanuts compared to the $40,000 Henry Cowan charges. According to *Who's Mailing What!*, a newsletter covering the direct-mail industry, Cowan is the highest paid copywriter in the world. *Direct Marketing* magazine reports that his income on the Publisher's Clearing House mailing alone (for which he receives a royalty) was $900,000 in a recent year.

Next to the movies and best-selling novels, direct mail is one of the highest paid markets for freelance writers. Although surprisingly easy to break into, most freelancers don't even know about it, and direct-mail writing is dominated by a few dozen writers who earn lush six-figure incomes writing only a few days a week.

I'd like to write a 3,000-word article on "Making Money as a Direct-Mail Writer." The article would tell your readers everything they need to know to start getting assignments in this lucrative but little-known specialty.

Here are the topics I would cover:

1. *The secret world of direct mail*. What is direct mail? Who is writing direct mail—and how much are they earning? Why has this market been a secret until now? I would interview some old pros as well as some new writers to get their perspective.
2. *A look at the market*. What are the various uses of direct mail (mail order, fund-raising, lead generation, cordial contact)?

3. *Getting started.* Learning about direct mail. Studying the market. Building your swipe files. Getting your first assignments.

4. *How to write direct-mail copy that sells.* Understanding the mission of direct mail. Tips for writing copy that will get results. How to present your copy to clients. Graphics and layouts for direct-mail copy. Differences in sales copy (direct mail) vs. editorial copy (magazine writing).

5. *Marketing your services.* Getting and keeping clients. How to market your services using: Portfolios. Meetings. Telephone calls. Letters. Advertising. Publicity techniques.

6. *Fees.* How to set fees. Table of typical fees. What others charge.

7. *Keeping up with the field.* Books. Publications. Professional organizations. Courses. Seminars.

This article will draw both from my own experience as a successful direct-mail copywriter (clients include Prentice-Hall, New York Telephone, Hearst, Chase Manhattan, Edith Roman Associates) and from interviews with top pros in the field—including Milt Pierce, Sig Rosenblum, Richard Armstrong, Don Hauptman, Andrew Linick and others. I know these people personally, so getting the interviews is no problem.

Also, I am a member of the Direct Marketing Club of New York and author of the forthcoming book *Direct Mail Profits* (Asher-Gallant Press).

May I proceed with the article as outlined?

An SASE is enclosed. Thanks for your consideration.

Regards,

Bob Bly

Sample Query Letter: *Amtrak Express*

Amtrak Express is an in-train magazine, similar in style and content to the in-flight magazines you read on airplanes. Here's a query that sold a business article.

Mr. James A. Frank
Editor
Amtrak Express
34 East Fifty-first Street
New York, NY 10022

Dear Mr. Frank:

Is this letter a waste of paper?

Yes—*if* it fails to get the desired result.

In business, most letters and memos are written to generate a specific response—close a sale, set up a meeting, get a job interview, make a contact. Many of these letters fail to do their job.

Part of the problem is that business executives and support staff don't know how to write persuasively. The solution is a formula first discovered by advertising copywriters—a formula called AIDA. AIDA stands for Attention, Interest, Desire, Action.

First, the letter gets Attention . . . with a hard-hitting lead paragraph that goes straight to the point, or offers an element of intrigue.

Then, the letter hooks the reader's Interest. The hook is often a clear statement of the reader's problem, his needs, his desires. If you are writing to a customer who received damaged goods, state the problem. And then promise a solution.

Next, create Desire. You are offering something—a service, a product, an agreement, a contract, a compromise, a consultation. Tell the reader the benefit he'll receive from your offering. Create a demand for your product.

Finally, call for Action. Ask for the order, the signature, the check, the assignment.

I'd like to give you a 1,500-word article on "How to Write Letters That Get Results." The piece will illustrate the AIDA formula with a variety of actual letters and memos from insurance companies, banks, manufacturers, and other organizations.

This letter, too, was written to get a specific result—an article assignment from the editor of *Amtrak Express*.

Did it succeed?

Regards,

Bob Bly

P.S. By way of introduction, I'm an advertising consultant and the author of five books including *Technical Writing: Structure, Standards, and Style* (McGraw-Hill).

Sample Query Letter: New Assignment From Current Editor

Once you know an editor, your queries for repeat assignments can be a little less formal—and you know the editor is already familiar with your work and reputation.

You may wonder why I gave my background in the P.S. when the editor has already done business with me. But she had only bought one previous article and didn't know me all that well, so I felt it would be beneficial to remind her of why I was exceptionally well qualified to write this particular article for her. It couldn't have hurt, because I got the assignment.

Ms. Kimberly A. Welsh
Editor
Circulation Management
859 Willamette Street
Eugene, Oregon 97401-2910

Dear Kimberly:

Thanks for publishing the article on mailing lists so quickly. I hope you get good reader response to it.

I'm writing because I have another idea that might be right for *Circulation Management.*

How about an article—"Do Premiums Work?"

Background: As you know, response rates are down all over. In an attempt to combat this, publications are offering more and more expensive premiums to attract first-time subscribers. *Sports Illustrated*, for example, is offering a videocassette on great sports flubs. *Time* recently offered a camera. And then there's *Newsweek's* successful free telephone offer.

Questions: Is there some point at which a premium ceases to be an added inducement and actually becomes a "bribe," overshadowing the primary offer and becoming the key reason why people respond to a mailing? If so, how does that affect the quality of the subscriber-base the magazine's circulation department is delivering to the publication's advertisers?

This would be the basis of my article, which would attempt to answer these specific questions:

- Do premiums still work? Are they still profitable? Or is their effectiveness declining as more and more publications jump into premium offers?
- Is there any limit to premium cost in relation to the cost of a one-year subscription? What is this limit? What's the "average" premium cost in publishing today?
- What works best—an information premium (printed report or book) or tangible item (telephone, clock radio, etc.)?
- Must the premium be related to the publication, the market or the theme of the mailing? Or do totally unrelated premiums work well as long as they have high perceived value?
- Once a subscriber is sold through a premium offer, must renewals also offer a premium?
- How do advertising managers feel about subscribers generated through premium offers? Is there a perception that a subscriber generated through a premium offer is worth less to an advertiser

than someone who buys the magazine without such a bribe? Any proof to back up this feeling?

To get the answers to these questions, I will interview circulation directors, advertising managers, direct response agencies, DM consultants and freelancers responsible for creating and testing premium-based packages. I see this as a feature article running 3,000+ words.

Kimberly, may I proceed with this article as outlined?

Thanks for your consideration. An SASE is enclosed.

Regards,

Bob Bly

P.S. By way of background: I'm a freelance copywriter specializing primarily in business-to-business direct mail. Publishing clients include Thomas Publishing, Hearst, Prentice-Hall and EBSCO. My most recent book is *Direct Mail Profits: How to Get More Leads and Sales by Mail* (Asher-Gallant Press). Magazine credits include contributions to *Direct Marketing, Writer's Digest, Cosmopolitan, Computer Decisions* and *New Jersey Monthly*.

WINNING BOOK PROPOSALS

The rule for nonfiction books is the same as the rule for articles: Query first.

One of the biggest mistakes a writer can make is to write the book before finding a publisher for it. The writer may spend months researching and writing a book, only to find that editors prefer to see a proposal rather than a completed manuscript.

Editors today don't have time to read unsolicited manuscripts—and if you want to be productive and profitable, you probably don't have time to write one. Editors prefer to review a brief outline of the book you propose to write. This saves them time and also lets them make suggestions or request changes before the book is written. In fact, submitting the completed book marks you as an amateur and actually diminishes your chances for a sale.

Here is a sample short book proposal. It took only a few hours to write and sold to the second publisher who looked at it.

THE ULTIMATE UNAUTHORIZED STEPHEN KING QUIZ BOOK

Hundreds of brain-teasing questions
on minute details and little-known facts
about the world's leading horror writer and his work

by
Robert W. Bly

Agent:
Tony Seidl
T.D. Media
515 E. Seventy-ninth Street, #16C
New York, NY 10021
Phone: (212) 734-3807

THE ULTIMATE UNAUTHORIZED STEPHEN KING QUIZ BOOK

by Robert W. Bly

OVERVIEW

With more than 150 million books sold, Stephen King is one of the most popular authors of all time. His movies gross in the tens of millions of dollars per picture. His TV miniseries get the major share of the viewing market and are typically run during Sweeps Week.

Other writers have readers; Stephen King has *fans*. More than a dozen books have been written about King and his work. He is mobbed whenever he speaks at conventions. There was even a Stephen King newsletter at one point, with a circulation in the tens of thousands. His books are so popular there is a Book Club that sells *only* Stephen King books. First editions of his novels have fetched over $2,000 at auction.

The Ultimate Unauthorized Stephen King Quiz Book taps into the King-mania market. It appeals to the legions of King fans who buy everything they can get their hands on by . . . and about . . . their favorite writer.

FORMAT

The book will be divided into five major sections—novels, the Bachman books (books King wrote under the pseudonym Richard Bachman), short stories, movies and TV, and personal and professional life.

There will be approximately fifty chapters, with 20 or so questions per chapter, for a total of 1,001 questions. Answers will be presented in a separate section at the back of the book.

ABOUT THE AUTHOR

Bob Bly is the author of more than thirty books including *The Ultimate Unauthorized Star Trek Quiz Book* (HarperCollins) and *Comic Book Hero: 1,001 Trivia Questions About America's Favorite Superheroes* (Carol). He has read every commercially published Stephen King book and is an avid fan.

TABLE OF CONTENTS

INTRODUCTION

PART ONE: THE NOVELS

1. Carrie
2. Salem's Lot
3. The Shining
4. The Stand
5. The Dead Zone
6. Firestarter
7. Cujo
8. The Dark Tower I:
    The Gunslinger
9. Christine
10. Pet Sematary
11. Cycle of the Werewolf
12. The Talisman
13. It
14. Eyes of the Dragon
15. Misery
16. The Tommyknockers
17. The Dark Tower II:
    The Drawing of the Three
18. The Dark Tower III:
    The Waste Lands
19. The Dark Half
20. Needful Things
21. Gerald's Game
22. Dolores Claiborne
23. Insomnia
24. Rose Madder
25. The Green Mile
26. Desperation
27. Dark Tower IV:
    Wizard and Glass

PART TWO: THE BACHMAN BOOKS

28. Rage
29. The Long Walk
30. Roadwork
31. The Running Man
32. Thinner
33. The Regulators

PART THREE: THE SHORT STORIES

34. Night Shift
35. Different Seasons
36. Skeleton Crew
37. Four Past Midnight
38. Nightmares and
    Dreamscapes

PART FOUR: TV AND MOVIES

39. Creepshow
40. Cat's Eye
41. Silver Bullet
42. Maximum Overdrive
43. Pet Sematary
44. Golden Years
45. Sleepwalkers
46. The Stand
47. And more . . .

PART FIVE: STEPHEN KING, UP CLOSE AND PERSONAL

48. Professional life
49. Personal life
50. Tabitha King
51. Nonfiction writings

52. Music and poetry
53. A potpourri of King trivia
54. A potpourri of King trivia
   part II

MISCELLANEOUS SAMPLE QUESTIONS TAKEN FROM DIFFERENT
CHAPTERS OF *THE ULTIMATE UNAUTHORIZED
STEPHEN KING QUIZ BOOK*

(Note: Questions will be placed into the appropriate chapters in the completed manuscript.)

1. How many rooms are in Stephen King's Victorian mansion? Where is it located?
2. What advance did Doubleday give King for his first novel, *Carrie*?
3. What adult fantasy novel did King write so his daughter Naomi, who dislikes horror, could enjoy reading one of his books?
4. What is "jaunting"?
5. How tall is John Coffey? How much does he weigh?
6. What type of word processor does King use? How many words does he write each day?
7. What feature film did Stephen King direct?
8. What are the call letters of the Maine radio station King owns? What format is the station?
9. What was the last Stephen King novel to feature the fictional town of Castle Rock, Maine?
10. What is the only Stephen King novel set in Colorado?
11. In what monster movie was the main character a young boy wearing a red "Stephen King Rules" T-shirt?
12. According to Stephen King, an aspiring horror writer should give up after receiving this many rejection slips from publishers and editors.
13. Which of his novels did Stephen King delay publication of because he thought it was too frightening?
14. What do Stephen King, Christopher Reeve, Ed Begley Jr. and Craig T. Nelson have in common?

15. How old was Stephen King when he sold his first novel? What was the title of the book?
16. Before he changed his last name to King, what was Stephen King's father's name?
17. What Stephen King character can start fires with her mind?
18. What kind of car was Christine?
19. What is the longest Stephen King novel?
20. Which of the following is Stephen King afraid of? (a) bugs (b) elevators (c) airplanes (d) the dark (e) raw oysters (f) rats

ANSWERS TO SAMPLE QUESTIONS

1. 24; 49 Florida Avenue, Bangor, Maine 04401
2. $2,500
3. *Eyes of the Dragon*
4. Teleportation of human beings over long distances
5. 6'8"; weight estimated to be between 280 and 350 pounds
6. Wang; 1,500 words every day of the year except Christmas, the Fourth of July and his birthday (September 21)
7. *Maximum Overdrive*
8. WZON; hard rock
9. *Needful Things*
10. *The Shining*
11. *The Monster Squad* (The leader of the squad—Sean Cranshaw—wears the shirt.)
12. 6,000
13. *Pet Sematary*
14. All 6'4"
15. 24 or 26, according to different interviews with King; *Carrie*
16. Donald Spansky
17. Charlie McGee
18. A 1958 Plymouth Fury
19. At 1,300 pages, *It*
20. a, b, c, d, f

CHAPTER 10

How to Get Lucrative Contracts From Corporations and Other Writing Clients

THERE IS NOTHING MORE DEMORALIZING
THAN A SMALL BUT ADEQUATE INCOME.

—EDMUND WILSON

The main problem with "traditional" freelance writing—novels, nonfiction books, articles, essays, plays, poems—is that it doesn't pay well. A recent survey conducted by the American Society of Journalists and Authors showed the median gross income of ASJA members who were full-time freelance writers was $25,000.

The pay scale in copywriting, however, is much higher. *The American Heritage Dictionary* defines a copywriter as "one who writes advertising copy." But freelance copywriters actually handle a much broader range of assignments: everything from company newsletters, annual reports and press releases to brochures, direct-mail packages, speeches and commercials.

How much can a freelance copywriter earn? *Creative Business*, a Boston-based marketing newsletter for advertising freelancers, estimates that the average freelance copywriter with five or more years' experience earns $50,000 a year; it has been my experience that many earn considerably more.

My experience is that an annual income of $85,000 is a realistic goal for a dedicated freelance copywriter, with gross earnings of $100,000–$150,000 or more a year being *very* possible. A number of freelancers I know even gross $200,000 a year or more.

WHAT IT TAKES

Freelance copywriting does not require a degree, certification, specific educational background or work experience. The main qualification is the ability to write good copy.

Take a look at some of the ads, brochures and mailings that cross your desk or enter your mailbox each day. Can you write similar material? If so, you can earn money as a freelance copywriter.

Many freelance copywriters have had previous experience in advertising. Some have worked as writers at advertising agencies or public relations firms. Others have experience as technical writers, promotion writers, advertising managers or corporate communications specialists.

Yet, many enter this field successfully with no previous experience and simply learn as they go. A novice can get some writing experience (and portfolio samples) by taking a course in copywriting, doing volunteer writing for a worthy cause or doing some copywriting—for low or no pay—for a friend or relative.

GETTING STARTED

The first step is to decide what types of materials you would like to write and then identify your potential clients. Will you write ads, brochures, pamphlets, direct-mail packages? Or do you prefer speeches, video scripts, newsletters or slide shows?

Will you write for nonprofits, government agencies, corporations, small businesses, ad agencies, PR firms? Will you be a generalist, or will you specialize in a particular industry or area, such as annual reports or medical writing?

Writers who are relatively inexperienced often start as generalists and then either continue that way or specialize once they've completed several projects in a specific area.

More experienced writers, and those with expertise in a particular field, may find it easier to specialize right from the start. If you've worked as a financial planner, for example, and are switching to a writing career, you'll have an easier time selling your services to banking and financial firms.

The roles of specialist and generalist are not mutually exclusive. You can have one or more areas of specialty while still handling other assignments. Richard Armstrong, a Washington, DC, copywriter, has several specialties, including magazine and newsletter subscription promotion, fund-raising, speech writing and political direct mail.

As a rule, specialists have an easier time winning assignments and generally command higher fees. Some of the most lucrative specialties include medical, financial, industrial, high-tech, annual report, direct-mail and speech writing.

You need to have a name under which you do business. This can be your own name (Bob Bly), a corporate affiliation based on your name (Bob Bly and Associates) or a made-up company name (The Center for Marketing Communication). My letterhead and business card simply list my name with a description of my services underneath:

> BOB BLY
> COPYWRITER/CONSULTANT

I see no advantage in using *and Associates* or a made-up company name: Clients want freelancers to handle writing assignments, and there's no need to create the illusion you're a company when you're not. In fact, doing so may create confusion—some might think you're an ad agency or a studio—and you could lose jobs that clients might prefer to assign to an individual freelancer.

Have a local printer design and print your letterhead, business cards and envelopes. Order five hundred of each to start; most freelancers end up changing their letterhead design two or three times, so you don't want to be stuck with an oversupply.

GENERATING LEADS

Success in this or any other business requires three talents: the abilities to generate leads, close sales and perform the contracted work satisfactorily.

Freelance copywriters use a variety of promotions to get potential clients to come to them. Direct mail is extremely effective. Send prospects a letter explaining who you are and what you do: Many will respond by requesting your resume or brochure, asking to see samples of your work or calling to discuss a potential assignment with you.

For more assertive writers, making telephone calls to prospective clients can also work. Once you make sure the person you're calling handles advertising or marketing communications for the company, ask what types of materials she's responsible for producing and whether she ever uses outside services to produce them. Then ask what it would take for you to be considered for such an assignment.

Whom do you contact? It depends on your market. At larger corporations, it may be the marketing manager, manager of marketing communications, or advertising or public relations manager. At small- to medium-size companies, ask for the president, general manager or director of sales and marketing. At advertising agencies, ask for the creative director or copy supervisor.

Where do you find names of companies or organizations that hire freelance copywriters? Ad agencies are listed in the *Standard Directory of Advertising Agencies*, available at your local library. Numerous other directories list companies by state and industry; again, check your local library. Mailing lists of creative directors, advertising managers and others who buy copywriting services are available from list brokers; one good source is Creative Access, (312) 440-1140.

CLOSING THE SALE

OK. Your mailing or cold calls have generated some initial interest in your copywriting services. What's next?

Some prospects may want to see a portfolio of samples or meet you in person. Follow up on these with a series of phone calls, or perhaps an occasional mailing, so you can contact each prospect about once every four to six weeks. You'll gain "top-of-mind awareness" and eventually be called when an assignment comes up.

Other prospects with more immediate needs may ask you to quote a price. Copywriters charge by the hour or by the project. Hourly rates range from $40 to $150 and up, depending on the region of the country and the experience of the writer. Project rates depend on the length and complexity of the job.

If the client accepts your fee, send a short letter of agreement stating what the job is, describing the work involved and confirming the agreed-on price. Have the client sign the letter and return a copy to you.

Some writers like to get partial payment in advance, ranging from 10 to 50 percent of the total project fee, with the balance paid on completion. A typical arrangement is one-third up front, one-third on completion of the first draft and one-third on delivery of the final manuscript.

If the client says your fee is too high, ask what his budget is, then restructure your estimate by reducing the scope of work. For example, if the client can't afford to pay $4,000 for an eight-page brochure, and has a budget of only $2,000, suggest that you instead write a four-page brochure.

Here are some typical fees for a variety of common copywriting jobs:

Ad
full-page .... $750-$2,000
fractional .... $300–$1,000

Annual report $8,000-10,000

Booklet .... $1,000–$2,500

Brochure
full-size (per 8½″ × 11″ page) .... $400–$700
small (one 8½″ × 11″ page) .... $600–$1,500

Catalog
per page .... $400–$600
per item .... $100–$175

CD-ROMs
per minute of presentation .... $150–$250

Concepts, strategies,
marketing planning .... daily or hourly rate

Direct-mail package
to generate mail orders .... $2,500–$6,000
to generate sales leads .... $1,000–$3,000

Feature articles
ghostwritten, (1,000–3,000 words)........ $1,000–$3,000

Labels and product packaging
per package or label
depending on size .... $200–$1,000

Newsletter, promotional
per page .... $400–$750

Press release (1–2 pages) .... $25–$800

Sales letter (1–2 pages).................................... $500–$1,500

Scripts
     radio commercial... $250–$700
     TV commercial.. $500–$1,500

Slide presentation (20–30 minutes)............... $1,500–$2,500

Speech (20 minutes) .... $1,500–$3,000

Video tape (8–12 minutes running time)...... $2,000–$3,000

Web sites
     per page.. $400–$600

Miscellaneous (manuals, reports,
     business plans, proposals, employee
     communications, etc.) .... daily or hourly rate

MEETING CLIENT EXPECTATIONS

Before you begin the assignment, ask questions to assess what the client is looking for. Does she like long, chatty, conversational copy, or should you keep your words to a minimum? Should the tone be friendly and folksy, or formal and professional? Does the client want technically sophisticated copy, or should it be simple, light reading?

Make sure you understand what points are to be covered. In annual reports, catalogs, corporate capabilities brochures, direct-mail packages and other copy-heavy assignments, it's wise to submit an outline before you begin writing. The client can then add missing facts, delete unnecessary text or reorder some of the points.

For obvious reasons, clients prefer copywriters who are cooperative, professional, diligent, easy to work with, and who meet all their deadlines. If you act like a prima donna, clients simply won't use you again. So put your customers first. Find out what they need from you, and give it to them.

If you feel your copywriting skills need improvement, there are many courses and books available on the subject. You might want to get a copy of my book *The Copywriter's Handbook.*

Although you'll always want to find new clients, marketing and selling take time and money. For this reason, you should aim to have a significant amount of your business come from existing clients. After seventeen years in business, about 80 percent of my income comes from repeat clients. You should make a similar percentage your goal.

How do you get repeat business? Several factors contribute:

1. **Do good work.** Always do your best on every assignment. Only satisfied clients will use your service again.

2. **Provide great service.** Meet your deadlines. Be pleasant and easy to work with. If you give clients a hard time, you won't get repeat business.

3. **Charge fairly.** Fees should be reasonably consistent from assignment to assignment. Don't suddenly double or triple your fees because you think the client won't notice or care. He will.

4. **Make sure the account is current.** As freelancer Milt Pierce told me, "The client who owes you money will never give you another job." Make sure all invoices are paid on time.

5. **Select repeaters.** A repeater is a client who has a need for continuing service, as opposed to a one-shot client who needs copy only once in a while. Ad agencies and big corporations are more likely to be repeaters; small businesses are more likely to be one-shots (but there are numerous exceptions).

6. **Ask for the next order.** When you finish an assignment successfully, ask your satisfied client, "What else can I do for you?" Doing so will often generate an assignment the client might not have considered giving you.

7. **Create new assignments for yourself.** The late consulting guru Howard Shenson once told me, "The most profitable marketing you can do is spend a half hour a week, on your own time (not the client's), coming up with new projects and proposing them to current clients." Whenever you have an idea for a writing project, send or fax a short note to your client; then follow up with a phone call. In many cases, you'll get a go-ahead.

8. **Let the client know you do other things.** One reason clients may not assign more projects to you is they aren't aware you can do them. When you finish that newsletter for your corporate client, don't forget to tell him you also

do magazine articles, press releases, speeches and booklets. The answer will frequently be, "Oh, I didn't realize!"—followed by a request for a cost estimate on a new job.

9. **Ask for referrals within the organization.** When you've established a good, solid working relationship with a client, ask whether managers in other departments or divisions might also benefit from your services. Then contact those people and say, "Mr. Client suggested I get in touch with you," and make a pitch for business. The fact that you're already doing good work for their organization will result in an extremely high closing rate.

You can also ask for referrals to potential clients at other companies. Just ask for the names of colleagues in noncompeting organizations who might be able to use your work. Follow up on each referral, and you'll get plenty of new business.

How much money can you *really* make following my guidelines? It depends on your level of experience, how hard you work and whether you're a diligent marketer. Some beginners charge modestly and build their incomes slowly, while others start with high rates and have all the work they can handle. Most of us fall somewhere in between.

Your annual income during the first year could easily be $30,000–$40,000 or more. In my first year, 1982, I grossed about $39,000, which was especially satisfying in comparison to my 1981 salary of $26,000, when I worked as an advertising manager for a small engineering firm.

Within a couple of years, you could easily reach $50,000–$85,000 a year or more! I hit six figures in my third or fourth year and have stayed there since.

To make $100,000 a year, you must bill about $2,000 a week, or $8,934 a month. If your average project fee is $1,000, that means doing two projects a week. If your average project fee is $4,000, it means a project every two weeks.

Is this possible? Yes. Say you specialize in ads, radio commercials, billboards and other short-copy assignments and your average fee is $1,000. How long does it take you to write an ad? If it takes a full day, you can work two days a week, bill $2,000 and gross $100,000 a year.

Does that mean you spend the other three days in leisurely pursuits? Not at all. Most freelance writers find that only 50 to 60 percent of their work time is actually "billable"—that is, spent doing research, writing or other activities a client will pay for.

The remaining hours are spent selling and marketing their writing services and tending to the countless details of running a small business: everything from bookkeeping, taxes and bill paying to photocopying, going to the post office, learning new software and filing.

"Your advice is all well and good for experienced writers," a lot of freelancers at my seminars tell me. "But I'm a beginner, I've never worked as a copywriter, have no experience and no portfolio. These techniques can't possibly work for me! Who would hire me?"

The answer is a strange secret I discovered years ago: In any business, many people *will* hire beginners. And you can get started by working with these people.

If you doubt me, think about brain surgery. Every practicing brain surgeon has, at some time in the past, performed a "first operation"—which means someone hired that brain surgeon to do surgery *when she had never previously performed the operation!* If brain surgeons can get hired with no experience, surely freelance writers can.

Sophisticated clients, such as big ad agencies and corporations, probably will go with experienced writers. But many small- and medium-size firms are open to the idea of hiring beginners when it's convenient and affordable to do so. Perhaps your rates are lower than the ten-year veteran's. Or perhaps it's more convenient to hire you because you're only a ten-minute drive from headquarters, your schedule is more flexible or you're more accommodating.

If you do enough self-promotion, you'll eventually reach the right person at the right time, and you'll get the job. You're bound to happen on at least one person with an urgent need for free-lance copywriting. Many times you'll find the person you wrote or called simply didn't know how to go about finding a writer; your mailing piece or phone call—conveniently—found him at a time of need.

Whatever the reason, it's a fact that a large percentage of clients are willing to work with beginners. At this point, you must take my word for it. But if you start your marketing and selling campaign now, you'll soon discover the truth of this strange secret for yourself.

TWENTY-TWO SECRETS OF SUCCESSFUL SELF-PROMOTION

1. Never tell anyone that you are not busy and that you are looking for work. (Clients want to hire those who are successful, not those who are hungry.)
2. Always put your name, address and phone numbers on every piece of promotion you produce. This makes it easy for potential new business to reach you.
3. Write a book. It positions you as an expert.
4. If you don't have the time to write a book, write an article.
5. When you write that article, try to sell it to more than one publication. (You can change the title and a few of the examples to tailor it to each publication's readers.)
6. Regularly mail reprints of your articles to your prospects and clients. Attach a note or short cover letter to personalize the mailing.
7. Advertise your services in magazines aimed at advertising professionals. Try a variety of journals and different ads until you find which ads give the best results. Also, try both classified and display formats.
8. Use direct mail to generate new business leads. A successful mailing of only a hundred letters can often yield five to ten highly qualified new prospects.
9. Create a package of literature describing your services, background, fees, methods, clients and so forth. Mail the package to people who request more information in response to your ads and mailings. Such a package is extremely useful in prescreening leads.
10. Some copywriters, such as the late Paul Bringe, have had great success using self-published newsletters to promote their services. Newsletters help build recognition and establish credibility with a select audience (the people who receive the newsletter) over an extended period of time.
11. Don't skimp on letterhead, envelopes and business cards.

The letterhead design and paper quality can convey an image of class and success.

12. Package your copy so that it looks expensive. Type on high-quality paper, mail flat and protect copy with cardboard, tissues and so forth. You can charge more if the product looks better.

13. Use a word processor. It will allow you to produce flawless manuscripts as well as dramatically increase your productivity.

14. Offer to speak and give seminars before trade associations and professional groups. Make sure potential clients will be among those in attendance.

15. Teach a course in advertising, marketing or writing at a local college or adult education program. This establishes you as an "instant expert" in the field.

16. Network. Don't be a recluse—be social. Attend meetings, seminars, luncheons. Volunteer to work on a committee. Become visible in the advertising community.

17. Recycle your material. A lecture can become the basis for an article or series of articles. The articles can be turned into a book. Using your basic material over and over makes it possible to get broad exposure and still have time to devote to your copywriting business.

18. Be selective. Not every opportunity to speak, lecture, write or participate is worthwhile. Focus on those promotional activities that will give you the most return on your time and effort.

19. Keep your name in front of clients and prospects by giving a "premium." Most will appreciate your thoughtfulness. And the right premium—one that is kept in the office for years—serves as a daily reminder of you and your service.

20. Let people know about your recent successes. If your latest piece of copy was a rousing success, get extra copies and send them to prospects and clients in similar fields. Include a cover note that says, "Here's what I've done recently—let me do the same for *you!*"

21. Save letters of praise you receive from clients and build a "kudos" file. Selected quotations from these letters—or even reprints of the letters themselves—can dramatically add to the selling power of your next ad or mailing. (Be

sure to get permission first before you quote someone in print!)

22. Keep written records of past promotions and their results. Only by measuring the success or failure of promotional experiments can we learn which promotions work for us and which will bomb.

CHAPTER 11

The Four Rs:
Making Money From Referrals, Repeat Business, Reprints and Resales

THE PROFESSION OF BOOK WRITING MAKES
HORSE RACING SEEM LIKE A SOLID, STABLE BUSINESS.
—JOHN STEINBECK

In this chapter we explore four lucrative ways to make extra income from existing clients and writings: referrals, repeat business, reprints and resales.

REFERRALS

The easiest way to get new clients is through referral from existing clients, prospects, colleagues and even competitors. Yet, asking for referrals is often neglected in favor of other marketing techniques such as cold calling, letter writing and proposals.

"Without question, selling through referrals is the most powerful way to build your business, not to mention the most enjoyable," writes sales trainer Bill Cates in his book *Unlimited Referrals*. "Your buyers would rather meet you through a referral. The endorsement and testimony of others make them feel more comfortable opening their door to you and giving you their business."

How do you go about getting referrals? You do it by calling your best customers and asking them for referrals.

Although this can be a separate call, it's better if combined with a call for another purpose—to keep in touch, check on customer satisfaction, follow up on a job you submitted or check on the status of a project. Here's how it might go:

YOU:	Mike, can I ask you a question?
PROSPECT:	Sure, go ahead.
YOU:	You seem pretty satisfied with the work I have done for you—am I right?
PROSPECT:	Yes, very.
YOU:	Would you be comfortable recommending my writing services to colleagues of yours who are not direct competitors with your firm?
PROSPECT:	Of course.
YOU:	Which of these people could I get in touch with to let them know about our product and service and how it can help them?
PROSPECT:	Joe Doakes at Hummingbird Industries.
YOU:	And do you have Joe's phone number?
PROSPECT:	(555) 555-1111.
YOU:	Joe Doakes at Hummingbird. May I use your name when I call him?
PROSPECT:	Certainly.
YOU:	Great. I'll call Joe. Who else do you know who might be able to benefit from our products and services?

You then repeat the cycle, ending with, "And who else?" until the prospect gives you all the referrals he is going to give you right now. By asking, "And who else?" you will probably get two or three referrals instead of the one the prospect was going to give you. Three is probably the limit for one call—the prospect will run out of ready names and get tired of giving the referrals— but ask until he says, "That's it."

I recommend you send a thank-you note to customers who give you referrals. A small, tasteful gift is optional. (I send a copy of one of my books.)

Keep the customer up-to-date if anything comes from the referral. If you get business out of it, send another thank-you and a slightly better gift (my choice is a gift basket).

You can ask these same customers for more referrals later. Just don't do it too frequently. Once every four or five months seems about right. If you do something particularly good for them, such as solve a problem or complete a successful project, by all means ask for a reference as you bask in the glow of their praise.

REPEAT BUSINESS

Most writers concentrate on new markets. Here's how to win lucrative ongoing repeat business from existing clients and editors. Repeat assignments are easier to get and take less time to complete.

While salespeople tend to focus on pursuing new business, there is a potentially more lucrative source of revenue you can exploit: getting additional orders from your existing customers.

Because many salespeople love the thrill of the chase, and because they often get bigger commissions for bringing in new customers, soliciting repeat sales and reorders from active accounts is often ignored at the expense of pursuing new business.

Not every teleseller makes this mistake. Stockbrokers, for example, know the value of working existing accounts. If you have an account with a brokerage, you get frequent calls from your broker offering new ideas for companies he wants you to invest in. But telesellers in some other industries are not as savvy. For example, the company that sold me my computer has never contacted me to offer any upgrades or new services, despite the fact that there are many they have I would want—a bigger memory, better CD-ROM drive, higher resolution laser printer or home page design. A mistake? I think so.

Have a plan for periodically recontacting active customers to remind them of your existence and give them news of any special offers, discounts, new services or new ideas for writing projects they might benefit from. Doing so will substantially increase reorders and repeat sales from your database of existing clients.

In particular, let existing customers know of new services you are offering, such as Web pages or CD-ROM scripting. This cross-selling will get existing customers to give you assignments they would have never thought to call you for before.

Experience shows that an active customer is five to ten times more likely to buy something from you than a prospect you cold-call from a prospecting directory or telemarketing list. That means "working your database" can yield five to ten times the response of a new business or customer acquisition effort aimed at a similar number of prospects.

How frequently should you keep in touch with existing customers? It's different for every business, but for freelance writers, a contact every quarter—a call or mailing once every three months, for a total of four in a given year—makes sense. It's frequent enough so the customer doesn't forget about you. But infrequent enough so you're not pestering customers or spending an inordinate amount of time and money making these contacts.

If possible, make most of the contacts phone calls. You can increase frequency of contact by adding one, two or three mailings a year or by substituting a mailing for one or two of the four annual phone calls. The mailing need not be elaborate. Remember, this is just to keep in touch and keep your name before the customer. A simple postcard or short sales letter is more than sufficient.

"Seek a reason to keep in touch with your existing clients so they don't fall into a dormant cycle," writes Loriann Hoff Oberlin in her book *Writing for Money.* "It takes much less effort to sell a previously satisfied client on a new writing job than a customer unfamiliar with your work. Send correspondence and clippings your clients might appreciate and schedule lunch meetings periodically to discuss your client's changing needs." In an article in the Institute of Children's Literature newsletter, *The Institute Newsline*, Elizabeth Hoekstra notes, "Good organization is key to positive communication with an editor. A quick reference to your files and submission records will tell you if, when, and what you have submitted to a publication previously."

REPRINTS
I earn an extra $5,000–$10,000 each year selling photocopied reprints of previously published articles I've written, copies of my out-of-print books, and audio- and videocassette recordings of my speeches and seminars, all via mail order. You can, too. Here's how:

1. Whenever possible, make sure you maintain reprint and mail-order rights to all your works.
2. Get extra tearsheets of published articles. Store in hanging files. Number each file. Keep a master index so you can easily look up and retrieve any piece by its code number. Make and store multiple copies of each piece. Copies should be of high quality with no blurs or smudges and easy to read.
3. Buy extra copies of your books from your publishers. When

the book goes out of print, buy the remainders and store them in your house if you have the room.

4. If organizations that hire you as a speaker professionally video- or audiotape your presentation, keep reproduction rights and have them give you copies of the masters in exchange for the right to tape you.

5. If you are a guest on a radio or TV show, get a tape master of your appearance. Before accepting the engagement, inform the producer that in exchange for appearing on the show, you maintain duplication rights.

6. If you give a talk where you will not be taped, arrange to have a professional video- or audiotape it at your expense.

7. Take these tapes to a duplicator and have copies made with neat-looking but inexpensive laser labels. Use a numbering system and make a master list of tapes with number and title.

8. Make sure your contact information, including name, address and phone numbers, appears on everything you write or produce. Solicit reader feedback by asking for questions, comments and suggestions. Encourage readers to contact you for more information or to establish a dialogue on your topic.

Soon you will have a line of "information products"—article reprints, books, audiocassettes, videotapes—that you have written or presented. You will also find yourself receiving frequent queries from readers who have questions or want to buy additional books and other materials you have written.

The greatest profit opportunity for selling these information products to your readers is through a minicatalog. The catalog can list article reprints, books and tapes, including title, description and price. It can also include a coupon the reader can use to order items.

Such a catalog need not be elaborate. You can print it in black ink on white or colored paper. You don't need to illustrate it with drawings or photos.

One of these minicatalogs should be included in every outgoing order you ship to your mail-order customers. The beauty is that it promotes your entire product line at virtually no cost—there is no postage or envelope to pay for since it is mailed with the product shipment. The only cost is the few pennies per catalog for printing.

For a small home-based business selling information products by mail, including a minicatalog in all product shipments can double your annual gross sales with no added marketing cost.

You can promote your information products in other ways, of course. For instance, you can periodically mail your minicatalog or other special offers to your list of mail-order customers. But the cheapest, easiest way to sell back-end products is by enclosing minicatalogs with products being shipped and sending them to anyone and everyone who writes, calls or E-mails you. If you don't do this, you are missing out on a large share of the profits your writing business can generate.

Reprint Sales Inc. actively markets reprints for publishers and others with information it owns the copyright to. For information, contact RSI, 60 East Forty-second Street, #3810, New York, NY 10165, phone (800) 567-7706.

RESALES

There are some writing projects that, while not lucrative based on the initial payment, can pay off handsomely when the writer retains rights and resells the same material to multiple markets, getting paid each time. Carol Andrus, for instance, earned an incredible $33,000 from one article, selling it to sixty-seven different publications.

Recycle your articles. Sell first rights only with articles, retaining all other rights. Rewrite and resell these articles in other markets. Do variations. Most writers do an enormous amount of research for one article or book then drop that topic. If you can amortize the time spent on that research over four or five related projects, your writing business will be much more profitable. "Why should you limit yourself to one article, one approach, one publication . . . and only one check?" asks Donald Nicholas, president of Blue Dolphin Communications, Inc. "You can make your hard work pay off better by finding topics that will satisfy more than one buyer. The more ways you can 'slice' the topic, the more money you will make."

Recycle your material. One writer of paperback westerns writes many novels a year for different series. He keeps all books on a hard drive. Often he pulls chapters from different books into new books, changing names, places and some of the narrative to fit the new story. In this way he can produce many more novels a year.

You may be thinking he's a hack. But he enjoys his work and makes a nice living in a field where most are struggling to pay the rent.

Recycle your articles and books. If you write on related topics, research materials collected but not used for one article or book can find their way into the next piece. Subjects given only limited space in the current project can be expanded and made into a series of follow-up works.

Don't let your out-of-print material stay out of print. Get the rights back and resell them to other publishers for a new contract and advance. You can revise the piece and create a new version much faster than you can write an entirely new book or article from scratch. Yet the advance you get for a revised book edition will be 50 to 80 percent of the advance you'd be paid for a brand-new book, so it's very profitable.

When my book *Secrets of a Freelance Writer* was published in July 1988, I didn't expect the publisher to go out of business four months later. (After all, it had been in business for 150 years.) People began complaining to me that they couldn't get the book in bookstores, and bookstores couldn't get it from the publisher. Finally, I received a letter from the publisher telling me it was having "losses and cash-flow deficits" and looking to sell its assets. In other words, it was going bust.

But even more shocking was the request that I buy back the rights to my own book—for $2,500! Naturally, I had assumed the rights reverted to me. After all, it was in my contract. But the publisher felt differently.

A book represents a great investment of time, effort and energy—an investment rarely covered by your advance alone. Unfortunately, most books go out of print too quickly to pay substantial royalties.

But having the book go out of print does not put an end to its value. The physical inventory—the remaining unsold books themselves—has value to the author, both as a product that can be marketed and sold on its own and as a promotional tool (for consultants, doctors, psychologists, speakers, experts in various subjects and others with professional practices in the fields his book covers).

Even more important are the rights to reprint and republish the work. Even if you never sell the book to a new publisher, you still want to be able to use the material—as chapters in other books, as articles, lectures, speeches, cassette programs, perhaps even in self-published material. If you don't have full and clear ownership of these rights, your material may remain unread and unused forever.

To make sure you retain the rights to your book after it goes out of print, the publisher should copyright the book in your name and not its own. Although copyrighting the book in the author's name is standard practice, numerous smaller publishers (and a few larger ones) will make themselves the copyright holder—unless you insist otherwise.

Include a contract clause that states that rights revert to you when the book goes out of print. In 1982, for example, I published a dictionary of computer words with a small press. When the press went out of business, I checked my contract and found that I had neglected to insist on a clause dealing with rights reversion (often called the "termination" clause in a standard publishers contract). Now the books are out of print, the former owner of the publishing house won't return my phone calls and my rights to reuse the material are probably lost forever.

Make sure the contract defines "out of print" so both you and the publisher know when you can request reassignment of rights. One publisher's contract says the book is out of print when "subsequent to one year from publication date, no earnings have been payable to the author during two consecutive accounting periods (12 months)." After that, the publisher must republish, resell or actively market the book within six months, or rights revert to the author.

Be careful of tricky clauses. Another publisher's contract says that rights don't revert to the author until the work is out of print "in all forms of media." This means that if the book goes out of print yet the publisher continues to sell a cassette version, a videotape or even a small pamphlet based on the book, I can't offer the book itself to another publisher.

Also, make sure the contract specifies what happens to the remaining inventory of books and the original camera-ready copy when the book goes out of print. Getting the copies is important if you intend to sell them or use them as promotional giveaways, or simply want them as mementos. Getting the plates is even more important because a new publisher can reprint your book directly from the existing plates or films, saving enormous amounts of time and money. And this, frankly, is a selling point when marketing the book to a new publisher.

Choose a reputable publisher with a good track record. This, I admit, can be difficult. For instance, in the early 1980s, I published six books with a small, entrepreneurial publishing firm that was a successful pioneer in computer books. When the computer book market went soft, the company went out of business and my six books went out of print.

I vowed to stick with major publishers. Then, after I published two books with a firm that had been in business since 1839, it folded in 1989 and two more books were out of print.

Meanwhile, my friend Roger Parker has completed some successful and lucrative books for a small publisher I had never heard of. His books continue to sell like gangbusters, and both he and the publisher are making a lot more money in publishing than I am right now.

Still, a large, established publisher is probably less likely to disappear than a small press with only a couple of titles in its catalog.

The best way to protect yourself from your book going out of print is to help the publisher sell it so there is a constant demand for it. Some suggestions:

1. When filling out the author's questionnaire, give the publisher complete information on the book, its selling points and any resources or media outlets for promotion. The staff at the publishing house gets this information from your completed author's questionnaire, not the book itself (which they don't have time to read). So don't take this document lightly.

2. Don't limit yourself to the space provided on the author's questionnaire form. If you're detailed in your answers, there won't be sufficient room for your replies. I type the questions and answers on my word processor, which gives me more room and allows me to insert entire sections of my book proposal into the appropriate sections of the questionnaire.

This gives the publisher's staff the same powerful material that sold my editor on the book in the first place.

3. Volunteer to write promotional copy for the publisher. Write your own catalog blurb and press release, and give it to your editor and publicist. Usually they will be only too happy to use what you supply and have you do the work.

4. Cooperate with the publicity and marketing departments. These days the most common complaint among authors is that publishers don't do enough to promote books. So when the publisher *does* get you a speaking engagement or book you on a talk radio show, don't be difficult. And let everyone know you are eager and available to do more of the same. Getting publicity for an author makes the publicist look good, so she will work with you if you encourage it and if your book is promotable.

5. Conduct your own marketing campaign. Politely find out what the publisher intends to do—and what it won't do. Then, consider taking up some of the slack yourself. If you have written a book on management, for example, and have some contacts at major corporations, see if you can sell the book in volume as a training tool or premium. Give seminars or lectures at which the book can be sold to attendees. This won't move large quantities, but it will help spread the word about your book.

6. Keep at least a dozen copies on hand. If the book suddenly goes out of print and you can't buy the remainders, you'll need these copies to send to prospective new publishers. And once you find a new publisher, the production department will probably need two or three clean copies of the book to print from, assuming you can't get the plates or films.

7. Keep up with the publishing industry. Subscribe to *Writer's Digest* and *Publishers Weekly.* If you read or hear rumors that your publisher is in financial trouble or is a target for acquisition, call your editor and buy at least a hundred copies of your book (at your author's discount, of course). Once a publishing house's money problems are bad enough to become public rumor, financial collapse—which can result in inaccessibility of its inventory—can happen faster than you think.

Another warning sign that your publisher is having financial difficulties is late royalty payments and statements.

But sooner or later, despite your best efforts, your book will go out of print. Either the publisher will notify you or royalty statements will indicate that the book isn't being sold anymore. If you've protected yourself by including the contract clauses I suggested, you're in good shape.

Not sure what your contracts say? Go to your files and check all contracts for your existing books. There's a good chance your contracts contain these clauses. If you don't have a clause reverting the rights of your out-of-print book to you, the going will be tougher, but not impossible. Some publishers—especially financially sound ones—will be reasonable and give you the rights. Others—usually small ones going out of business—may not respond to your request at all.

When your book goes out of print, immediately send a letter to the publisher requesting that all rights revert to you. If your contract contains a reversion clause, say so.

Also, consider buying the remaining inventory of books and the printing plates or films, but at a reasonable price. Include a sentence in your letter that indicates your interest without making you seem too eager. For example: "If you are interested in selling the remaining inventory and the plates, I may be a customer."

If all is well, the publisher should respond by offering you the remaining inventory at a reasonable price (I'll discuss pricing later). You should get the books, the films or plates (if available), and a letter stating that all rights have officially reverted to you.

A far more serious problem arises when the book goes out of print because the publisher is going out of business. You might think that because the book is out of print, the rights automatically revert to you. But beware, "There appears to be a general misconception in the publishing industry that if a publisher fails to remit royalties or becomes the subject of either voluntary or involuntary court supervised liquidation proceedings, authors' contractual rights revert to the authors," stated the publisher in a letter to me concerning my books. "We believe that the rights under the authors' contracts do *not* [italics mine] revert to him. In fact, in such recent proceedings as the Stein and Day bankruptcy case, authors' contracts were sold to the highest bidder.

Therefore, you should not rely on any automatic right of reversion."

One publisher, now out of business, sent me a notice offering to sell me the rights to my two books, *Secrets of a Freelance Writer* and *The Copywriter's Handbook*, for $2,500 apiece—$5,000 total.

My immediate reaction was to get my attorney to threaten a lawsuit, which was a mistake. A company hounded by creditors isn't afraid of one more complaint. My lawyer got out of it, and my agent took over. In the final deal, the publisher granted me all rights to both books in exchange for a payment of $2,000 ($1,000 per book) plus forgiveness of back royalties (which I never would have seen anyway). I could have gotten it cheaper: I believe those authors who negotiated early instead of fighting as I did paid around $250 per book for rights.

Conclusion? If the publisher offers to sell you the rights, re-spond immediately with a much lower figure and begin negotia-tion. The authors who act first can get back the rights at the lowest price. Later, when the publisher realizes how badly it needs cash, it becomes more demanding and less open to negotiation.

Determine whether to accept the publisher's final offer based on what the book means to you—personally, emotionally and financially—as well as its sales potential. With my children's book, *Ronald's Dumb Computer*, the book is financially unim-portant to me and I never bothered to pursue the rights. But *The Copywriter's Handbook* is an ongoing promotional tool for me and a major source of new consulting business, so getting back the rights was crucial—and well worth the $1,000 I paid.

My story has a happy ending. My editor moved to another publishing house. She got in touch and expressed interest in republishing *Secrets of a Freelance Writer* and *The Copywriter's Handbook* if I could get the rights back. My advance from the new publisher more than covered what I paid the original pub-lisher to recover the rights, and new editions of both books are now in bookstores.

When the original publisher offered to sell me the rights to my books, it also asked me if I wanted to purchase the remaining inventory. While most book contracts offer the remainders to the author at manufacturing cost, this publisher wanted cost plus $1 per book. This was $3.16 per book for 629 hardcover copies of *The Copywriter's Handbook*, with a cover price of $17.95, and $3.19 per book for 406 paperback copies of *Secrets of a Freelance Writer*, with a cover price of $9.95. With shipping, handling and taxes included, this meant I'd write an additional check for $3,575.10 in exchange for 1,035 books with a retail value of $15,330.25—assuming I could sell them.

In my case, I wasn't especially worried about being able to sell the books. I use *The Copywriter's Handbook* as a premium, giving it to clients and prospects for my consulting and copywriting services. In addition, I receive several calls each week from people wanting to know where they can get a copy. As for *Secrets of a Freelance Writer*, I knew from running a test ad in *Writer's Digest* that I could sell the book profitably as a mail-order item.

However, by the time I decided to buy the books, the publisher's inventory was frozen for legal reasons. Eventually, I bought the books at an even lower price from a remainder house (a distributor that buys and sells inventories of out-of-print books).

Make an offer and get the books shipped to you right away. Otherwise, you may never get them.

This assumes, of course, that you want the inventory. You may not. Storing hundreds or thousands of books presents problems in itself. The best place is the garage, attic, basement or spare bedroom, but you may not want to live with the clutter. The alternatives—warehouses or other storage facilities—are not inexpensive. I got a quotation from a "fulfillment house," which would not only store the books but also handle incoming mail orders and ship books to customers for me. Storage alone for the two thousand books was in the range of $50–$100 per month—which would quickly eat into my profits. I keep my books in my basement.

Selling the inventory is a challenge. But, being a writer, you may be able to find creative and profitable ways to do it. Many authors sell their books by mail.

The selling method you use determines the maximum you can afford to pay for your out-of-print books. If you sell them at seminars, for example, where selling costs are low, you can pay up to 50 percent of the retail price and still make a handsome profit because your only advertising cost is holding up a copy of the book from the podium.

But if you want to sell the book through mail-order advertising, you need a higher profit margin to cover the costs of advertising (classified is best) and shipping books to customers. The most you can afford to pay is 25 percent of the retail price, and you really should be looking to pay 10 to 20 percent of retail, maybe less.

For most trade paperbacks, this comes to $1–$3 per copy. When selling the books mail order, add $2 to the retail price for shipping and handling. This helps relieve some of the burden of your high selling costs.

Assuming you are successful at selling your books, the inventory will soon be gone. Then what?

If the rights belong to you, you have two choices. You can sell the book to another publisher, or you can publish it yourself.

The author who wants to self-publish his out-of-print book has a big advantage over other self-publishers; namely, the book has already been designed and set into type—eliminating thousands of dollars in typesetting and composition costs.

Ideally, your printer should print from the publisher's original plates or films. But in most instances, the printer can produce an acceptable finished product using existing copies of the published book as his camera-ready artwork. For this, he will need two clean copies in good condition.

How many copies should you print? Most self-publishing experts I talked to recommend a first print run of three thousand copies. Printing fewer copies drives up the cost per copy, while printing more could leave you with a warehouse full of books if they don't sell.

For a 128-page trade paperback, trim size 5½″×8½″, a book production house quoted me a price of $6,488.09 for three thousand copies, or $2.16 per book. I could probably have gotten a lower price going directly to a printer and handling the production details myself. Be sure to go to a printer specializing in books.

Self-publishing offers you the advantage of control over jacket design, pricing, marketing and distribution. You might want to get into the bookselling business this way. I didn't. And where would I store three thousand books? So, instead, I chose to resell the rights to the publisher where my editor now worked.

Will you be able to resell your book to another publisher? It may be difficult. Publishers are more interested in something new than something old. Unless your book was a big seller, most editors won't get excited about it. But if you query publishers, you may find one looking to fill a slot in its catalog with a book just like yours. Or maybe an editor who praised the book in the past would be happy to acquire it now. If your original editor has moved to another publishing house, he would be your best bet for a resale.

What kind of advance can you expect? Probably 50 percent or less of the advance you would get for the book if it were new. On the other hand, it's easy money; unless your book must be revised and updated, there's almost no work involved for you.

If there's one piece of advice to follow above all else, it's *act quickly*. Those authors who take immediate action and persist until the deal is made suffer least and profit most when their books go out of print.

PART FOUR

GETTING PAID BETTER

You now write faster, write more and sell more of what you write. The final step in maximizing your income is to get paid more for each assignment you do. This section helps you find and sell to better-paying markets while asking for—and getting—top dollar.

CHAPTER 12

Where to Find (and How to Reach) Better-Paying Markets

SOME PEOPLE MAKE THINGS HAPPEN.
SOME WAIT FOR THINGS TO HAPPEN,
AND THEN THERE ARE THOSE WHO SAY—WHAT HAPPENED?
—ANONYMOUS

Instead of trying to squeeze more money out of modest-paying sources, writers who want to make a lot of money should target the better-paying markets to begin with. These include the following:

- book publishers who pay the biggest advances and highest royalties
- magazines who pay the biggest fees
- corporate clients and assignments that pay best
- other lucrative markets for writers (from greeting card companies to graphic designers producing annual reports)

This chapter profiles three of the most lucrative, but often overlooked, markets for writers: annual reports, direct marketing and the speaking and training business.

ANNUAL REPORTS

Writers don't produce annual reports for the glory or fame or to obtain literary and artistic fulfillment. They perceive, quite correctly, that annual reports are a lucrative writing assignment for which freelance writers are frequently hired—and they want to get their share of the loot.

Writing a large annual report for a major corporation is a

lucrative assignment, with fees ranging from $8,000 to $11,000 or more per project. Even for a small annual report for a medium-size corporation, you can charge $4,000–$6,000 or more.

On a word rate, figure annual report copy at anywhere from $1 to $2 a word. That includes revisions, and there are normally lots of revisions on this type of assignment.

Pages can be light or heavy on text, but figure 300–400 words of text maximum per page. On a per-page rate, annual report writers charge $400–$600 per page.

The advantage of large assignments such as annual reports is that if you get a few assignments, you are well on your way to making your income goal for the year.

For example, if a corporate writer does half a dozen annual reports per year, those six assignments alone could bring him $50,000–$60,000 in fees.

By comparison, some corporate writers I know charge only $300 for press releases. To earn $60,000 at this rate, you'd have to write two hundred press releases! That's a lot of assignments to handle.

If you can get one, two or three annual reports for clients and do them annually, that's a solid base from which to build a profitable freelance writing income.

One writer I know wrote, for many years, the annual reports of six companies every year. This brought him $50,000 a year in income. The assignments occupied him full time for about four to five months; the rest of the year he was free to vacation or pursue other projects.

Who publishes annual reports? Companies who sell stock on any exchange are public and are required to produce a comprehensive financial report every year. Although some privately held companies may do an abbreviated version of the standard annual report, 99 percent of annual reports are done by publicly owned companies, as required by the Securities and Exchange Commission (SEC).

Freelance corporate writer Maryclaire Collins writes in her book *How to Make Money Writing Corporate Communications* "Companies that publish these reports for the public often produce them in a slick, colorful format that incorporates a significant amount of narrative about the company's products and performance. This calls for writing that seamlessly integrates a discussion of financial matters with company braggadocio. While some companies staff individuals who specialize in writing the annual report, others might call on freelancers, or opt for a consulting agency that specializes in this type of writing."

The annual report summarizes a company's performance for the past year and promises great things for the year ahead. Annual reports are generally divided into two parts. The first tells the company's story in narrative form (for large firms, this narrative might consist of several separate subsections, each devoted to one of the firm's various operating companies, divisions or subsidiaries). The second part, sometimes called the management discussion, consists mainly of numbers reported by the corporation's accounting firm.

In an article in *Writer's Digest*, annual report writer Stephanie Ferm of SM Communications notes: "Today's typical report encompasses more than the obligatory chairman's letter, product reviews and financial highlights. Many now include lively company histories, employee profiles, or features on corporate philanthropic commitments. Some major conglomerates have recently added proactive reports that reinforce corporate initiatives on such social issues as the environment, health care and education. The most innovative of the lot are experimenting with videos, newsletters, newspaper formats and computer disks to supplement or enhance their financial reports. For the past two years, Marvel's annual report has been in the form of a comic book."

Freelance writer Loriann Hoff Oberlin, in her book *Writing for Money*, describes the writer's role in annual report publishing as follows: "What they [employees and stockholders] demand [in an annual report] is an honest account of business. They want to know where and how the organization has helped others, what makes the company special, what makes it better than others in the industry. The public likes to learn this year's success stories, how major problems were tackled, and whether the company was a good steward of private and public money. Finally, people want to know what's in store for the future, and the organization's place in that large picture."

According to an article in the newsletter *Creative Business*, over $5 billion is spent each year on annual report production. About 20 percent of that, or approximately $1 billion, is spent on creative services: writing, design, illustration and photography.

There is a lot of opportunity for you in this market. According to the *Creative Business* article, there are around ten thousand publicly owned corporations that must produce annual reports in accordance with SEC guidelines. The good news for you is these companies are open to trying new writers. Each year, three companies out of every ten choose a different vendor to create their annual reports.

The best way to become familiar with annual reports is to get your hands on a bunch of them and read them carefully. There are two ways to get copies of annual reports. If you buy stock in a company, even a single share, you'll automatically receive an annual report from that company once a year. Many shareholders throw them away without reading them. You should start a reference library of them.

If you are not sure you want to buy stock, you can call a stock broker anyway. Tell him you are thinking of buying the stock of company X, and could he send you an analyst's report along with a company annual report.

Or you can call the corporation directly. Ask the operator for the investor relations department. When you are connected, simply state that you want a copy of the company's latest annual report. It will be sent to you without charge.

Another alternative: Pick up *Forbes* or *Fortune* magazine. In many issues, free annual reports from companies advertising in the issue can be obtained simply by completing and mailing a return postcard included with the magazine.

Read the annual reports as a writer, not a shareholder or consumer. Study them for tone, style, content, organization, length and format. Make notes on the topics covered, the various sections and the number of words and pages devoted to each.

Write the contents of several reports in outline form. Note the similarities between reports. These are the same sections you will have to write when you are given an annual report assignment.

One section that is usually up front and given a lot of emphasis and attention is the letter to the shareholders. Signed by the chairman, president, CEO or another top executive, the letter, usually two to three pages long, sums up the year's activities and presents an overview of what the reader will find in the report.

Occasionally clients will write their own annual reports in-house but farm out just the president's letter to a freelancer. The fee for writing such a letter should be around $1,500—certainly not less than $1,000 and probably not more than $2,500.

Writing the president's letter is not difficult. To get a feel for the style, read half a dozen or so president's letters from the annual reports you have collected. Key one or two of them into your word processor.

When doing the assignment, ask your client (I'll discuss shortly who the clients are and how to find them), "What are the main points you want to get across in the president's letter? What's the best thing that happened to the company this year? What's the biggest problem the company had, and what has been done to resolve the problem or improve the situation?" The answers to these questions will guide you in organizing and composing the letter.

Look at the last one or two annual reports the client has done. Count the pages. Yours will probably be around this length. Ask the client to make sure.

For publicly owned Fortune 500 corporations, who do the biggest, most elaborate reports, length can be anywhere from thirty to forty pages or more.

You will write all descriptive narrative—the bulk of the report. The financial stuff in the back, usually printed in finer type, is prepared by the client's accountants. You have nothing to do with this—you don't even edit it. So don't worry about it.

Doing an annual report usually entails multiple meetings with the client, numerous telephone calls for fact-checking and follow-up questions, reading through and digesting a mound of printed material the client has provided, writing a detailed outline and writing a first draft plus several revisions.

Writing an annual report takes many weeks of work. If your billing rate is $75 an hour, and you are charging the client $9,000, you should not be surprised if you spend well in excess of one hundred billable hours on the job.

Annual reports pay well, but they are a labor-intensive assignment over which the client is likely to be fussy and demanding. You will earn every dollar you get.

The corporate communications managers will have overall responsibility for producing the annual reports. Some will hire writers directly to produce the copy, then hire designers separately to do the layout. Others will give the entire job to their PR firms, ad agencies or graphic design studios. The agencies or studios will either have staff copywriters write the reports or will hire freelancers, like you, to do them. I suspect the majority of annual reports are in fact written by freelancers, whether hired directly by the corporation or indirectly through an agency.

Information for writing the annual report will come from two primary sources: interviews (in person or via telephone) with company personnel and source documents provided by the client.

Although interviews can uncover fresh information and additional insight not found in other printed materials provided by the client, I recommend you gather as much written material as you can. While interviews may yield ideas, themes and slants, the nitty-gritty details and facts can usually be extracted from previous documents.

The source material you collect can include any or all of the following:

- last year's annual report
- any outline or preliminary layout developed for this year's report
- copies of the corporate capabilities brochure
- product and service brochures, equipment spec sheets, other product literature
- the company catalog
- all back issues of the company newsletter or magazine for that year
- copies of significant speeches and presentations made by key company executives
- videos and CD-ROMs
- copies of all press releases issued that year by the company public relations department
- a list of company personnel you should interview and, if known, the topics you should discuss with them

There is no "right" way or official process, since no two assignments are the same. Annual reports shape up and come together in different ways. But the following steps (although not always in this order) are usually involved:

1. **Initial project launch meeting.** Once you get the assignment (which may in itself require an initial meeting with

the prospect without compensation), you will meet again with the communications manager who will bring in various subject matter experts, executives and other corporate personnel for you to interview. This can go anywhere from two hours to a full day. Discuss in advance how long this process will take and your schedule availability so there are no misunderstandings.

During this meeting the client will provide you with loads of background material (if it hasn't already been sent). More will be sent as it is requested or someone comes up with it. Expect frequent E-mail, fax, phone and mail contact with the client throughout the process.

Cameron Foote, an experienced annual report writer, says that good questions to ask annual report clients include, "What would you like to see your annual report accomplish better?" and, "Has a specific focus or theme for this year's report been established, and if so, upon what is it based?"

2. **Rough outline.** You will have one or two weeks to digest this material, ask additional questions and prepare a rough outline or table of contents for the annual report to submit to the client for approval.

3. **Secondary research.** Since the project fee is so big, you have enough revenue on the project to afford to put in a little extra time on your own. I suggest you do this by going to the library, getting online or hiring a researcher. Look for articles on the client company, its industry or its technology. If you find an interesting relevant fact you can manage to work into your copy, the client will be impressed (as long as you footnote it and provide the reference material for backup).

4. **Primary research.** The more you dig into the background material, the more questions you will have that are unanswered by it. If the client is close, you may want to set up an additional half day of interviews to get answers. Alternatively, you can do these interviews by phone or E-mail. Primary and secondary research together should take about a week and can be done while the client is reviewing the outline.

5. **First draft.** After you get the bulk of the information you

need and the client's approval of your outline, write a first draft. Allow one to two weeks for this.

6. **Review.** Many different people at the client company will meticulously review your draft. All will have comments, many of which conflict with one another. The communications manager—your liaison with the client company—is the person to go to when you need to resolve such issues. Review of your draft will take at least a week.

7. **Revision and second draft.** You incorporate the comments, revise the copy and submit your rewritten draft, which again goes around for review. This takes another week.

8. **Final draft.** You may spend another week polishing, fine-tuning, filling in blanks, adding photo captions, etc. Finally the client approves the copy and you are finished.

Here are some additional suggestions to help you create annual reports your clients will love:

1. Research is critical. Facts make annual reports readable, believable and even interesting. Spend a lot of time up front gathering critical source materials. Ask your research questions early so you get the key facts in time.

2. Expect lots of reviews, comments and rewrites. The annual report is a big document encompassing a lot of activity. It's important, and many people are involved. You may have heard the expression, "A moose is a cow designed by committee." Annual reports are, by their nature, committee projects.

3. Be extremely polite to everyone within the client organization with whom you come in contact during the researching and writing of the annual report. Part of what your client expects from you is to be well represented by you in front of his senior management. If someone is difficult with you, be polite in return (but immediately tell the client afterward).

4. Be flexible about revising your copy in terms of style, tone, content. The annual report is designed to tell the story the company wants to tell, not the story you think it should tell. More so than almost any other marketing or corporate communications document, the annual report is tailored to the objectives of the client company.

5. Be organized. Divide your research materials into files corresponding with the various sections of the annual report. If the report covers multiple divisions, product lines or markets, edit carefully to minimize redundancy between the various sections of copy.

6. Since the annual report goes to many different audiences (including stockholders, stock brokers, analysts, vendors, customers, employees, senior management, suppliers, business partners, the press and the business community in general), keep the language simple. Write in plain English so everyone can understand.

7. Sometimes large chunks of the previous annual report or other source documents can be lifted and incorporated into your annual report as is or with some minor editing. Identify and scan these sections early so when it's time to write, you already have them on your PC as computer files, eliminating boring, tedious rekeying of text. You'll save a lot of time and effort and get the job done faster.

8. For a project of this length, you may want to hire a proofreader to review each draft being submitted to the client. You will get worn out looking at this copy over and over again. For a nominal fee, a proofreader provides a welcome set of fresh eyes. Expect to pay $10 to $15 an hour for proofreading.

9. The most important question to ask your client at the beginning of the assignment and throughout is, "What are the main messages you want to communicate?" If the annual report says what the client wants it to say, he'll be pleased. If it doesn't, he won't.

After you have completed the client's annual report, it doesn't hurt to ask, "When does the process start for next year?" You can try to get a commitment (even if not firm) now. If not, call well in advance of planning for next year so you can be considered for the assignment early.

Get extra copies of the annual report. Distribute them to potential new annual report clients with a note explaining that you wrote this report and can do theirs too.

Send copies to existing clients for whom you have done other work but have not done their annual reports. Let them know you offer this additional capability of annual report writing and that companies have already used you in this capacity.

Ironically, although the annual report is probably the most expensive marketing document a corporation produces, it also has one of the shortest life spans: Within a year, it's obsolete, replaced by a new report.

Yet, much of the copy in the annual report that describes the company—its organization, products, markets, technologies and services—remains consistent from year to year and is of interest all year to potential customers of the firm.

For this reason, many corporations will produce elaborate "corporate capabilities brochures" in addition to (or, if they are privately held, instead of) annual reports.

A corporate capabilities brochure is similar to the "front end," or descriptive, portion of the annual report, except it is a bit more general and not tied in with a specific year. A company might have one corporate capabilities brochure covering everything or have multiple brochures (for different divisions, markets or product groups).

Writing a corporate capabilities brochure is similar to writing an annual report; therefore, if you can do one, you can do the other. Offer your services for writing capabilities brochures to clients for whom you've satisfactorily completed annual reports.

Also: Don't stop at doing annual reports and corporate capabilities brochures. The communications directors who hire you may also need product brochures, newsletters, ghostwritten articles, speeches and multimedia presentations. If you can do this work as well, let them know. It could mean many more projects for you!

DIRECT-MAIL WRITING

Next to the movies, TV and best-selling novels, direct mail is one of the highest paid markets for freelance writers. Although surprisingly easy to break into, most freelancers don't even know about it, and direct-mail copywriting is dominated by a few dozen writers who earn lush six-figure incomes writing only a few days a week.

Direct mail is unsolicited advertising or promotional material (that is, material the recipient has not requested) sent to an individual or company through the mail. The general public and press call it "junk mail," although professionals in the industry abhor that term.

The best way to get a feel for the form and style of direct mail is to pay extra attention to the "junk mail" you receive this week and next. Instead of throwing it away, read it. Study this mail as carefully as you would analyze an article in a magazine in which you want to be published.

Which mailings grab your attention? Which turn you off? Start collecting samples of direct-mail packages that interest you and save them in a "swipe file." You'll turn to this swipe file for inspiration and ideas when writing for your clients. One hint: Any mailing you receive repeatedly is probably a winner (if it wasn't successful, the advertiser wouldn't keep mailing it).

If you want proof that direct mail is big business today, just look in your mailbox. If you're like most people, you're getting more unsolicited advertising materials in the mail than ever before.

Other facts that demonstrate direct mail's fast growth:

1. According to *DM News*, direct mail has become the leading medium among national advertisers. It accounts for 29.2 percent of all advertising expenditures (vs. 26.6 percent for television).
2. Direct mail now generates over $120 billion in direct sales revenue and accounts for 15 percent of consumer purchases in the United States.
3. Mail order is growing at twice the rate of retail sales. Nearly half the adults in this country buy products through the mail.

Yet, despite this demand, there are relatively few writers competing in the field. Some writers, naturally, consider themselves journalists or article writers and aren't interested in commercial writing assignments of any type, no matter how lucrative. But I suspect the real reason for the shortage is that most freelance writers simply aren't aware of what a gold mine direct-mail copywriting can be for them.

How much, specifically, can you earn? One writer, just in her second year as a direct-mail freelancer, confided in me that she bills clients approximately $7,000 a month for her services. Many direct-mail writers have annual incomes of $125,000 or more.

Some superstars even top the $200,000 a year mark. As a beginner, you can realistically expect to make $50,000 a year or more as a freelance direct-mail writer, and annual income in six figures is not unreasonable.

Who hires direct-mail writers? Any company who promotes its products or services by mail. One way to build a list of prospects is to keep track of the names and addresses of companies who send *you* direct mail. Often the person whose signature appears at the bottom of the sales letter is the one who hires freelance direct-mail writers.

Here are some of the types of companies who hire freelance direct-mail writers:

1. **Publishers.** Magazine publishers use direct mail to gain new subscribers, renew current subscribers and get bills paid. Because their income is so dependent on the success of their mailings, magazine and newsletter publishers pay top dollar for direct-mail copy, with fees for a single package ranging from $3,000 to $15,000 and up. Some publishers will even pay the writer a commission or royalty for a successful mailing, although this is rare. Book publishers also need direct-mail packages and direct-response ads to sell their products, although fees here can be lower, since book publishing is generally not as profitable as magazine publishing.

2. **Financial services.** According to the Maxwell Sroge Company, insurance is the leading mail-order product in the United States. For this reason, advertising managers at insurance companies are constantly looking for new writers who can sell insurance by mail. Other financial services organizations, especially banks, also do a lot of direct-mail promotion. Contact the advertising manager, and offer your services.

3. **Fund-raising.** Nonprofit organizations depend on mail-generated contributions to stay afloat, so creating a successful mailing is of key concern to them. Although fund-raising doesn't pay as well as commercial assignments, you can still get $2,000 or more to write a fund-raising direct-mail package. And these packages are usually shorter and less complex than the packages used to sell insurance or magazine subscriptions.

4. **Mail-order products.** There are many other products sold through direct-mail packages, catalogs, and mail-order advertising. These include home furnishings, housewares, gifts, clothing, collectibles, sporting goods, crafts, foods, records and tapes. And the companies selling these products need writers to create mailings.

5. **Lead generation.** In addition to generating direct sales, direct mail can also be used to generate sales leads for follow-up by mail, telephone or a sales call. Companies who use direct mail to generate inquiries rather than mail-order sales include industrial manufacturers, high-tech companies and service firms, such as PR agencies, accountants, management consultants and home improvement contractors.

   Although lead-generating direct-mail writers command lower fees ($500–$1,500 a letter and $2,000–$3,000 for a complete package are typical), the mailings are simpler, and this area of direct mail is easier to break into. Plus, the use of direct mail by "nontraditional mailers" (companies who don't use a lot of direct mail or sell through mail order) is perhaps the fastest-growing segment of the direct-mail industry.

6. **Ad agencies.** Ad agencies—both general ad agencies as well as those specializing in direct mail—are a big market for freelance copywriting services. You will find more than forty-four hundred ad agencies listed in the *Standard Directory of Advertising Agencies.* Also known as *The Agency Red Book,* this directory is available in the reference areas of many local libraries.

The easiest way to get started is to write simple sales letters for local clients. For example, you can write a letter for a new restaurant inviting people to a grand opening. Or perhaps a small consulting firm will hire you to write a letter to generate interest in its services.

The idea is to start small with basic sales letters rather than complete direct-mail packages. Why? Established, big-volume users of direct mail—magazine publishers, insurance companies, mail-order houses—usually won't hire a beginner and prefer a writer who can show samples of previous packages written for other big-name clients.

But the small companies, on the other hand, have no such prejudices. Indeed, they may not even think of the letter you're writing for them as "direct mail." To them, it's just a letter. Yet, by writing these simple sales letters, you gain valuable experience and samples for your portfolio.

Eventually, you show these proven successful letters (try to find out sales results) to larger firms, and one will surely try you out on a mailing package. You do the package, add it to your sample portfolio and build your business from there.

Here are some other techniques for breaking into the direct-mail business:

1. **Offer your direct-mail services to current clients.** Maybe you're doing press releases for the local animal shelter or an ad campaign for a high-tech software publisher. Suggest to these clients that direct mail is another effective way to promote their causes or generate more sales. Then write the letters for them.

   It's always easier to get people who know you to trust you with something you haven't done before. It's much harder to convince a stranger to be the guinea pig for your first direct-mail effort.

2. **Offer to work on spec.** A major publisher or other big mail-order firm might hire an unknown writer on spec. In this arrangement, you tell the client, "Let me write a direct-mail package for you. Pay me only if you like it." You may find some takers for this offer. And even if they don't use your package, you've created a sample you can send to other potential clients.

3. **Volunteer.** "Volunteer to write whatever you can," advises direct-mail writer Suzanne Becker Ramos. "Do fund-raising letters for local good causes or sales letters for your uncle's store." Writing copy for friends, relatives, or worthy causes is an excellent way to build a portfolio of real-life direct-mail letters that have been tested in the mail.

4. **Take a course.** Much of my own involvement in direct mail came about as a result of taking Milt Pierce's Direct Response Copywriting Workshop at New York University, and I strongly urge you to take a course in direct-mail copywriting at a local college or university.

Not only will you learn the basics of direct mail and build your writing skills, but you'll also make contact with a working direct-mail professional—the teacher—who can help introduce you to the right people in the local direct-marketing industry. (Before signing up for the course, make sure the teacher is a professional freelance direct-mail copywriter and not an academic.)

5. **Find a mentor.** The direct-mail industry is fairly close-knit, and a lot of business comes from referrals, contacts, friends and word of mouth. Try to establish a relationship with an experienced direct-mail writer or other professional who can serve as your guru and guide you through the field.

    "Try to find a mentor, or, at least, someone with more experience than you—someone who likes you, is willing to be helpful, and believes in your ability," says Suzanne Ramos. "Stay away from naysayers—you need self-confidence and a bit of brashness in this business."

6. **Become more involved in direct marketing.** Join a local direct-mail club or association. Attend meetings. Try to talk with as many people as you can. And become involved in the organization. You might volunteer to serve on a committee, for example. Subscribe to one or more magazines covering the direct-marketing field, and read them from cover to cover. *Direct Marketing, DM News, Direct, Who's Mailing What!* and *Target Marketing* are all excellent. If you see an article that interests you, start a correspondence with the author. You never know where it may lead.

If you follow this advice, you will soon be faced with the pleasurable task of creating your first mailing piece. The following tips can help make the job easier:

1. **Don't panic.** After all, a direct-mail package is basically a letter, right? And you've written plenty of letters. So there's nothing terribly mysterious or difficult about the task at hand. Just keep a cool head and let common sense be your guide.

2. **Start small.** I recommend you start with a simple one-page lead-generating sales letter than a big, complex mail-order package. Why? As a novice, you'll find writing a mailing with just two elements (letter and reply card) less

intimidating than a job with many different inserts, brochures, letters and forms.

3. **Do your homework.** Don't write off the top of your head.
First, gather and read all you can about the client's product
or services. Be sure to ask for copies of previous letters,
ads, brochures, press releases and catalog descriptions of
the product. Go through this material, reading carefully and
taking notes. If you're missing a key fact or don't understand
something, call the client and get the information. The job
of writing a successful mailing is much easier with the facts
at your fingertips.

4. **Write person-to-person.** Pretend your prospect is sitting
across the table from you. What would you say to convince
her to buy your product or request more information on
your client's services? This sales pitch, put into writing, becomes the basis of your letter.

5. **Keep it simple.** Sometimes, complex and elaborate mailings will do better than simple, uncluttered ones—and
sometimes the opposite is true. I advise beginners to keep
their first mailings simple. Once you're comfortable with
the format, you can experiment and get more elaborate.

6. **Do the best you can.** Don't worry about how long the job
takes to complete. Your first letters will take longer because
you are learning direct mail as you go. Once you become
comfortable with the format, future assignments will go
much faster.

The important thing right now is to concentrate on doing the
best job possible and not worry about how much you are earning
per hour. You want to write a letter that gets good sales results
for your client because this generates repeat business for you
and builds your reputation as a writer whose copy is successful
in the marketplace.

Here are seven basic copywriting techniques that can dramatically improve the effectiveness of the direct-mail copy you write:

1. **Start with the prospect—not the product.** Your readers'
primary concern is not with the product per se but with
what the product can do for them. Direct-mail experts are
fond of saying that people don't buy products; they buy
solutions to problems. So instead of beginning your sales

letter with, "Our telecommunications system," start with, "Your telecommunications needs," or, "Is your current phone system obsolete?" Start with the prospect and her concerns—not with the product. Talk about the customer's lawn—not your grass seed.

2. **Have a clear offer.** The offer is what you send the prospect when she responds to your mailing. In a mail-order package, the offer consists of the product, the price, the payment terms, the guarantee and any premiums (free gifts) included with the product.

   The offer—and how it is phrased—can make a dramatic difference in direct-mail results. In one test, three identical packages were mailed, the only difference being the *phrasing* of the offer. The three offers were as follows:

A. HALF PRICE!

B. BUY ONE—GET ONE *FREE*!

C. 50% OFF!

   Each statement conveys the same offer, but B generated 40 percent more orders than A or C. Apparently, people would rather get something for free than get half price or 50 percent off.

   Always try to use the word *free* in your offer. If you can't, at least stress money savings and discounts. And always offer a 30-day money-back guarantee with all products sold through the mail.

3. **If the client doesn't have an enticing offer, create one for him.** In lead-generating mailings, where the purpose is to generate an inquiry rather than a mail-order sale, a common mistake is to have a weak offer or no offer. Many such mailings start strong but end with a lame, "So, we would be delighted to do business with you and hope for a mutual relationship soon"—or some other such nonsense.

   A lead-generating mailing needs a strong call to action. It must tell the reader what to do next and then give her a reason to do it.

   One effective technique is to offer a free booklet, report, article reprint or other useful item that (1) relates to the service you are offering and (2) would be of genuine interest to the reader. For example, freelance direct-mail writer Richard Armstrong offers prospects a free booklet, "Six Questions to Ask *Before* You Hire a Freelance Copywriter—and One Good Answer to Each."

In many lead-generating campaigns, the goal is to set up a sales meeting with the prospective client. If this is the case, why not think of this event as a *consultation*, not a sales meeting—which it is. Then stress this offer in your letter. For example: "Want to improve the effectiveness of your trade show displays? Call us right now to arrange a free, no-obligation analysis of your exhibit needs, including a *free* design sketch of a new MOD-TEK display that highlights your products as no other exhibit can."

4. **Ask a provocative question.** One easy and effective way to begin your sales letter is to ask a provocative question. Questions, if phrased correctly, can be a powerful opening technique for grabbing attention and arousing curiosity.

The most effective question openings are those that deal with a timely, important or controversial issue or ask something to which the reader genuinely wants the answer. Some examples:

WHAT DO JAPANESE MANAGERS HAVE THAT AMERICAN MANAGERS SOMETIMES LACK? *(Economics Press)*

IF YOU WERE TO FIND OUT TODAY THAT YOU HAD ONLY A SHORT TIME TO LIVE WOULD YOU FEEL COMFORTABLE WITH THE AMOUNT OF LIFE INSURANCE THAT YOU HAVE PROVIDED YOUR FAMILY? *(United Omaha)*

An example of a typically *ineffective* question lead is:

DO YOU KNOW WHAT XYZ COMPANY IS UP TO THESE DAYS?

Remember, the reader is interested primarily in her own needs, not in your company or your product.

5. **Be specific.** Write copy that is factual, concrete and specific. As in article writing, vagueness and generalities make for weak direct-mail copy. For example, instead of, "Our new wealth-building plan can make you *rich!*" say, "Now you can earn $5,498 a day in the seminar business!" In one mailing I

received, which offered a business opportunity, the brochure featured a photo of the writer holding up a check. The copy said, "I'll send you a check for $4,154.65 for selling just one order!" This is what I mean about being specific.

6. **Narrow the focus.** Always encourage clients to pursue narrow market niches whenever possible. The more you can identify the specific needs of your target reader, the better you can address those needs in your copy.

   One of my clients creates customized computer systems for small businesses. He had been using, without much success, a mailing whose theme was, "A system tailored to your specific business needs." The new mailings I devised, which were much more successful, targeted certain groups of businesses that represented good prospects for him—lawyers, accountants, liquor stores. In these mailings, my client could promise specific solutions to the problems frequently encountered in managing these businesses.

7. **Use a provocative teaser.** A teaser is copy printed on the outer envelope. Its purpose is to get the reader to open the envelope by creating an interest in the information inside. This is done by arousing curiosity or promising a reward. Some examples:

1986 SURVEY ON DIET AND CANCER
IMPORTANT: THE ENCLOSED SURVEY IS RESERVED IN YOUR NAME. YOU ARE REQUESTED TO COMPLETE AND RETURN YOUR SURVEY.

CAN 193,750 MILLIONAIRES BE WRONG?

CHEMLAWN HAS A $10 GIFT FOR YOU.

YOUR TELEPHONE BILL REFUND IS COMING . . .

Another effective technique is to use a blank white outer envelope with no teaser, logo or company name. By making the package resemble a letter, you increase the likelihood that the reader will at least open the envelope.

How should your direct-mail copy be presented to clients? Mine is printed on plain white computer paper; I don't put it in presentation folders or print it on special sheets labeled "Copy," as some other writers do. Sales letters are typed single-spaced, as they will appear in final form, while brochures and other copy that will be typeset are typed double-spaced. Proofread to ensure an error-free manuscript.

There is a wide range in fees charged for mail-order packages—anywhere from $750 to $9,000 or more. That's quite a range.

How much should you charge? As a beginner, you might charge near the low end of the fee spectrum. For a one-page sales letter, for example, a fee of $500–$750 is not unreasonable. For a magazine publisher's mail-order package, a beginner might charge $1,500 to $2,500, while a seasoned professional would get $3,000–$5,000 or more.

My feeling is that, at the beginning, it's more important to get prestigious clients and plum assignments than it is to charge big fees. Once you build a client list and a track record of having written successful direct-mail packages, you can increase your fees according to what the market will bear.

A survey of seventeen established direct-mail copywriters, conducted a few years ago, revealed that they charged the following fees for direct-mail copy:

Complete direct-mail package	$3,000–$7,500
One-page letter	$400–$850
Two-page letter	$600–$1,000
Four-page letter	$1,200–$2,500

Even the successful pros of this business are constantly on the lookout for new clients and projects. Just because you're on top now doesn't mean you can stop marketing. People change jobs, companies move or take their business in-house or to an ad agency, firms go out of business or cut back on promotion or another writer comes along who can do the job cheaper. Every client you have now may leave you, someday. So you must be able to generate new business when you need it.

What are the self-promotion techniques used by freelance direct-mail writers to get new business? Not surprisingly, direct mail is one. Freelancer Bob Schulte told me his self-promotion mailing package generated $15,000 in new business in a short period of time. I have created a simple one-page letter and reply card offering more information on my freelance service, and this mailing generates a 7 to 10 percent response whenever mailed.

I've also been successful with small classified and display ads in various direct-mail and general advertising magazines, both local and national. And I've also gained visibility by publishing how-to articles in these magazines—something I strongly urge you to do, too.

My friend Milt Pierce gets a lot of business through networking, personal meetings, lunches with potential clients and participation in various direct-mail activities and clubs, including the Direct Marketing Club of New York.

Don Hauptman prefers to use publicity—primarily through article writing but also by giving talks and lectures to various advertising and marketing groups. Bob Matheo is a big believer in print advertising.

Direct mail doesn't have to be your whole life. You can, if you wish, devote only a small portion of your time to commercial assignments, with the rest of your effort concentrated on whatever you like best, whether it's magazine articles and nonfiction books or short stories and novels.

But whether you go at direct mail full-time or part-time, you'll do better by becoming a part of the industry. Again, this means joining some direct-mail clubs, keeping up with the industry through trade journals, and constantly trying to become more educated by studying the direct mail you receive at home, reading books on the subject, attending seminars and sharing results and ideas with friends and colleagues.

How would you like to receive a check for $500 or $3,000 or $5,000 or more for a single writing assignment you can do in just a few days in the comfort of your own home? Become a direct-mail writer, and it can happen to you on a fairly regular basis. You'll enjoy the challenge of writing copy that sells. And the money you earn will also be a source of constant delight.

SPEAKING, TRAINING, WORKSHOPS AND SEMINARS

A few weeks ago I taught a writing seminar to a group of twenty-five logistics professionals employed by the U.S. Army. My fee: $6,000. The week before, I taught a shorter version of the seminar at a medical equipment company. For less than a day's work, I received $3,500 plus expenses.

The point: Writers can earn significant fees teaching their writing and marketing skills to others. In fact, with fees ranging from $100 to $4,000 a day, *teaching* writing often pays better than doing the writing itself. Here are some steps you can take to get into the lucrative speaking, consulting, training, seminar and workshop business.

Surveys frequently cite writing and other communications skills as key factors contributing to the success of corporate managers and support staff. Yet many executives will tell you their employees are poor writers. This has created a steady demand for in-house corporate seminars in writing skills. According to the American Society for Training and Development, American corporations spend $55 billion a year for formal workplace training programs.

Fortune 1000 companies are the most likely candidates to hire you for this work. Some midsize companies also buy writing seminars. But as a rule, the smaller the firm, the less likely it is to have a formal training program or budget.

In-house communications seminars are needed in such topics as business writing, technical writing, grammar and presentation skills. Specialty subjects, such as how to write reports, manuals or proposals, are also in demand.

If you write on a subject of interest to businesspeople—stress reduction, time management, leadership, success, selling, management, the Internet—you may find a ready market for in-house training seminars on these topics as well. Recently, I got an inquirer from a major integrated circuit manufacturer looking for speakers to train employees in "active listening skills."

Contact corporations and offer your services as a writing consultant. Write to training managers. Or call vice-presidents, supervisors and department managers whose employees may need improved writing skills. Prepare an outline of your course and a biography highlighting your credentials to send prospective clients who request more information. Design these materials so they can be faxed or E-mailed if there is immediate interest.

Training managers typically won't be interested in your writing program unless they've gotten requests from managers in their companies for seminars on that topic. Most collect information for future reference. Send them your literature and follow up periodically by mail, fax and phone. Don't call too often, or you will be perceived as a pest. Two to four times a year is just about right.

Managers and supervisors may not be thinking about a training program, but if they feel lack of writing skills is a problem in their organization, your offer will interest them. Stress the benefits of better writing: clear communication, elimination of confusion, increased customer satisfaction, increased sales and greater productivity.

In corporate training, the client hires you on a per diem basis and sends employees to the training session you conduct. The client provides the bodies, room and refreshments. You teach the seminar and supply course materials. Class sizes typically range from ten to twenty-five students. Seminars, which take one or two days, are usually held in a conference room at the client's offices.

Day rates vary, but the corporate market is lucrative. Pay ranges from $500 to $4,000 a day, depending on your reputation, the demand for your course and the client. Most writers who do corporate training average from $1,200 to $2,000 per day. But some earn considerably more.

If the client is out of town, you'll have to travel. You don't get paid an extra fee for your travel time, but the client reimburses you for all expenses, including airfare, lodging, meals and other out-of-pocket expenses. I use the travel time to work on my program and prepare for the upcoming class. On the trip home, I tally my expenses, prepare an invoice, write the client a thank-you note and work on writing projects I've brought with me.

The client does not hand you a textbook or outline and say, "Teach this course." As an independent trainer, you present a program of your own design. You must supply the complete content including handouts.

Putting together a writing course is not at all difficult. Courses are organized in a similar fashion to books, except where books have chapters, courses have modules.

Therefore, if a manager at a local company asks you to present a seminar on business writing to her employees, go immediately to the bookstore and buy two or three books on the subject. You can pattern your course outline after the table of contents in these books. I've written two books you can use: *The Elements of Business Writing* and *The Elements of Technical Writing*.

Your course should be designed as a series of modules covering various writing-related topics. The outline for my "Effective Business Writing" course, aimed at corporate managers and support staff, lists the following eight modules:

1. Overview—elements of effective business writing; tasks of the business writer (letters, memos, proposals, reports, E-mail).
2. Fundamentals of Grammar—grammatical rules, punctuation, abbreviation, capitalization, spelling.
3. Principles of Composition—active vs. passive voice, simple vs. complex language, how to write concisely, tenses, style.
4. Words and Phrases—how to eliminate sexist language, redundancy, jargon, wordiness, clichés and other ills; correct meaning and usage for commonly misused words.
5. Principles of Organization—organizing business documents, executive summaries, writing the lead, use of headings and subheads.
6. Principles of Communication and Persuasion—how to get your reader's attention; using facts, opinions and statistics to prove your case; determining the level and depth of information content; how to get the reader on your side; how to get the reader to take action.
7. Principles of Tone—informal vs. formal language, finding and using the appropriate tone, using contractions, substituting positive words for negative words.
8. Special Writing Concerns of Corporate Employees—how to write for a specific audience; tips for making a boring topic interesting; working with uncooperative collaborators; the editing, revision and approval process.

Additional topics I've covered in my business writing seminars include editing, rewriting, research, outlining and prewriting planning. In technical writing seminars, I have a module on illustrating writing with tables, graphs, charts, diagrams and other visuals.

You can adjust the course to the customer's training objectives and class schedules by mixing and matching modules and topics within each module. Some modules, such as grammar and persuasion, can be complete seminars by themselves.

Most trainers include a set of handouts for each student as part of the cost and pay the photocopying out of their own pockets. Some bind their handouts in workbook format and charge the client an additional $10–$25 for each student receiving a workbook. If you've written a book on the topic of your seminar, give the client the option of offering copies to each of the attendees. In the corporate world, the client will buy copies for the trainees and distribute the book to them; it is inappropriate to "pitch your products" from the platform as you might at a public lecture or association meeting.

Make your seminar entertaining as well as informative. Consider using videos, cartoons, humor, props, overheads, flip charts, games, team exercises and other techniques to maintain attendee interest. Plan a lot of activities for the students. Ask them to submit writing samples in advance. Photocopy the samples (but first cover the authors' names), make photocopies for the class and have the class edit these samples as group exercises. Seminar attendees want to see their own company's documents used as the primary examples for review and critique.

Be creative in your presentation. Seminar leader Terry Smith, author of *Making Successful Presentations*, gets seminar attendees to participate by offering anyone who asks or answers a question a mystery prize in a sealed envelope. Smith tells the attendees that the prize may be worth one million dollars or more! Inside each envelope is a lottery ticket.

In a seminar on effective phone communication, I had students practice conversations using toy phones. Sound effects, including dial tones and phones ringing, made the presentation fun and lively.

Remember, although you love writing, most of the people in your seminar don't. In many instances, seminar attendees are forced to go to your course by their managers. A few may resent being sent. Others may resist your trying to teach them a skill they don't admire or care about. The more you can entertain as you train, the more enthusiastic your class will be—and the more they'll learn.

Keep in mind your trainees are busy adults with many things to do. Do not be disturbed if class members have to pop in and out to attend meetings, make calls or check messages. Do not act annoyed when they do.

Arrive at least an hour early. This gives you time to prepare the room and meet some of your students before class starts. Talk with students before the seminar and during breaks to get their feedback on how the day is going.

Offer some type of follow-up or support service. This can be included in the fee or sold for an extra charge. One writing trainer offers free telephone support for thirty days after the seminar. Another offers an editing-by-fax service for trainees to fax in their work for comment and review.

Another market for your seminars and talks is aspiring and professional writers. Aspiring writers want you to reveal the secrets of how to get published. They also want help becoming better writers. A large part of what they buy when they attend a seminar is hopes and dreams. If you can motivate them and give them hope that their work can be published, they'll be satisfied. If you can actually help some of the attendees get into print, they'll rave about you for life.

Experienced professional writers don't want a basic writing course. They attend programs that teach them how to sell more of their work and get more assignments at higher fees. Or they may want to learn how to break into new markets.

Every writer has marketing and sales skills within his specialty or markets—and you can share these with other writers for a profit.

For instance, if you are successful at writing annual reports, can you teach other writers how to get these lucrative assignments? Or can you give a half-day seminar on how to make money editing medical monographs for doctors and pharmaceutical companies?

There are several venues available. You can teach an adult education course for a community college or university. This can be a one-day Saturday program or an evening course. Most evening courses are one or two sessions per week for two to twelve weeks.

Other organizations that offer seminars include high schools, YMCAs, writers groups, libraries and bookstores. Programs run usually one to two hours and are held in the evening.

Fees are usually modest. Some seminar sponsors pay a flat rate of a few hundred dollars at most. Others pay you a percentage of the registration fees, ranging from 15 to 50 percent. That's risky: If attendance is high, you can earn a handsome day rate. But if few people show, your earnings can be minimal.

Some writers promote and sponsor their own writing seminars. While the rewards can occasionally be great, this option entails the greatest out-of-pocket expense—and the greatest risk. It also requires a knowledge of seminar marketing, direct mail, newspaper advertising and other promotional methods.

Most writers who market their own seminars have audiocassettes, videos, books, reports and other materials to sell to attendees. Income from these "back of the room" sales can sometimes make a marginal seminar profitable.

Another outlet for giving seminars to writers is writers conferences. *Writer's Digest* runs ads and announcements for upcoming writers conferences. Almost every conference features writing and marketing workshops led by professional writers. Write to conference directors, and offer your services.

Pay here is usually a modest honorarium, although a famous author can command higher fees. The perk is free conference attendance with all or most expenses paid. My wife and I once enjoyed a lovely Florida vacation at no charge when I spoke at a writers conference in Orlando. I ask for other favors to compensate for the low pay—for example, free usage of the conference's mailing list or a free ad in its member publication.

Writers don't just teach writing. They can also teach the subjects they write about. A cookbook writer, for instance, can teach cooking classes. A computer book author can give seminars in how to use a program or surf the Net.

When you write and publish books and articles on a topic, you are perceived as an expert. Many authors get calls from companies, associations and schools asking them to conduct programs on the topics of their books. If you want to generate more of these inquiries, include a description of your program, address and phone number in the bios that run with your articles and books. My $6,000 Army contract came because someone in the Army had found my phone number in the back of my book *The Elements of Business Writing*.

Speakers' fees vary widely. Beginning speakers often speak for low or no pay at small local meetings for such organizations as real estate offices, chambers of commerce and civic groups.

Authors of books and articles who are not celebrities or

best-sellers can get $500–$1,000 or more for a short talk at a luncheon or dinner meeting.

Best-selling authors, top professional speakers and celebrities command $3,000–$5,000 or more per talk.

An overlooked opportunity for teaching writing is in community centers and the school systems. Writers are called on to present workshops to children in public schools and adult education classes in community centers. The pay, $20–$40 an hour, isn't bad. A writer can earn $1,000 or more for a single four-day workshop.

How do you get into the school system? Teaching credentials and college courses in education are not required. Schools look for writers who have real-world credentials, such as published articles and books.

If you're interested in pursuing this type of work, contact your State Council of the Arts. In most states, this is the government agency providing grants for writers to teach writing in schools. Another organization that puts writers into classrooms is Teachers and Writers Collaborative in Manhattan.

As with corporate training, you must provide your own program: The schools don't hand you a text and a course that's ready to teach. Incidental expenses, such as commuting, typically come out of the writer's pocket.

The amount of money you can make as a speaker depends largely on your fame. If you are a best-selling author, you can command $1,000–$3,000 or more for a one-hour talk. If you are unknown, payment will be nominal. One published poet I met routinely charges $30 for a one-hour poetry reading at colleges, libraries or bookstores.

When and why would someone hire a writer as a speaker? Several examples: At an advertising convention, the association hired Ray Bradbury to talk about creativity in a keynote address. And a group of printers recently retained a writer specializing in the Internet to tell its members how cyberspace will affect the printing business.

If you write on topics that are appropriate for a business audience, there are thousands of associations who hire speakers. One good reference source is the *Directory of Association Meeting Planners and Conference/Convention Directors*. Updated annually, the directory lists more than 13,600 association meeting professionals. Listings indicate professional speaker usage as well as size and number of meetings, destinations, lengths and schedules.

Local groups, and local chapters of national groups, typically pay no fee or a small honorarium. There are exceptions.

National associations pay significant fees to speakers who give talks at national meetings: $1,000–$3,000 for a talk ranging from an hour to half a day. Sometimes the pay is even better. I know one meeting planner who paid an author $6,000 for a one-hour talk. Best-selling authors, such as John Naisbitt and Tom Peters, can command $10,000–$25,000 or more per talk, but they are the exception, not the rule. The top fee for noncelebrity speakers is about $5,000.

Is the seminar and workshop business for you? It depends on your personality and what you enjoy. All writers are communicators and teachers, but some are comfortable only when there is a printed page between them and their audience. If you are introverted and dislike public speaking, you may still be able to make money teaching—but you simply may not want to.

On the other hand, if you are as comfortable at the podium as you are in front of the word processor, consider giving teaching and speaking a try. It's a nice change of pace from the isolation of writing. So are the fat paychecks—and the applause when you finish.

CHAPTER 13

How to Negotiate Higher Fees, Advances and Royalties

No matter what accomplishments you make,
somebody helps you.

—Althea Gibson Darben

C hapter thirteen is a brief lesson on a topic covered in virtually every selling seminar but very few writing seminars:
how to negotiate better fees and get paid more money.

You'll learn how and when to ask for more money, how to
gain the best position for negotiating, when to back down and
accept the offer and when to pass. As a result, you will be able to
increase your fee per project 10 to 25 percent in a short time using
these simple methods. Also covered in chapter thirteen: how to
find and work with agents, reps, packagers and others who can
market and sell your services and negotiate deals for you.

SETTING FEES FOR COMMERCIAL WRITING PROJECTS

One of the toughest questions beginning *and* experienced writers wrestle with is, "How much should I charge?"

You probably have a standard fee, or range of fees, you want
to charge (or have been charging) your clients. But is it the *right*
fee?

The amount of money you charge and how you present this
fee to your potential clients plays a big role in determining
whether you make the sale and get the project.

Charge too *little*, and you diminish your prestige and importance
in the eyes of your client. You also diminish the perceived value
of your services and dramatically reduce your own earnings.

A low fee may get you a contract you might otherwise have lost, but will you be happy doing the work for so little money?

People who sell products don't worry about this too much because they can usually make it up on volume. But when you are selling your services as a freelance writer, you are also selling the finite amount of time you have available to perform these services. In fact, time is your only moneymaking resource, and there's a sharply limited inventory. So you can't afford to give your time away too cheaply.

On the other hand, charge too *much* and you may price yourself out of the market, losing out on jobs to other service providers who charge less.

Here are four important factors to consider when determining what to charge the client:

1. **Your status.** Are you a beginner or a pro? Are you well known in your field and highly recommended, or are you still waiting to be discovered by the masses? Are you a novice, learning your craft as you go, or are you really a master at what you do?

   And do you just *think* you're good, or do you have the client list, testimonials, referrals and track record to back up the big fees you want to charge?

   Because of their status, experienced writers with lots of credentials generally can command higher fees than beginners. But ability is even more important, so a highly talented novice is worth more to clients than a hack, no matter how long the hack has been working.

   Still, as a rule, those who are less experienced set their fees at the lower end of the scale; pros, at the higher end. But be careful about underpricing yourself. Beginners have a tendency to set their fees at the absolute bottom of the scale, reasoning that they do not have the experience or credentials to justify higher rates. I used this strategy myself when starting out, and I suppose it makes sense. However, clients will probably take you more seriously if you put your fees in the range at medium to medium-high. I have found that the less a client pays for a job, the less she respects the work and the person who produced it.

   One beginner I know charged, during his first year, fees

that it had taken me four years to get up the nerve to charge, and he had absolutely no trouble getting them despite the fact that he was young and lacked heavy experience. So I may have lost a lot of money by charging too little for too many years. I hope you don't make that same mistake!

2. **The going rate for your type of service (i.e., what the market will bear).** Unless you are the number one great guru of your industry, or the most in-demand writer in your town, or the only person in the world who can write authoritatively and engagingly about investing in penny gold stocks, your rates will have to be *somewhat* reflective of what the standard rates are for your type of service. And even if you are the great guru, there's still an upper limit to what most clients can afford or are willing to pay you.

   In some industries, pricing is fairly standard. Some service fields are regulated; in others professional societies or codes of behavior set fee guidelines.

   On the other hand, the writing business has no such standards, and writers' fees, as one professional put it, "are all over the lot."

   For example, in my business—direct-mail copywriting—fees for writing a sales letter range from $100 to $20,000 and up!

   The variation in fees in many fields is tremendous. However, by talking with a few prospects, you quickly get a sense of the upper and lower limits you can charge.

   You may find, for example, that some clients expect to pay $1,000 for a speech, while others are willing to spend $3,000 or even a bit more. But no one expects to get it for $200, and no one is willing to go above $5,000. After a few initial conversations and meetings with potential clients, you'll get a good idea of what the market will bear.

   The important thing to remember is that you are not locked into an hourly or project rate because you quoted it to one client. You can experiment with different rates until you find the right *range* for your services and your market.

3. **The competition in your local area.** Call some of your competitors, and ask them what they are charging. Many will gladly tell you. If not, you still need to get this information, so it's acceptable to do so undercover. Call or have a

friend call a few of your competitors. Describe a typical project, and get a cost estimate. See if they have published fee schedules or price lists, and ask them to send you copies.

Finding out the competition's fees is a real help in closing sales. You learn just where to price yourself in relation to other firms offering similar services.

You'll also benefit by asking your competitors to send you their brochures and other sales materials. By reviewing these materials, you can learn much about their sales and marketing approach.

4. **Your current financial need.** How much do you need the work and the income? In some situations, when cash flow is slow, you may feel financial pressure to get the work. At other times, you may not need the money but, psychologically, you need to close the deal in order to feel successful and good about yourself.

Your need to get the work should not really be a consideration in setting your fees. But, practically speaking, it is for most of us.

If you've got a million bucks in the bank or dozens of top corporations are knocking at your door, begging you to make space for their projects in your busy schedule, then obviously you don't need the work, and this helps at the bargaining table. If the job isn't right or the prospect gives off bad vibes or haggles over your fee, you can walk away without regrets.

If, on the other hand, the rent check is three weeks overdue and you haven't had a phone call or an assignment in the past two months, you may be willing to take on a less than ideal project or client who, if he senses your neediness, may use this to his advantage in price negotiations.

Ideally, you should negotiate each project as if you don't really need or want the work. But when you're hungry or just starting out, this isn't always possible or even wise.

Sometimes, you need the ego boost that comes with landing a project, being busy with work or getting your writing published. For many writers, "psychic" wages can be as important as the green, folding kind.

Before giving a cost estimate to the corporate prospect, ask,

"Do you have a budget for this project?" If the answer is, "Yes," say, "Can you share it with me?" About half of your prospects will tell you what they have budgeted for the project, and you can work up your own cost estimate with this budget in mind.

If the prospect says he does not have a budget, ask, "Do you have a dollar figure in your mind of what you would *like* it to cost?" Again, many will tell you, providing guidance for your cost estimate.

If the prospect can't or won't tell you what he wants to spend, you are on your own. Quote a fair price, one that seems affordable yet allows you to earn your desired rate for the work being performed. After giving a few price quotations, you will quickly get a feel for the acceptable fee range for different types of writing projects.

NEGOTIATING WITH PUBLISHERS

The above discussion applies primarily to commercial assignments—brochures, newsletters, manuals and similar projects—done under contract to corporations, small businesses and other organizations.

Can you similarly negotiate with magazine editors and book publishers? In theory, yes. However, it is easier to negotiate fees with a commercial client than with an editorial client. Corporate clients are accustomed to negotiating prices for a wide range of services, including writing services. Magazine editors, on the other hand, often have set per-piece or per-word rates they pay, and they are hesitant to pay more than this fee for the first assignment they give you. Once you have written a couple of pieces for them, they may be open to negotiating a higher rate.

Most magazines, however, pay for articles within a limited fee range. So if you want to make more money writing articles, start with easier markets, then go after the higher-paying publications once you've gained experience.

Book publishers may be open to negotiation on a book contract, depending on how much they want the book. Book contracts have many different terms and conditions aside from just the advance and the royalty, so if the publisher is not willing to give a higher advance or royalty, you may be able to get more from the contract on other points. For example, most book contracts give the author six free copies; I have negotiated to get over a hundred free copies on some contracts. I then made a nice profit selling the books through mail order and at seminars and talks.

My rule of thumb is that if the publisher won't budge on the advance, ask for another percentage point or two in royalties. If the publisher won't budge on royalties, negotiate more favorable terms on other contract points. This can range from a bigger author's discount on buying your own book to a greater percentage of the revenues from book club and article reprint sales. (For a complete discussion of book contract terms, see my book *Getting Your Book Published.*)

Another good strategy for getting more money from book publishers is to do a simultaneous submission, which means sending your book proposal to more than one publisher at a time. Most publishers find this acceptable, as long as you make them aware of the multiple submission.

The advantage of simultaneous submission is the possibility of getting more than one offer. If two or more publishers want your book, you have more leverage in negotiating for a higher advance and royalty. When only one publisher wants your book, and especially if you are eager to have the book published, your leverage is greatly diminished.

A final tip for any negotiation: If you want to negotiate and ask for more money, you have to be willing to walk away from the job if the client or publisher refuses. If the job or project is a "must have" to you, take what is offered. Hold off on playing negotiation hardball until you are at a place in your career where you feel comfortable enough to turn down a deal that is not rich enough for you.

AGENTS, REPRESENTATIVES, PACKAGERS

If you have an agent, the agent can do all the negotiation for you. Traditional literary agents handle book contracts only; they don't do magazine articles, plays, poems, stories or corporate work.

Authors, being nervous about upsetting the publishers, are unlikely to push for more favorable terms. Agents, on the other hand, are expected to do so, and *can* do so without damaging the author-editor relationship. Agent Scott Waxman told me, "You are likely to get more money when you use an agent."

And in an interview with *Fast Company*, agent Stefanie Henning observed, "It's very hard for people to negotiate good deals for themselves. An agent serves as an outside 'business affairs' person." *The New York Times Book Review* reports that Irma Rombauer, author of the best-selling *Joy of Cooking*, signed a contract with Bobbs-Merrill that "cost her and her heirs perhaps millions of dollars in royalties."

A literary agent acts as your representative, aggressively selling your book ideas, proposals and manuscripts to publishing houses. As the author, you are responsible for coming up with ideas, although an agent may sometimes bring an idea or publishing opportunity (e.g., a publisher looking for a writer to produce a specific title) to the author.

The basic function of an agent is *sales*. A good agent is one who is able to sell your writing and get you the best deal in terms of advance, royalty, publisher, promotional budget and quality of editor and publisher.

The agent collects a percentage of all advances, royalties and other income (e.g., sale of serial rights, movie rights, etc.) generated by your book.

In most contracts, there is a clause specifying that the advance and royalty checks go first to the agent, who deducts his commission and then sends you a check for the money owed you. You need not worry about this clause. The agent will add it for your approval and signature. You do not pay any fees to your agent until he makes a sale for you, at which time the agent receives a commission as discussed above.

Agents typically absorb phone expenses, postage, travel, lunches with editors and other expenses involved in marketing books and running their agencies. However, it is traditional for the author to pay for the cost of photocopying book manuscripts and provide the agent with as many copies as required (usually three or four for simultaneous submissions to multiple publishers).

There are book entrepreneurs known as packagers who can also make publishing deals for you. A book packager comes up with an idea for a book or book series, sells it to a publisher, puts together a team (writer, artist, editor) to produce the work and may even deliver typeset camera-ready pages or disk to the publisher. Although packagers often get 40 to 50 percent of your advance and royalties vs. an agent's 10 to 15 percent, they may be a good option for you if you like to write but don't have a lot of ideas of your own.

How do you go about finding an agent? The best place to start is with your own personal contacts. If you don't know someone who has published a book, chances are a friend of a friend, or a relative of a friend, may know someone. Ask that author for a referral. Does he have an agent he can recommend to you? Does he have any suggestions on which agents to contact?

Or, go to a bookstore or library and look at recent books on topics similar to the book you want to write. Now, read the acknowledgments at the beginning of the book. Many authors will thank their literary agents by *name* in the acknowledgments. Write down the names of these agents, look them up in a directory, such as *Guide to Literary Agents* or *Literary Market Place*, and contact them.

This technique of looking for agents in book acknowledgments works well because agents, like other people, have their own particular interests, and an agent will be more receptive to your idea if it fits with the type of books she likes to work with.

The best way to contact an agent is to send a brief letter of introduction. Explain where you got his name and who you are, and briefly describe the type of book you want to write. If you have writing credentials or are an established expert in the subject matter of your proposed book, say so. Close your letter by offering to send the agent a book proposal, outline or other background material that describes your proposed book in more detail.

There are only a few hundred agents but hundreds of thousands of writers and wanna-be writers. Agents are inundated with material from writers seeking representation, and most feel you need them more than they need you. "For the unpublished writer, 'selecting' an agent is somewhat of a contradiction in terms," writes Connie Goddard in a special supplement to *Writing for Money* newsletter. "You don't so much select an agent as one selects you or your manuscript." Therefore, be polite and respectful, not bullying or difficult, when approaching potential agents.

"A coauthor and I had interested a New York agent in seeing a proposal," reports Florida freelancer David Kohn. "We sent one. My coauthor was new to the business, and said that he just wanted to see the agent's resume so he could be comfortable that he was dealing with a pro.

"When dealing with most professionals, asking for a resume is a reasonable request. Not with agents. At least, not with this agent. Her assistant's tone turned glacial when I told her what I wanted. Soon after, the manuscript was returned, unread."

Author James Cross Griblin notes that some agents require that you sign a one- or two-year contract with them. But others operate on a more informal basis: If you're satisfied with each other's performance, you continue. If not, you are both free to part company.

MORE WAYS TO GET PAID MORE FOR YOUR WRITING

Even with increasing your billable hours, you can still work only so many hours in a given week—which puts a very real limit on your income.

Let's say you are working fairly consistently and efficiently now and still want to double your freelance income. Here are some suggestions:

1. **Raise your fees.** The quickest way to boost your income and feel good about yourself is to raise your fees.

   Most freelancers do not charge enough and could be charging much more. *Fear* prevents them from doing so.

   Afraid of losing current clients? Then don't raise your fees to them. Instead, simply quote the higher fee to all *new* clients that call.

   A healthy fee raise is a wonderful ego boost. And, rather than being draining (as is working too much), it has the effect of energizing you.

   Another advantage of raising your fees is that it weeds out the cheap clients and results in a better class of client using your service.

   Probably it's best not to raise your fee on any particular item on your price list more than 25 percent at one time. The exception is if you are significantly underpriced. In that case, maybe you can double your fee.

2. **Subcontract for others.** Another possibility is to subcon-

tract for other writers or for companies that broker, agent or represent freelance writers.

One such agency is Paladin, with offices in San Francisco, New York City and Chicago. These "freelance agents" match freelancers with potential clients. In exchange, they get 20 percent of the money the client pays you.

Or you can subcontract for other writers, consultants or small one-person freelance advertising or PR agencies, handling overload work for them. Generally you charge them your regular fee and they mark it up when presenting the bills to their clients. Some contractors may ask for a discount ranging from 15 to 25 percent to allow them to mark up and make a profit on your copy.

The advantage of subcontracting is that it eliminates the need to do marketing, sales and client hand-holding, freeing your time to work on billable assignments.

Another agency that finds work for writers (mostly direct mail but also in other categories) is Copywriter's Council of America Freelance, CCA Building, 7 Putter Lane, Middle Island, NY 11953-0102, phone (516) 924-8555. Write for membership information.

3. **Subcontract your work to other writers.** As I've said, there are only so many hours in the day, and you will eventually reach the point where you are too busy to take on new business and must actually turn down lucrative, attractive assignments because you don't have the time to handle them. It's a shame to turn good business away. Is there any solution?

One is to take on the work, then "farm it out," or subcontract the work, to other freelancers.

For example, let's say Corporation X asks you to write five brochures in three weeks for $2,000 a brochure. Rather than refuse the job or only accept part of it, you say yes to the whole assignment.

Then, you write one brochure and hire four other writers to write the four other brochures. You pay them a fee lower than your contract with the company and pocket the difference. If you pay them $1,000 a piece, you make $4,000 on their work plus $2,000 for the one you wrote, or $6,000 total on the job.

In this unethical or immoral? No. You have spent time marketing and selling to the client. You spend time contacting the client. You may have to edit or revise the work if it does not meet your standards. You are responsible for collecting and making payment. You are adding your time, expertise and consulting services, not to mention providing the other writers with guidance and direction. It is fair and reasonable for you to get paid for doing this. My feeling is that your cut should be 20 to 50 percent of the total fee, with the writer you subcontract to getting the balance.

4. **Hire employees.** As you get busier and busier, time becomes your biggest problem. Your income is limited by the finite amount of time you have each workday—time that is rapidly eaten up doing client work, talking on the phone and handling a million other tasks.

Instead of dividing yourself this way, you can "multiply" yourself by hiring a staff, having them do the work and making a profit on the work they do.

There are two basic types of employees. The first type is a secretary or other "personal assistant"—someone who handles the tedious (but important) details of your work life, freeing you to do more profitable work.

Freelancer Sig Rosenblum has for years had a full-time secretary."I only make money writing and thinking for my clients," he says. "Everything else is a waste of time and better handled by a secretary." Rosenblum dictates his direct-mail copy into a tape machine for transcription by his secretary. He then edits the printout and has her make corrections on her IBM Displaywriter. His hands never touch a typewriter or computer keyboard!

Joan Harris, another direct-mail writer, has hired a full-time account executive, Mary Bruce. Harris provides her clients with a full ad agency and consultation service, and Bruce handles a lot of the details of the various projects, leaving Harris freer to do creative work and deal with clients.

In addition to the personal assistant, the second type of employee you can hire is the "clone." The clone is someone who has similar skills to you and does what you do, under your direction, for your clients. For example, if you write software manuals and you get large annual contracts from several clients, you may hire a staff of software writers who do the work as your employees.

Whether you hire personal assistants or clones or a combination, having employees is one way to free yourself from your personal time constraints and multiply your earnings. Let's say you make $50,000 a year working alone. Then you hire a staff writer. The staff writer handles $50,000 worth of work; you pay $25,000 salary, so you make $25,000 a year on the writer.

You can continue to multiply yourself this way almost infinitely, taking on as much work as clients will give you. For example, there's no reason you can't hire a staff of ten writers, paying $250,000 in salary and making $250,000 clear income on their work—with little effort of your own. Then, you expand with a staff of 15 . . . 20 . . . 25 . . . it's up to you.

5. **Work on a royalty or commission basis.** This is not for beginners. But at some point, you might consider working for a commission, royalty or percentage of sales rather than a straight fee. Such deals can sometimes be negotiated for clients requiring direct mail, ads, Web sites and other such materials.

This is possible only with a client you trust and when the services you render can be measured against some tangible, quantitative objective, such as response (to an ad, mailing or promotional event), increased sales or some other result (such as number of articles generated by a PR campaign).

Gary Halbert, a successful direct-response writer, charges some of his clients a fee equal to 5 percent of gross sales of the products he creates ads and mailings for. One of his clients is Ernest Borgnine's wife, Tova, a perfume manufacturer.

Roger Parker, a successful New Hampshire writer and consultant, created a seminar on desktop publishing. Although he gets paid over $1,000 a day by his client, a seminar promoter, to give the seminar all over the country, Parker also wisely retained all rights to the material. As a result, he gets paid a commission whenever *other* teachers hired by the firm give his basic seminar, raking in handsome fees while he relaxes at home.

Think about whether you can perform a service or create a product that can pay you a commission or royalty, earning you money without your direct effort. This is a great way to relieve the burden of having to work every day for your living.

6. **Contract for retainer fees.** As your business progresses, you will find that many clients come to you for advice as well as writing. For these clients, you might suggest a monthly retainer arrangement. Here's how it works:

Let's say your consulting fee is $150 an hour or $1,200 a day. The client agrees to buy two days of your time each month for a specified period—three, six, twelve months or more (one year is typical). The retainer guarantees your availability to the client and entitles the client to up to two days (sixteen hours) of time. In exchange for this, the client sends you a $2,400 retainer check at the beginning of each month.

If the client uses less than the amount of hours contracted for, he does not get a refund, nor do hours "carry over" into the next month. If the client uses more than the sixteen hours, he pays for each additional hour at your rate of $150 per hour.

The retainer provides an often-absent degree of regularity and security in an otherwise uncertain freelance world. For example, having five clients on monthly retainer at $1,000 a month gives you a regular income of $5,000 a month or $60,000 a year.

CHAPTER 14

Secrets of the Superrich:
What Does It Take to Make $100,000 a Year or More as a Writer?

I AM OPPOSED TO MILLIONAIRES,
BUT IT WOULD BE DANGEROUS TO OFFER ME THE POSITION.
—MARK TWAIN

A few best-selling authors and top screenwriters earn seven-figure incomes, but there's no path that guarantees best-sellerdom. In between these extremes, there is a small and select group of freelancers who regularly earn six-figure incomes equivalent to what doctors, airline pilots, attorneys, accountants and other professionals are paid.

This chapter discusses some of the interesting and innovative ways in which "nontraditional" writers earn lots of money. When people say, "freelance writer," they think, "books and articles." But there are many writers who have never written an article for a major magazine or published a book and have become millionaires.

How do they do it? Here are some of the "superstar" writers I know who are not best-selling authorities but earn six figures year after year:

- a technical writer who makes $100,000 a year doing systems documentation
- a direct-mail writer who makes $200,000 a year traveling the globe teaching businesspeople to market their products and services more effectively
- a former humor writer who earns $2,500 a day teaching business writing to corporate executives

- a writer who specializes in the construction industry and earned more than $200,000 last year
- a freelance writer who has earned over $2 million writing about—and teaching others to be—better organized
- a writer who has become a self-made millionaire self-publishing his writings and selling them via mail

The classic "writer starving in a garret" image is a self-created condition, not a marketplace necessity. Many writers earn handsome incomes allowing them and their families to enjoy comfortable upper-middle-class lives; a few even become rich.

RULES OF THE OFFICE, REVISITED

In chapter one, I made reference to my "Rules of the Office"—a list of rules I have that I must follow in order to be financially successful as a writer. But I only discussed one of the rules. Here's the entire list, along with a short comment on each rule and how you can apply it to your own freelance writing business:

1. **Meet all deadlines. Set priorities. Do first things first.** Make to-do lists so you know what you have to do each day, every day, to meet all your deadlines. When you get assignments, do some of the initial work—reading, research, outlining—as soon as you get them. That way, even if you procrastinate or other things come up, when you finally sit down to work on them again, you'll be pleasantly surprised at the progress you've already made.
2. **Make sure meetings are "working meetings."** Don't be too eager to meet with editors, publishers, corporate clients and others who contact you about your writing services. Define the agenda and objective of the meeting in advance so you can decide whether it's worth taking the time to attend.
3. **Confirm everything in writing; call to make sure faxes, E-mails and FedExes were received.** At times clients and editors will complain that they did not receive materials you sent them. Therefore, after sending a manuscript, call to notify the client, telling her when it was sent and how. Having been so notified, she can't say she never got it and didn't know you sent it—because you told her.
4. **Return calls promptly.** When you are in the office, return

business calls within the hour. If you are away from your office, change your voice mail message to indicate you are out and when you will be back and able to return calls. If you cannot have a long conversation with the caller, call back and set up a time to talk at length later that day or the next day. People today are impatient; don't make them wait to hear from you—or they may call someone else.

5. **Bill on time. Get paid on time.** Send out all invoices within a week. If the invoice is not paid on time, follow up with letters and phone calls until you get a check. The older a debt gets, the more difficult it is to collect.

6. **Learn to say no. Don't overbook or overcommit.** Don't take on so much work that you burn out, suffer illness or miss deadlines.

7. **Engage in positive self-talk.** Many writers are filled with self-doubt. Realize and tell yourself that you are a good writer, worth the money your clients pay you (and more).

8. **Invest your money.** Get a financial planner or a broker you can trust to help you manage your investments. Ignore sales calls from brokers trying to sell you good deals over the phone. Have a financial plan and stay with it.

9. **Early research + organized scanned files = success.** When you get an assignment, do the bulk of the research within a few days of your receipt of the contract. If the client provides materials you can use in your copy and they are not in electronic form, get them on disk or E-mail, or scan them yourself. This will eliminate time wasted re-keying boilerplate copy that you will use as is or with slight edits.

10. **Don't underquote or quote in haste.** If you're not sure whether your quote will be within the client's budget, ask the client, "What is your budget?" Often he will tell you. If he doesn't have a budget, say, "Did you have a dollar amount in your mind you wanted to spend?" Don't feel compelled to come up with a price on the spot. Tell the client, "Let me work up an estimate and I will get back to you within twenty-four hours"—and then do so. This gives you the time to think things through and consult your colleagues and even your competitors for their advice on what to charge.

THE FIFTH SECRET OF MAKING
A LOT OF MONEY AS A WRITER

In addition to practicing the four principles in this book—writing faster, writing more, selling more, charging more—many high-earning writers are successful because they work in nontraditional areas. The entrepreneurial or clever writer can break out of the $25,000-a-year trap by taking advantage of a fifth principle: supply and demand.

The principle works as follows: When supply outweighs demand, pay scales are low. That's why most article and book writers don't earn much money. When demand outweighs supply, writers can charge a premium. That's why specialists doing work in areas most other writers have not discovered earn the big money.

You will make more money as a specialist and be more in demand. Think of it this way: If magazine editors get many thousands more submissions than they can possibly use, the supply outweighs the demand. So why should they pay top dollar?

On the other hand, if regulatory agencies require more and more corporations to publish quality manuals, the demand will be high. And since few writers know about this requirement, the supply is low. Therefore, you can charge a premium price by meeting this need, if you can find out what companies need and deliver it to them.

The best specialties are those that (1) are in demand, (2) don't have a lot of competition and (3) are important to the client organization. Here is a partial list of writing specialties that fall into this category:

- annual reports
- pharmaceuticals, health care and other medical writing
- direct mail
- infomercials
- high-tech marketing communications (brochures, catalogs, ads and other promotions for technically sophisticated products and services)
- employee benefits
- executive speeches
- banking and financial services
- chemicals and industrial equipment

- telecommunications, data communications, wireless communications and networking
- Web sites and other Internet marketing
- CD-ROMs

Many of the best specialties are undiscovered or known only to a handful of writers fortunate enough to stumble upon them. Sometimes the quirky writing assignment you view as an oddball opens a whole new field for you. Gary Blake, for example, was a magazine and public relations writer when a training company asked him to teach a seminar to New York state employees on clear writing. He discovered an untapped market teaching writing to corporate employees and now makes a handsome living doing primarily that—a field he got into largely by accident.

PROS AND CONS OF BEING A NONFICTION WRITER IN THE INFORMATION AGE

Is the "information explosion" a good thing for nonfiction writers and other information marketers? Actually, it's a mixed blessing. Thanks to the Internet and recent publishing explosion, more source information is available to you more readily than ever. But on the downside:

- People have too much to read and not enough time to read it.
- More and more information is competing for their attention.
- There is a proliferation of low-cost/no-cost information sources eating into the market for your expensive information products.

Fortunately, you can still succeed in writing and selling information. It's tougher than it was in yesteryear, I think. So here are some rules and guidelines formulated specifically for information marketers competing in the Information Age:

1. **Narrow the focus.** Although the most profitable product may be one with wide appeal, such as Joe Karbo's *The Lazy Man's Way to Riches* or Bob Kalian's *A Few Thousand of the Best Free Things in America*, "gold mine" concepts such as these are difficult to come by. Today we live in an age of specialization. People have narrow, specific areas of interest and eagerly seek the best information in these niche areas.

Match your own interests and expertise with the information needs of an identifiable market and you're on your way.

How big must this market be? Jerry Buchanan, publisher of *TOWERS Club USA Newsletter*, a how-to newsletter for information marketers and self-publishers, says that "any group large enough that some magazine publisher has seen fit to publish a magazine about them or for them" is large enough for your purposes.

2. **Seize a subject.** The tendency of the typical magazine writer or book author is to wander from subject to subject to satisfy a never-ending curiosity about all things. But the information marketer must behave differently. You must latch onto a narrow niche or topic, make it your own and produce a series of information products that meet the needs of information seekers buying materials on this subject. Not only does this increase profits by giving you more products to offer your customers, it also helps establish you as a recognized expert and authority in your field.

Steve Sarnoff, editor of *Sarnoff's Samurai Strategies*, a financial newsletter on gold futures, says the key to making a lot of money writing is to "become an expert in something." Dan Poynter, author of *The Self-Publishing Manual*, says, "Book subjects are becoming more focused, with books targeted to specific groups of people."

3. **Plan the "back end" before you start marketing.** Many entrepreneurial direct-response advertisers dream of duplicating the one-shot success of Joe Karbo and of getting rich from a single mail-order book. But it rarely happens. This "front end," or first sale, can be profitable, if cost-effective marketing techniques are used. But the real profits are in the back end—selling a related line of additional information products to repeat customers.

I advise clients to come up with and plan this back end of related products before launching a direct-response campaign. Otherwise, precious opportunities for repeat sales will be lost if they can only offer a single product to eager, information-hungry buyers. Example: If you write a book on adoption and many readers contact you for more information, make up a catalog sheet to send them. The sheet offers reprints of articles you've written on the topic (to which you, of course, have retained reprint rights). You can easily charge $2–$4 or more for such reprints.

4. **Test your idea.** If you want to sell your writing via mail order, test your concept with classified ads. Most information marketers want to immediately mail thousands of direct-mail packages or place full-page ads.

That's fine if you can afford to risk $5,000–$25,000 on an untested idea. However, I prefer to test with small classified ads first. By doing so, I can determine the product's sales appeal and potential for under $200.

Your ad should seek inquiries, not orders. Reason: There is not enough room in a small ad to give all the details required to generate an order. You do better by stating your sales proposition succinctly, then offering free information to any potential buyers who want the details. All requests for information should be immediately fulfilled with a powerful direct-mail sales letter, circular, order form and reply envelope.

What should all this cost? A successful classified ad will bring in inquiries at a cost of $.25–$1.00 per lead. A good sales package will convert 10 to 35 percent of these leads to sales. I have run classified ads that pulled up to seventeen times their cost in product sales.

5. **Use the important "bounce-back" catalog.** A bounce-back catalog is a circular containing descriptions and order information for your complete line of related information products. When a customer orders your lead product, you insert the bounce-back in the package and ship it with the order. Ideally, he sees the catalog, scans it, orders more items and his order "bounces back" to you.

The bounce-back catalog doesn't have to be long or elaborate. For my mail-order business, the catalog is printed on two sides of a single $11'' \times 17''$ sheet in black ink on colored paper, which is folded once vertically to form four panels.

Additional sales generated by bounce-backs can range in dollar amount from 10 to 100 percent of the front-end sales generated by your original ad or mailing. The only cost is a penny or two to print each catalog sheet. There is no postage cost because the catalog gets a "free ride" as an insert in your product shipment. (Tip: When you fulfill a bounce-back order, send out another bounce-back catalog—and another—until the customer has bought every item in the catalog.)

6. **Create low-, medium- and high-priced products.** Different buyers have different perceptions of what information is worth and what they will pay. You will get more sales by testing a variety of prices for your lead item and by offering a number of different products reflecting a broad range of prices.

My front-end product in my how-to line of information products on "how to succeed as a freelance writer" is a $12 book. The back-end consists of a series of $7 and $8 reports, a second book for $20 and a six-tape cassette album for $49.95. Dr. Jeffrey Lant, who sells business development products and services, has products ranging from a $4 report to a $4,800 consulting service.

Recently, I sent an inquiry to a well-known and successful marketer who specializes in selling information on how to make money as a speaker. I didn't buy because the only alternatives were a large cassette album or a one-year newsletter subscription, both of which are fairly expensive, and I wasn't ready to make that kind of commitment to the subject. Most buyers prefer to sample your information with a lower-priced product, such as a book, single cassette or inexpensive manual in the $10–$50 range.

7. **Let your buyers tell you what products they want you to create.** Always put your name, address and phone number in every information product you produce, and encourage feedback from readers. Many readers become advocates and fans, calling, writing and establishing a dialogue with you.

Welcome this. Not only can you solve their problems and answer their inquiries by telling them which current products to buy, but their questions can suggest new products. Most of my back-end reports were written to answer specific questions readers asked me repeatedly. Instead of having the same telephone conversation over and over, I can simply sell them a report that contains the answers they seek. It saves time and generates revenue.

8. **Be the quality source.** Your strongest advertisement is a good product. A clever or deceptive ad can certainly generate brisk sales, and returns may not be excessive even if your product is poor, but customers will feel cheated and will not favor you with repeat business.

A good product will have people actively seeking you out and will bring in a small but steady stream of phone calls, letters, inquiries and orders generated by the product itself and not the advertising. You will be shocked at the enormous effort some people expend to locate the source of quality information products that are well spoken of by other buyers.

If you decide to self-publish all or some of your writings, I recommend the following books to you:

Buchanan, Jerry. *Writer's Utopia Formula Report.* Rev. ed. Vancouver, WA: TOWERS Club U.S.A., Inc., 1987.
    TOWERS Club U.S.A., Inc., P.O. Box 2038, Vancouver, WA 98668-2038. Phone: (206) 574-3084. The best book I ever read showing how to sell information from small classified and display ads.

Kalian, Bob. *Mail Order Success Secrets.* White Plains, NY: Roblin Press, 1993.
    Roblin Press, 405 Tarrytown Rd., Suite 414, White Plains, NY 10607. Phone: (914) 592-4431. How to sell books and other information products by mail. Charmingly written, with solid advice.

Kremer, John. *1001 Ways to Market Your Books.* 4th ed. Fairfield, IA: Open Horizons Publishing Company, 1993.
    Open Horizons Publishing Company, P.O. Box 205, Fairfield, IA 52556-0205. Phone: (515) 472-6130. The company has other excellent books for book publishers and others who self-publish books and other "information products" and sell them via mail order.

Lant, Jeffrey. *How to Make a Whole Lot More Than $1,000,000 Writing, Commissioning and Selling "How to" Information.* 2nd. ed., rev. Cambridge, MA: JLA Publications, 1993.

JLA Publications, 50 Follen St., Suite 507, Cambridge, MA 02138. Phone: (617) 547-6372. Detailed, information-packed guide to successful self-publishing. Recommended.

Nicholas, Ted. *How to Publish a Book and Sell a Million Copies.* Chicago: Enterprise/Dearborn Financial Publishing, Inc., 1993.
Dearborn Financial Publishing, Inc., 155 N. Wacker Dr., Chicago, IL 60606-1719. Phone: (312) 836-4400. Nicholas Direct, Inc., 1511 Gulf Blvd., Indian Rocks Beach, FL 34635. Phone (813) 596-4966. A basic primer on how to self-publish a book and sell it by mail order through direct-response ads and direct mail. Nicholas is a successful self-publishing entrepreneur and one of the top direct-response ad copywriters of all time. His self-published, self-promoted *How to Form Your Own Corporation Without a Lawyer for Under $75* has sold over a million copies.

Powers, Melvin. *How to Self-Publish Your Book and Have the Fun and Excitement of Being a Best-Selling Author.* North Hollywood, CA: Wilshire Book Company, 1984.
Wilshire Book Company, 12015 Sherman Rd., North Hollywood, CA 91605-3781. Phone: (818) 765-8579. Check your local library or *Books in Print.* Comprehensive, with lots of detailed information and examples of books and book promotions that worked.

Poynter, Dan. *The Self-Publishing Manual: How to Write, Print and Sell Your Own Book.* 9th ed., rev. Santa Barbara, CA: Para Publishing, 1996.
Para Publishing, P.O. Box 4232, Santa Barbara, CA 93140. Phone: (800) PARA-PUB. Poynter is considered the "dean" of self-publishing, and his book is the "bible"—detailed, specific and informative.

Vitale, Joe. *Turbocharge Your Writing!* Houston, TX: Awareness Publications, 1988.
Joe Vitale, Awareness Publications, P.O. Box 300792, Houston, TX 77230-0792. Phone: (713) 434-2845. I recommend this book to anyone faced with the challenge of writing a book. Vitale is also available to work with au-

thors on book proposals, manuscripts, self-publishing and selling to a major publisher.

TIPS FROM THE PROS

Here's more advice from top writers and editors on how to succeed as a freelancer:

1. **Develop your skills.** "Study published authors with whom you feel a rapport," Elmore Leonard told *USA Weekend*. "Imitate them—the way they paragraph, punctuate. . . . Concentrate on developing your skill and you'll find a way to get published."

2. **Don't underestimate yourself.** Bob Higgins, presenter of the Living on Purpose Seminars, says to accept the fact that some editors and clients will like your work and others will not. "So what?" says Higgins. "We all have the capacity to change the world."

3. **Do what you love.** "Focus on what you love," says Martha Stewart. "Whatever you're passionate about deserves to become a priority. Think about what you want to accomplish. Days can slip by at an astonishing rate—but only if you let them."

4. **Give your customers what they want.** *Dilbert* creator Scott Adams didn't become really rich until he put his E-mail address (scottadams@aol.com) in his strip. "I decided to figure out from my customers what they wanted," said Adams in an interview with *Reader's Digest*. The E-mails he received told him his readers favored cartoons in which he mocked the corporate world. "The business-oriented strips were being hung on walls, so I switched emphasis to 80 percent business and technology—and that's when the strip took off."

5. **Say old things but in a new way.** "Tell a really good story that's honest," advises Emily Heckman, an editor at Bantam Books. "Having an authentic voice is crucial. Successful nonfiction book authors put language and structure to concepts we intuitively know to be true, speaking about them in a way that is utterly fresh and new."

6. **Stay positive.** "It's easy to get depressed about the capricious nature of publishing," says Emily Bessler, editor in

chief of Pocket Books. The only way to stay on track is to "keep the faith and believe in your own muses."

TWENTY-TWO MORE SECRETS FOR BOOSTING YOUR WRITING PROFITS

Judith Broadhurt has published an in-depth study of freelance writers earning $60,000 or more a year. Based on her research, she has come up with the following suggestions (reprinted with her permission) to place your own earnings in this category:

1. **Honor the first commandment of successful freelance writing: Know thy market!** "It is better to send one, two or three queries tailored to magazines that you know publish articles like the one you're proposing than to send a rather generic query to twenty magazines because they might."

2. **Reslant and resell.** "Try to resell every story at least three times, but make sure you honor the rights clauses in your contracts. Use the initial research and interviews from every magazine story you can to either reslant the story to sell it to a different magazine, or to sell it as a reprint, unchanged. Resell sections and chapters of books as magazine stories or special reports. You'll double, at least, your chances of survival as a freelancer if you don't start from scratch every time. Maximize profits on the reporting and writing for each assignment."

3. **Get a steady gig.** "Just as houses need to be built on solid foundations, you need a base to support your freelance writing. For some, that's a part-time job until they're making enough to let it go. Even then, most who survive, much less thrive, in this business have publications they write for repeatedly, who call them for assignments or give go-aheads on ideas pitched to editors in casual phone calls; write columns; or do good-paying work, such as corporate/ PR writing, tech writing or direct-mail copywriting, to enable them to take on less lucrative projects. For some, trade magazines provide that base. Trade magazine stories don't pay as well as consumer (newsstand-type) magazines, but they usually lead to a stream of assignments and are far quicker to research and write."

4. **Practice rigorous self-discipline.** "If, because you work from home, you sleep in, take too many long lunches or leisurely walks or think freelancing is mainly a great way to spend more time with your kids, keep your day job or consider another career. Many freelancers need baby-sitters or daycare providers during their working hours, just as those who work in offices for others do. To keep up and to keep the mind-set that reminds you you're working and this is business, you must adhere to a schedule and routine. Yes, you can set your own hours, but once you do, stick with that framework."

5. **Remember the 80/20 rule of marketing.** "When you're just starting out as a freelancer or in slow periods later, you need to spend 80 to 100 percent of your time on things that will generate income or on marketing. One query out a day or a follow-up call, at least, is a good goal, and minimum if you have no assignments. Even when you've got a flow of assignments and are well established, the most successful people still set aside one day a week or an hour or two a day to keep in touch with editors, send out proposals and submit expense reports in order to protect their cash flow. That prevents the sudden realization, after completing current projects, that they've let the flow dry up. Let it lag, and you'll face a dry spell of up to six months before cash starts coming in again. Repeat: If you don't market continually or do something to keep work coming in, it's deadly."

6. **Keep an eye on the cash flow constantly.** "Calculate your monthly expenses, all of them, and keep enough assignments going so you have at least 2½ to 3 times that monthly amount out in receivables at all times. Minimum. If you have to hustle and work sixteen-hour days and weekends for six months to make that happen—which you probably will—do it, because the payoff is not only the money but the relief from anxiety. Nothing makes creative juices dry up faster than wondering where next month's housing payment is coming from."

7. **Edit one-third and you'll make your story three times better.** "OK, maybe only twice as good as the draft version, but unless you're an experienced wire service or newspaper reporter (and even if you are), most of us need to edit to

make our stories lean and clean. Some of the most experienced and best writers routinely run through five or six rewrites or revisions. And remember the time-honored advice to writers: 'Kill your darlings.' Meaning: If you're enamored of a phrase or word, that's probably the one that's overwritten or self-indulgent. Cut it."

8. **Do thorough, reliable research.** "You can be a truly creative writer, but if editors can't trust your research and feel confident in your ability to track down information and sources, resourcefully, word will get around among editors, and you will not get repeat assignments."

9. **Ensure absolutely accurate reporting.** "Editors also want to know that you double-checked facts, know how to conduct a good interview, use quotes accurately and well (too many is as great a mistake as too few), and know how to tell a story that holds the reader's attention and one that can stand up against any critical responses from readers as at least fair, balanced and accurate."

10. **Don't make editors edit.** "The less editing your story requires, the better editors will like you and the more often they'll call. It typically takes a time or two writing for a particular publication and working with a given editor to be able to mold stories that fit what she wants. But you can increase the likelihood of this early on in three ways: (1) make sure you're thoroughly familiar with the magazine's style or voice, content and audience; (2) get thorough instructions from the editors about what they want from your story; and (3) keep in touch with editors before deadline and right afterward, especially if the story takes an unexpected turn because you discover something none of you had anticipated in the course of your research and reporting."

11. **Meet deadlines and keep editors informed.** "Many editors would rather work with a mediocre writer whom they know they can count on to meet deadlines than an artiste who pleads writer's block or sick relatives. They've heard all the excuses numerous times. Plan for the unexpected, and if you have to pull an occasional all-nighter to meet a deadline, do it. But you'll stay saner and your work will be better if you finish your final draft in time to let the story

gel, then hone it one last time, yet still meet the deadline."

12. **Cultivate relationships, because that's what this business is based on.** "Editors give most assignments to writers they've already worked with, either in their present positions or wherever their last stops were in the perpetual game of musical chairs that editors play, or to writers recommended to them by other writers or editors. Thus it pays to cultivate relationships with both editors and writers and to continually expand and nurture your network. That network of other writers is also critical for reducing the isolation inherent in freelancing, as well as for obtaining tips and input from others who understand the nature of your work, much as those with other jobs do with co-workers."

13. **Become and stay computer savvy.** "A year or two ago, it gave you a competitive advantage to be reasonably adept at using computers and online networks. Then it became a question of maintaining your foothold where you are. Now, you're steadily losing ground if you don't know your way around online and aren't able to file stories and do research by modem."

14. **Get it in writing.** "Most tales of woe writers tell would have turned out differently if they'd simply had a written agreement that made the content and conditions of each assignment clear and covered all the bases, including rates, rights, payment policies and deadlines. Although few newspapers use contracts for freelance assignments, if a magazine doesn't offer one, send your own letter of agreement. That's a good idea for newspapers, too."

15. **Know your rights and take a stand.** "You absolutely must understand what you're signing and keep informed about issues that affect your livelihood, such as electronic rights, or E-rights. Almost all contracts are negotiable, and if you ask for changes, the other party will know you're a pro, not just someone desperate for a byline or a check. Learn the basics and subscribe to the American Society of Journalists and Author's Contract Watch, if you're online. And you're already online or will be soon, right? If not, reread item thirteen."

16. **Develop a viable mixture of work.** "Very few freelancers make it by doing just one kind of work, such as magazine

writing or books. Only you can decide what works best for you, and you learn that only by trial and error and learning when to cut your losses or let loose of something less lucrative so you can free the time to move up to the next level, even if that means a temporary loss of income. But bear in mind that one key to success for most businesses is diversification. Or, as your mother taught you: 'Don't put all of your eggs in one basket.' A good image to keep in mind is that a stool won't stand with less than three legs. The trick is balance. With too many things in the works or pulling you in different directions, you become frazzled and fragmented, rather than focused. With too few, your position is too tenuous."

17. **Allow yourself daydreaming and downtime.** "Don't forget to take time to exercise and just daydream or do simple tasks that let your mind wander. Physical health fosters mental health, which is as essential to your work as meeting deadlines and mastering your computer. And what is tempting for you to think of as downtime is really the time you need to reflect, reevaluate and solve problems, even if that's just how to start or structure a story, think of new story ideas or let ones already floating around in your mind develop."

18. **Know your limitations.** "Don't take on more work than you can handle in a normal work week, but do learn when you're experienced enough to hire others to help you with research or background interviews. Even then, always check their work, because it's your reputation and livelihood that are on the line."

19. **Don't work for less than you need to earn to make ends meet.** "First, you've got to figure out how much that is. Factor in all of your overhead, from phone to insurance to savings, and be realistic about how much of your time each month is what lawyers and ad agencies call billable hours. Consider, too, what the going rates are for the type of project and where you live, because regional rates vary. Don't sell yourself, nor other writers, short. It rarely pays off to do that. Position and conduct yourself as a pro, and people will think of you as one and pay you pro rates."

20. **Keep your expenses and debts low.** "Freelance income

is often erratic, so you can't afford to live on credit cards or spend all of what comes in when it comes in. Prudent folks set aside 20 percent or more of everything they make for taxes and savings, as a cushion. Pay cash. Think: The new sofa or suit I want will cost me only x number of stories. Now all I have to do is get those assignments and get the checks."

21. **Maintain a system for story ideas.** "Clip newspaper and magazine stories that give you even pieces of story ideas or sources to interview for other stories. Set up topical files to gather information for story and book proposals, and keep a paper or computer file called 'Ideas' that you feed continually. Then when you're stuck or have a spare hour, use it to draft a query. Then get that query in the mail!"

22. **Adopt an attitude of gratitude.** "As much as writers grouse about the vicissitudes of the freelance writing life, there are many who envy our creative and intellectual challenges, freedom and autonomy. If you'd prefer the security of a "regular job," get one, or keep the one you've got. If you know, in your gut, that this is what you should be doing, be thankful that you are, and get on with it, or at least set a time limit on negative thinking or take a break. Like it or not, you're partly in the sales business, too, and any successful salesperson will tell you that your own attitude is as important as what you're selling and to whom."

DOES BEING PROLIFIC PAY? AND IS IT FOR YOU?

I'm a competent writer, but there are many more skilled and talented. What has saved me is my ability to be productive and prolific, coupled with good agents and my own sales ability.

By getting a lot of assignments and being able to do them fairly quickly, I have maintained an income in the six figures, despite the fact that I'm not a star or best-selling author. So for me, being busy has paid off, financially and professionally. If you are a young writer, creating literature may seem more important than commerce to you. But believe me, as you get older and—as many of us do—take on the financial obligations of a family and a mortgage and college tuition for the kids, money becomes more of an issue, and most writers don't have enough of it.

What's best for you? Only you know. I like being busy and having many different projects and having many books and articles published. So that's the way I operate. The tips in this book can get you there if that's your goal, too.

Or maybe you shudder at all this activity and prefer, like poet Donald Hall, to sit and revise your poem six hundred times. You won't make a fortune, but you just might make art. More power to you.

APPENDIX A • SAMPLE DOCUMENTS

Brief Author Bio

BUSINESS-TO-BUSINESS/HIGH-TECH/DIRECT RESPONSE

Bob Bly is an independent copywriter and consultant with more than fifteen years' experience in business-to-business, high-tech, industrial and direct marketing.

A winner of the Direct Marketing Association's Gold Echo award and an IMMY from the Information Industry Association, Bob has written copy for such clients as ITT Fluid Technology, Medical Economics, M&T Chemicals, Wallace and Tiernan, PSE&G, Brooklyn Union Gas, Samsung, Sony, Ascom/Timeplex, G.E. Solid State, Graver Chemical, Plato Software, IBM, AT&T, Agora Publishing, McGraw-Hill, Louis Rukeyser's Wall Street, CoreStates Financial Corporation, Swiss Bank, Value Rent-a-Car, Hyperion Software, GeorgeTown Publishing, Alloy Technology, EBI Medical Systems, Citrix Systems, AlliedSignal, The BOC Group, John Wiley and Sons, DataFocus and Graver Chemicals.

Bob is the author of over thirty books, including *The Advertising Manager's Handbook* (Prentice Hall), *Business-to-Business Direct Marketing* (NTC Business Books) and *The Copywriter's Handbook* (Henry Holt & Co.). Other titles include *Targeted Public Relations* and *Selling Your Services*, both from Henry Holt & Co., and *Keeping Clients Satisfied*, from Prentice Hall. His articles have appeared in *Business Marketing*, *Direct*, *Computer Decisions*, *New Jersey Monthly*, *Writer's Digest*, *Amtrak Express*, *Science Books and Films* and *Direct Marketing*.

Bob has presented marketing, sales, writing and customer service seminars for numerous groups, including the Publicity Club of New York, Women in Communications, Direct Marketing Association, Independent Laboratory Distributors Association, American Institute of Chemical Engineers, American Chemical Society, Business Marketing Association, International Tile Exposition, Direct Marketing Creative Guild, Women's

APPENDIX A • SAMPLE DOCUMENTS

Direct Response Group, Direct Media Co-op and American Marketing Association. He also taught business-to-business copywriting and technical writing at New York University.

Bob writes sales letters, direct-mail packages, ads, brochures, articles, press releases, newsletters and other marketing materials clients need to sell their products and services to businesses. He also consults with clients on marketing strategy, mail-order selling and lead-generation programs.

Bob Bly holds a B.S. in chemical engineering from the University of Rochester. He is a member of the American Institute of Chemical Engineers, Business Marketing Association and Software Association of New Jersey. For a *free* information kit or a free, no-obligation cost estimate for your next project, contact:

Bob Bly
22 East Quackenbush Avenue
Dumont, NJ 07628
phone: (201) 385-1220
fax: (201) 385-1138
E-mail: Rwbly@aol.com

APPENDIX A • SAMPLE DOCUMENTS

Direct-Mail Letter to Generate Leads
From Potential Corporate/Business Clients

Dear Marketing Professional:

"It's hard to find a copywriter who can handle industrial and high-tech accounts," a prospect told me over the phone today, "especially for brochures, direct mail and other long-copy assignments."

Do you have that same problem?

If so, please complete and mail the enclosed reply card, and I'll send you a free information kit describing a service that can help.

As a freelance copywriter specializing in business-to-business marketing, I've written hundreds of successful ads, sales letters, direct-mail packages, brochures, data sheets, annual reports, feature articles, press releases, newsletters and audiovisual scripts for clients all over the country.

But my information kit will give you the full story.

You'll receive a comprehensive "Welcome" letter that tells all about my copywriting service—who I work for, what I can do for you, how we can work together.

You'll also get my client list (I've written copy for more than one hundred corporations and agencies) . . . client testimonials . . . biographical background . . . samples of work I've done in your field . . . a fee schedule listing what I charge for ads, brochures and other assignments . . . helpful article reprints on copywriting and advertising . . . even an order form you can use to put me to work for you.

Whether you have an immediate project, a future need or are just curious, I urge you to send for this information kit. It's free . . . there's no obligation . . . and you'll like having a proven copywriting resource on file—someone you can call on whenever you need him.

From experience, I've learned that the best time to evaluate a copywriter and take a look at his work is *before* you need him, not when a project

APPENDIX A • SAMPLE DOCUMENTS

- moving toward the concept of a "virtual business"—90 percent outsourcing, with all business partners connected via the Internet
- a mini-directory of major national outsourcing firms with contact information and services offered.

By way of introduction, I am the author of more than one hundred magazine articles and thirty books, including *Keeping Clients Satisfied* (Prentice Hall) and *Power-Packed Direct Mail* (Henry Holt & Co.). My articles have appeared in *Cosmopolitan, Science Books and Films, City Paper, Computer Decisions, Direct, Amtrak Express, Chemical Engineering, Writer's Digest, Business Marketing, Direct Marketing* and *New Jersey Monthly.*

I can have this article on your desk in three to four weeks. Shall I proceed as outlined?

Sincerely,

Bob Bly

APPENDIX A · SAMPLE DOCUMENTS

Sample Book Proposal

SELLING YOUR SERVICES:
PROVEN STRATEGIES FOR GETTING CLIENTS
TO HIRE YOU (OR YOUR FIRM)

A GUIDE FOR

- consultants
- freelancers
- independent professionals
- contractors and vendors
- service firms
- and anyone else who works in a service or service-related business

by
Robert W. Bly
22 East Quackenbush Avenue
Dumont, NJ 07628
(201) 385-1229
November 16, 1989

APPENDIX A · SAMPLE DOCUMENTS

SELLING YOUR SERVICES:
PROVEN STRATEGIES FOR GETTING CLIENTS
TO HIRE YOU (OR YOUR FIRM)

There are dozens of books on selling, but these books focus on selling products—physical, tangible items—and are aimed at professional salespeople working on commission.

But there has never been a book on selling services, which is as different from selling products as night is from day.

Now *Selling Your Services* fills that gap, providing the hundreds of thousands of people in the service sector with proven strategies on how to sell.

WHY A BOOK ON SELLING SERVICES?

Selling services—which are intangibles—is fundamentally different and requires an entirely separate strategy from selling products—which are tangible. Among these key differences:

Selling Products
Sold by professional salespeople who don't see the customer once the sale is made and whose only concern is bringing back an order.

Selling Services
Frequently sold by the person who will actually render the service. This person must build a personal relationship with the buyer and has to select prospects with good personal chemistry; otherwise, the relationship will fail.

Products
Sale is finished once the order is taken and product is delivered.

Services
Getting a signed contract is only the first step. The client must be continuously sold and resold before, during and after service is performed.

APPENDIX A • SAMPLE DOCUMENTS

Products

Proof of satisfaction is easy to demonstrate and is achieved when product is delivered. The product salespeople, therefore, are not selective and will sell to basically anybody with money to buy.

Services

Satisfaction is subjective. Therefore, service sellers must be sure to screen prospects and select only those prospects who seem a good fit with the seller's personnel and type of service.

Products

Prospects are qualified according to whether they have the money and authority to buy.

Services

Prospects are qualified according to whether their specific problems can be solved in a satisfactory manner by the service offered.

Products

Salesperson is primarily concerned with closing the sale and does not worry about whether the prospect will become a difficult account— because salespeople do not have to personally deal with customer complaints (in most cases).

Services

Salespeople will not pursue sale of difficult prospect, since the salesperson is also the one who will have to cope with this person while rendering service.

Products

Pricing is fairly standard and easy to calculate.

Services

Pricing differs with each client and project and frequently requires intensive up-front effort in order to prepare a quotation or proposal.

Products

Visits from salespeople are always free.

APPENDIX A · SAMPLE DOCUMENTS

Services

Some service providers view visits in preparation of bids or proposals as consulting work and may want to charge for these services (e.g., lawyers who charge a small initial consultation fee to listen and decide whether to take your case).

Products

Salespeople use volume discounts and price bargaining as a prime negotiations tool for closing sales.

Services

Prices not greatly flexible because service business is labor-intensive and firm cannot lose money on initial contract in exchange for promise of future business—as is often done in product selling.

Products

Salesperson is viewed by prospect as a salesman and is not expected to be an expert.

Services

Salesperson is viewed by prospect as a consultant, and the prospect's image of the service firm is dependent largely upon how well this consultant performs in initial meetings.

Products

Salesperson is paid commission, creating a powerful incentive to sell as much product as possible.

Services

Salesperson must also render services sold (or at least part of them), so can be hesitant to sell unless she can handle.

Products

Product salespeople are trained to overcome objections and sell to the prospect despite his protestations that he does not want to buy.

Services

In service selling, an objection is not necessarily something to be

APPENDIX A • SAMPLE DOCUMENTS

overcome but, rather, serves as a warning signal that the person might be a bad match for your service and that the meeting should end.

Products
Customer is buying an off-the-shelf item that is mass-produced and not tailored to his specific needs.

Services
Customer is buying (and expects to get) a service that is highly customized and tailored to his specific needs.

America has made the transition from a product-producing to a service-providing economy. According to a recent article in *Executive Business Magazine*, 35 percent of the U.S. workforce was employed in manufacturing in 1970. This increased to 60 percent in 1987. The U.S. Bureau of Labor Statistics reports that approximately 21 million Americans were employed in manufacturing a decade ago, versus nearly 36 million in service businesses today.

Because of this shift from a manufacturing to a service economy, most books on selling—which focus on goods rather than service, information or ideas—are outdated and not applicable in today's sales environment.

Further, even manufacturing companies are becoming service sellers. As buyers see less and less difference between manufactured products, the factor that most influences their choice of vendor is service. Selling service has now become both a profit center in its own right (IBM, for example, is one of hundreds of manufacturers deriving substantial income from service) as well as an integral component of any hard-good product. So everyone—even salespeople who traditionally think of themselves as "merchandise movers"—is in fact a "service seller." The ability to provide and sell service is now critical to the success of every corporation, small business and self-employed entrepreneur in the United States.

MARKETS

Selling Your Services speaks directly to the needs of a number of large and easily identified target markets, both entrepreneurial and corporate:

APPENDIX A · SAMPLE DOCUMENTS

1. Consultants. Among self-employed professionals selling services, consultants are the most active and aggressive when it comes to sales and marketing; thus they will welcome a book that deals specifically with selling service (which consultants render) rather than product. *Selling Your Services* will have great appeal to the more than 100,000 current and would-be independent consultants who eagerly purchase such books as Herman Holtz's *How to Succeed as an Independent Consultant* (John Wiley and Sons; sales over 100,000 copies).

2. Entrepreneurs and would-be entrepreneurs. Because a service business can be started inexpensively in one's home or apartment, most of the 625,000 small businesses started each year are service businesses rather than manufacturing firms or distributors. This book would have strong appeal to both working entrepreneurs as well as those thinking about starting a business, that is, readers of such publications as *Inc.* (Circulation: 600,000), *Entrepreneur* (circulation: 200,000) and *Nations Business* (850,000). Dr. Jeffrey Lant, publisher of the Sure-Fire Business Success Catalog, has a list of more than 75,000 such people who are proven buyers of books on entrepreneurial topics.

3. Service and service-related firms. Perhaps the strongest markets are individual entrepreneurs, small firms, and medium- to large-size corporations that derive all or part of their income from selling services. This is the only book that presents proven strategies for getting people to buy services.

Dozens of industries and types of businesses and professions fall into this category, including the following:

Accountants	Barbers
Ad Agencies	Bed and Breakfasts
Architects	Builders, Contractors,
Attorneys	Remodelers
Automobile	Business and Management
Banks and Financial Services	Consultants
Institutions	Camps

APPENDIX A · SAMPLE DOCUMENTS

Career Training Firms

Child Care, Baby-Sitting, Preschool Centers

Computer Programmers, Custom Software Developers, DP Consultants

Construction Firms

Contractors

Dating Services

Dentists

Diaper Services

Doctors

Dry-Cleaning and Laundry Establishments

Editorial Services

Electronics Repair Shops

Engineering and Consulting Engineer Services

Environmental Testing Services

Executive Search Firms

Financial Planners

Franchise Owners

Freight Forwarders

Fund-Raising Consultants

Funeral Parlors, Morticians

Graphic Artists

Hair and Beauty Parlors

Health Spas and Exercise Clubs

Hospitals and Clinics

Hotels, Clubs, Restaurants

Insurance Agents

Interior Decorative, Design, Planning Services

Investment Agents

Maintenance and Service Firms

Metal Working and Fabrication Services

Musicians and Entertainment

Pharmacists

Photographers

Proofreaders

Psychiatrists and Psychologists (Therapists)

Real Estate Agents

Sewer and Drain Cleaning Services

Speakers

Stock Brokers

Tanning Salons

Tax Preparers

Telecommunications and Telephone Services

Temporary Employment Services

Training and Development Consultants

Transportation Firms

Travel Agents

Utilities

Veterinarians

Videotape Rental Stores

Watch and Jewelry Repair Services

Wedding Consultants

Word Processing Services

Writers

XRay, Ultrasound, NMR, Diagnostic Services

APPENDIX A · SAMPLE DOCUMENTS

This is just a sampling; obviously, the list could be much, much longer.

4. Self-employed professionals. This group includes graphic artists, photographers, writers, copywriters, publicists, proofreaders, secretarial services, attorneys, dentists, doctors, accountants and other white-collar workers who are self-employed and must market and sell their professional services. Most are involved in advising, consulting or rendering professional services from home offices equipped with computers, modems and fax machines. The finished product is frequently in the form of a written report or other printed material.

5. Blue-collar entrepreneurs. This group includes handymen, wallpaperers, painters, plumbers, locksmiths, landscape architects, lawn maintenance workers, roofers, carpenters and other tradespeople who provide a variety of services, usually related to home repair and maintenance, to the local community. Most work within a fifty-mile radius and run the business from a home office and pickup truck or van.

MARKETING AND PROMOTION

The most cost-effective way of promoting *Selling Your Services* is through the magazines in the selling field as well as the magazines and newsletters that reach protection readers in specific vertical industries and professions (e.g., veterinarians, attorneys, dentists, doctors, consultants, freelance writers, graphic artists, photographers). A press release can inexpensively be sent to these publications, while review copies could be targeted to those most likely to run a review or articles (these would be the selling magazines as well as magazines and newsletters that focus on marketing and selling in specific vertical industries, e.g., Cameron Foote's *Creative Business* for freelance advertising writers and artists or Howard Shenson's newsletter on marketing and selling consulting services). I can provide a list with the addresses and editors of most of the worthwhile publications.

Although the market is flooded with books on selling, *Selling Your Services* is one of the only books to focus on service selling. Therefore, it has a better chance of standing out from the crowd and is more likely

APPENDIX A • SAMPLE DOCUMENTS

to be of interest to program directors and editors—especially those whose publications deal with service fields. One technique might be to write short articles tailored toward specific industries and send them to these editors in exchange for a short blurb promoting the book. I would be happy to provide as many of these articles as needed.

Although the paperback would probably be too inexpensive to promote via stand-alone direct mail, there are several widely distributed catalogs of business books for which *Selling Your Services* would be a good selection. We could also test a postcard deck aimed at entrepreneurs, especially a higher-priced hardcover version. In addition, my survey of area bookstores shows that selling is a healthy category with many titles displayed; thus, *Selling Your Services* could do well in bookstores. And it should be slightly easier sell to the bookstore owners and buyers because it's not just another sales book but, rather, has a unique angle (i.e., it is a book about selling services, not products or goods).

COMPETITION

There are over a hundred books listed in *Books in Print* on topics of selling sales. But this book does not compete with most of them because it deals with selling services rather than merchandise. So for competitive analysis I eliminated

- books published before 1980
- books self-published or published by small or unknown presses
- books that are unavailable in bookstores and sold solely through direct mail
- books on general selling that focused on traditional selling (i.e., selling tangible items—goods, products, merchandise)
- books that focused on marketing only in an extremely narrow vertical market (e.g., a book on marketing your office practice).

This leaves us with the following books as primary competition:

1. *Minding Other People's Business: Winning Big for Your Clients and Yourself*, by Donald L. Dell (New York: Villard Books, 1989), 237 pp., hardcover, $18.95.

APPENDIX A • SAMPLE DOCUMENTS

Although this is an excellent book, it is mostly about dealing with and servicing clients rather than selling. Of its eight chapters, seven deal with client service, client relations and client contact. Only chapter two—"Getting Clients"—deals with selling or marketing services, and this chapter is thirty-one pages of the book's 237 pages.

In addition, the book has two major flaws: First, almost all the stories and examples deal with sports management and marketing, which is the author's field (his company ProServ, represents 250 professional athletes). Second, the constant name-dropping of celebrities in sports and other fields eventually turns off the average reader, whose business operates on a scale less grand.

By comparison, *Selling Your Services* is primarily about selling and marketing to get new clients, rather than servicing those clients you already have (although part five of my table of contents deals with this very important topic of serving the client to ensure satisfaction and more business after the initial sale is made). Also, I draw examples from a wide range of fields because as a consultant and teacher I have worked with firms in dozens of industries.

2. *Marketing Your Consulting and Professional Services* by Jeffrey P. Stone Davidson and Richard A Conner (New York: John Wiley & Sons, 1985), 219 pp., hardcover, $22.95.

This is a good book but too theoretical. It provides excellent coverage of marketing (e.g., creating a marketing plan, identifying lists of prospects, classifying prospects into categories, types of promotional vehicles available to reach prospects) but does not provide adequate instruction on selling (i.e., how to deal with and sell prospects over the telephone or in face-to-face meetings). For example, of the book's 219 pages, only one 16-page chapter (chapter nine) is devoted to personal selling.

Selling Your Services, by comparison, tells you what to say and when to say it in order to get the prospect to hire you. Actual dialogue the reader can adapt to his own situation will enable the reader to overcome

APPENDIX A · SAMPLE DOCUMENTS

virtually every objection he might hear, from, "I already use someone else," to, "We don't need any right now," to, "Your price is too high." Just as important, I will also tell when not to push a prospect to buy your service. Knowing how to select the right clients is as critical to success in any service industry as knowing how to overcome objections and close the sale.

FORMAT

Selling Your Services is organized to reflect the precise sequence of things the reader must do to successfully sell his services to the client— from generating a sales lead and making the initial contacts to making the presentation, preparing the price quotation and getting a signed contract.

The book is divided into five major sections and sixteen chapters. I see *Selling Your Services* as a medium-length, conversational, accessible guide rather than a treatise—a trade paperback (and possibly hardcover, for corporate and library sales) of approximately 200 pages. Target length would be between 65,000 and 75,000 words.

Although the book would be mostly straight text, there would be some graphics, consisting mainly of sample materials the reader could copy and use in his daily selling work. These would include sample contracts, proposals, price quotations, letters of agreement, telephone scripts, sales letters, promotional brochures, ads, press releases and other marketing documents.

TABLE OF CONTENTS

INTRODUCTION

PART I: Solid-Gold Prospecting: How to Generate Initial Interest in Your Services

CHAPTER 1: *Selling Your Services*: An Overview
Selling services vs. selling products: similarities and differences. The three-part service marketing strategy: inquiry generation/direct response,

APPENDIX A • SAMPLE DOCUMENTS

visibility/credibility building and inquiry fulfillment/marketing support. Selling services to consumers. Selling services to business.

CHAPTER 2: Sales Lead-Generating Techniques That Work
Inquiry generation/direct-response marketing techniques that work: sales letters, direct mail, telemarketing, cold calling, self-mailers, postcard decks, referrals, personal selling.

CHAPTER 3: How to Become Famous in Your Field
Gaining visibility and establishing credibility: articles, media coverage, books, speeches, seminars, professional groups, trade associations, presentations, publicity, monographs, special reports, networking, teaching.

CHAPTER 4: How to Create Marketing Documents That Sell
Inquiry authority/marketing support materials: capabilities brochures, service-specific brochures, sales kits and folders, overhead and slide presentations, videotapes, audiocassettes, booklets, bios, resumes, business cards, fliers.

PART II: Follow-up: How to Get Appointments With Prospects

CHAPTER 5: Proven Techniques for Prequalifying Your Prospects
Follow-up techniques that presell your prospect, identify areas of need and screen out nonprospects. Ranking prospects. Tracking sales activities.

CHAPTER 6: How to Get Your Prospects to Talk With You
Phone and mail strategies for getting past the secretary barrier.

CHAPTER 7: Getting the Initial Appointment
How to sell the meeting to your prospect—in thirty seconds or less.

PART III: The Initial Client Meeting: How to Use It to Achieve Your Goal

CHAPTER 8: Increasing Your Selling Efficiency
The initial meeting—fee or free? How to decide when to meet with clients gratis and when to charge for initial meetings. Plus: strategies to get clients to hire you by mail.

APPENDIX A • SAMPLE DOCUMENTS

CHAPTER 9: Consultative Selling
Why prospects want consultants, not salespeople. Why you should use the initial meeting to solve the client's problem, not sell.

CHAPTER 10: How to Handle Objections
Objections: how to use them as screening devices to eliminate potential problem clients and concentrate on your best prospects. How to answer questions and client concerns.

CHAPTER 11: Closing the Sale
How to move the client to the next step—a signed contract—in the shortest possible period of time.

PART IV. Getting the Project—Contracts, Proposals, Letters of Agreement

CHAPTER 12: How to Ask For—and Get—the Fee You Deserve
Price quotation: how to set and get your fees.

CHAPTER 13: The Written Agreement
How to put it in writing with contracts, proposals and letters of agreement

PART V: Continuous Selling: How to Keep Clients Sold After the Sale Is Made

CHAPTER 14: How to Increase Your Sales With Client Satisfaction
Tips on performing your service so the client is satisfied.

CHAPTER 15: Coping With Difficult Clients
How to spot and correct problems before they harm your client relationship.

CHAPTER 16: The Key to Successful Service Selling
The key: Don't give your client her money's worth—give her more than her money's worth. The little (but important) things you can do to make the client love you.

ABOUT THE AUTHOR

In his work as an independent marketing consultant, copywriter and seminar leader, Bob Bly has helped dozens of companies and hundreds

APPENDIX A · SAMPLE DOCUMENTS

of individuals sell more of their professional and consulting services through his articles, lectures and training sessions.

In addition, he has written sales letters, direct-response ads, brochures and other marketing documents that have generated millions of dollars in sales for such service-business clients as Value Rent-a-Car, Midlantic National Bank, American Medical Collection Agency, Advantage Presort Service, JMW Consultants, Medrecon and Fala Direct Marketing. His service-industry clients are in a variety of businesses ranging from car rentals, consulting and data processing to mail presorting, collection agencies and P.R. Firms.

Bob Bly is the author of seventeen books including *How to Promote Your Own Business* (New American Library), *Create the Perfect Sales Piece: How To Produce Brochures, Catalogs, Fliers and Pamphlets* (John Wiley and Sons) and *The Copywriter's Handbook: A Step-by-Step Guide to Writing Copy That Sells* (Henry Holt & Co.).

Bob's articles have been published in numerous magazines, including *Business Marketing, Executive Business Magazine, Amtrak Express, Writer's Digest, New Jersey Monthly* and *Cosmopolitan*.

Sample Contract

Some writers use simple contracts to confirm job assignments from clients. Here's one I have developed.

CONTRACT FOR WRITING SERVICES

From: Bob Bly   Phone: (201) 385-1220
     22 East Quackenbush Avenue   Fax: (201) 385-1138
     Dumont, NJ 07628

Date:

Client:

Job:

Fee:

Advance retainer required:

Balance due upon completion:

Notes:

Your signature below authorizes me to write copy for the project described above, for the fee listed. Revisions are included if assigned within thirty days of your receipt of copy and are not based on a change in the assignment made after copy is submitted. Payment due net thirty days upon receipt of invoice.

I will make every attempt to write copy that complies with all laws and regulations, but you agree to have your lawyer review all copy for compliance with all applicable laws and regulations in the United States, Canada and any other countries in which the promotion is used. You agree that your lawyer will work with me to make any necessary revisions required for legal compliance. You release me from responsibility for any legal or regulatory problems that may arise from the use of the copy I write for you.

Signed _____

Title _____ Date _____

APPENDIX A • SAMPLE DOCUMENTS

Please sign and return this form with your check for the amount listed under "Advance retainer required." This will give me the go-ahead I need to proceed with the assignment.

Note: If no retainer is required, you can save time by signing above and faxing the form to me at (201) 385-1138.

APPENDIX A · SAMPLE DOCUMENTS

Sample Invoice

INVOICE FOR SERVICES RENDERED

July 15, 1997

From: David Willis
15 Sunnyville Drive
Anyplace, USA 12345
(201) 555-5555
Social Security #000-00-0000

To: XYZ Corporation
Anytown, USA 12345
Attn: June Chapman, Advertising Manager

For: Copy for Ron Dempsey "Future of Computer Telephony" speech

Reference: Purchase order #1745

Amount: $3,000

Terms: Net 30 days

Thank You.

APPENDIX A • SAMPLE DOCUMENTS

Form for Keeping Track of Sales Leads

Date _____ Source of inquiry _____ Response via _____

Name _____ Title _____

Company _____ Phone _____

Address _____ Room/floor _____

City _____ State _____ Zip _____

Type of business or publication: _____

Type of projects: _____

For:

___ immediate project

___ future reference

___ project to be started in _____ (month/year)

Status:

___ Sent package on _____ (date)

___ Enclosed these samples _____

___ Next step is to _____

___ Probability of assignment _____

___ Comments _____

_____

_____

Contact Record:

Date _____ Summary _____

_____

APPENDIX B • SOURCES & RESOURCES

Books

Bly, Robert. *The Copywriter's Handbook: A Step-by-Step Guide to Writing Copy That Sells.* New York: Henry Holt and Company, 1990.

Collins, Maryclaire. *How to Make Money Writing Corporate Communications.* New York: Perigree, 1995.

Davis, Paul D. *How to Make $50,000 a Year or More as a Free-lance Business Writer.* Rocklin, Calif: Prima Publishing, 1992.

Floyd, Elaine. *Making Money Writing Newsletters.* St. Louis: Newsletter Resources, 1994.

Foote, Cameron. *The Business Side of Creativity.* New York: W.W. Norton and Company, 1996.

Holtz, Herman R. *How to Start and Run a Writing and Editing Business.* New York: John Wiley and Sons, 1992.

Javed, Naseem. *Naming for Power: Creating Successful Names for the Business World.* New York: Linkbridge Publishing, 1993.

Lee, Robert E. *A Copyright Guide for Authors.* Stamford, Conn.: Kent Press, 1995.

Reimold, Cheryl. *The Language of Business.* Atlanta: TAPPI Press, 1992.

Winchester, Jay. *Infomercial Writers Market Guider.* Wayland, Mass.: Blue Dolphin Communications, 1995.

Catalogs

Hollywood Scripts
5514 Satsuma Ave.
North Hollywood, CA 91607
(818) 980-3545

These folks sell copies of scripts from more than eight thousand TV shows and movies by mail. The catalog is free.

APPENDIX B • SOURCES & RESOURCES

Organizations

American Medical
Writers Association
9650 Rockville Pike
Bethesda, MD 20814-3998
(301) 493-0003

American Society of
Journalists and Authors
1501 Broadway, Suite 302
New York, NY 10036
(212) 997-0947

Authors Guild
330 W. Forty-second St.
New York, NY 10036
(212) 563-5904

Author's League of America
330 W. Forty-second St.
New York, NY 10036
(212) 564-8350

Editorial Freelancers
Association
71 W. Twenty-third St.
Suite 1504
New York, NY 10010
(212) 929-5400

Education Writers Association
1331 "H" St. NW, Suite 307
Washington, DC 20036
(202) 637-9700

Florida Freelance
Writers Association
P.O. Box A
North Stratford, NH 03590
(800) 351-9278

National Association
of Science Writers
P.O. Box 294
Greenlawn, NY 11740
(516) 757-5664

National Writers Union
873 Broadway, Suite 203
New York, NY 10003-1209
(212) 254-0279

Outdoor Writers Association
of America
2017 Cato Ave., Suite 101
State College, PA 16801-2768
(814) 234-1011

Society for Technical
Communication
901 N. Stuart St., Suite 904
Arlington, VA 22203
(703) 522-4114

Society of American Travel
Writers
4101 Lake Boone Trail,
Suite 201
Raleigh, NC 27607
(919) 787-5181

Society of Children's Book
Writers and Illustrators
22736 Vanowen St., Suite 106
West Hills, CA 91307
(818) 888-8760

APPENDIX B • SOURCES & RESOURCES

SWAN
Self-Employed Writers and
Artists Network
P.O. Box 440
Paramus, NJ 07653-0440
(201) 967-1313

Teachers and Writers
Collaborative
5 Union Square W., 7th Floor
New York, NY 10003-3306
(212) 691-6590

Periodicals

Children's Book Insider
P.O. Box 1030
Fairplay, CO 80440-1030
(800) 807-1916 or
(719) 836-0394

Children's Writer
The Institute of Children's
Literature
95 Long Ridge Rd.
Redding, CT 06896-1116
(203) 792-8600

New Writer's Magazine
Sarasota Bay Publishing
P.O. Box 5976
Sarasota, FL 34277-5976
(813) 953-7903

*The New York Times
Book Review*
The New York Times Company
229 W. Forty-third St.
New York, NY 10036
(212) 556-1234

Poets and Writers Magazine
Poets and Writers, Inc.
72 Spring St.
New York, NY 10012
(212) 226-3586

Publishers Weekly
Cahners Publishing Company
Printing and Publishing
Division
249 W. Seventeenth St.
New York, NY 10011
(800) 278-2991

The Writer
The Writer, Inc.
120 Boylston St.
Boston, MA 02116-4615
(617) 423-3157

Writer's Digest
F&W Publications, Inc.
1507 Dana Ave.
Cincinnati, Ohio 45207
(513) 531-2690

Writing for Money
Blue Dolphin
526 Boston Post Rd.
Wayland, MA 01778
(508) 443-8214

Software

Scriptor
(scriptwriting software)
Screenplay Systems, Inc.
150 E. Olive Ave., Suite 203
Burbank, CA 91502-1849
(818) 843-6557

INDEX

More Great Books for Writers!

1998 Writer's Market—Helping writers realize their dreams for more than 75 years. This newest edition contains information on more than 4,000 writing opportunities. You'll find all the facts vital to the success of your writing career, including an up-to-date listing of buyers of books, articles and stories, listings of contests and awards, plus articles and interviews with top professionals. *#10512/$27.99/1088 pages/paperback*

Writing for Money—Discover where to look for writing opportunities—and how to make them pay off. You'll learn how to write for magazines, newspapers, radio and TV, newsletters, greeting cards and a dozen other hungry markets! *#10425/$17.99/256 pages*

The Writer's Digest Guide to Manuscript Formats—Don't take chances with your hard work. Learn how to prepare and submit books, poems, scripts, stories and more with the professional look editors expect from a good writer. *#10025/$19.99/200 pages*

How to Write Fast (While Writing Well)—Discover what makes a story and what it takes to research and write one. Then learn, step by step, how to cut wasted time and effort by planning interviews for maximum results, beating writer's block with effective plotting, getting the most information from traditional library research and on-line computer bases, and much more. Plus, a complete chapter loaded with tricks and tips for faster writing. *#10473/$15.99/208 pages/paperback*

The Writer's Digest Guide to Good Writing—In one book, you'll find the best in writing instruction gleaned from the past 75 years of *Writer's Digest* magazine! Successful authors like Vonnegut, Steinbeck, Oates, Michener and over a dozen others share their secrets on writing technique, idea generation, inspiration and getting published. *#10521/$14.99/352 pages/paperback*

Freeing Your Creativity: A Writer's Guide—Discover how to escape the traps that stifle your creativity. You'll tackle techniques for banishing fears and nourishing ideas so you can get your juices flowing again. *#10430/$14.99/176 pages/paperback*

20 Master Plots (And How to Build Them)—Write great contemporary fiction from timeless plots. This guide outlines 20 plots from various genres and illustrates how to adapt them to your own fiction. *#10366/$17.99/240 pages*

Writer's Digest Handbook of Magazine Article Writing—This is your complete guide to every type of magazine article writing, featuring 33 chapters of writing and marketing instruction. *#10171/$13.99/248 pages/paperback*

Editing Your Newsletter, 4th Edition—Here is all the information you need to produce an effective professional publication, from postal regulations and printing technologies to infographics and more. *#10422/$22.99/160 pages/107 b&w illus./paperback*

Roget's Superthesaurus, Second Edition—With more than 400,000 words, including 2,000+ new and expanded entries, this one-of-a-kind reference goes beyond traditional sourcebooks, giving you notable quotations, slang, cross-referencing and even a "reverse dictionary." *#10541/$19.99/672 pages/paperback*

Other fine Writer's Digest Books are available from your local bookstore or direct from the publisher. Write to the address below for a FREE catalog of all Writer's Digest Books. To order books directly from the publisher, include $3.50 postage and handling for one book, $1.50 for each additional book. Ohio residents add 6% sales tax. Allow 30 days for delivery.

Writer's Digest Books
1507 Dana Avenue
Cincinnati, Ohio 45207

VISA/MasterCard orders call TOLL-FREE
1-800-289-0963

Prices subject to change without notice.   Stock may be limited on some books.

Write to this address for information on *Writer's Digest* magazine, *Story* magazine, Writer's Digest Book Club, Writer's Digest School, and Writer's Digest Criticism Service.   6555